THE ŚĀKTA PĪṬHAS

THE
ŚĀKTA PĪṬHAS

D.C. Sircar

Carmichael Professor and Head of the Department
of
Ancient Indian History and Culture,
University of Calcutta.

MOTILAL BANARSIDASS PUBLISHERS
PRIVATE LIMITED • DELHI

Second Revised Edition: Delhi, 1973
Reprint: Delhi, 1998, 2004

ISBN: 81-208-0879-7

Also available at:

MOTILAL BANARSIDASS

41 U.A. Bungalow Road, Jawahar Nagar, Delhi 110 007
8 Mahalaxmi Chamber, 22 Bhulabhai Desai Road, Mumbai 400 026
236, 9th Main III Block, Jayanagar, Bangalore 560 011
120 Royapettah High Road, Mylapore, Chennai 600 004
Sanas Plaza, 1302 Baji Rao Road, Pune 411 002
8 Camac Street, Kolkata 700 017
Ashok Rajpath, Patna 800 004
Chowk, Varanasi 221 001

Printed in India
BY JAINENDRA PRAKASH JAIN AT SHRI JAINENDRA PRESS,
A-45 NARAINA, PHASE-I, NEW DELHI 110 028
AND PUBLISHED BY NARENDRA PRAKASH JAIN FOR
MOTILAL BANARSIDASS PUBLISHERS PRIVATE LIMITED,
BUNGALOW ROAD, DELHI 110 007

Dedicated to the
Sacred Memory of the Late
Professor Louis Renou

Prācyavidyodadherindorujjvalajñānakarmaṇaḥ /
Sūreḥ Śrīhemacandrasya Rāyacaturdharasya ca //
Bhāṇḍārakaravaṁśābjadevadattasya dhīmataḥ //
pratnalipipragalbhasya svalpajñenāntavāsinā //
kavervaidyāgragaṇyasya Yajñeśvaryasya satpituḥ /
mātuśca Kusumādyāyāḥ kumāryāstanujanmanā //
Dīneśena kṛtiśceyaṁ Kāyasthena samarpyate /
Luvireṇusudhīndrāya vedavidyāvivasvate //

FOREWORD

The Śākta Pīṭhas by Dr. D. C. Sircar, which is limited and precise in scope but has a wide appeal, brings honour to the young historian of Calcutta. Its basis is a critical edition of the *Pīṭhanirṇaya* or *Mahāpīṭhanirūpaṇa* which is a short treatise of the late period describing the fiftyone pilgrim spots associated with the Mother Goddess under some of her various names. Each one of the *pīṭhas* is mentioned along with a particular form of the Goddess and that of Śiva associated with it.

The said text passes as a chapter of the *Tantracūḍāmaṇi* and resembles some others, so that a plausible edition, based on six manuscripts and four source materials which Dr. Sircar's diligence has succeeded in grouping together, was philologically realisable. The editor adds a reconstructed text, based mainly on a Bengali version, and furnishes other useful matters in appendices, one of them containing an index of the *pīṭhas* with necessary identifications of the localities.

But what doubtless deserves much more attention is the erudite study in the introduction, wherein the author recapitulates what is known or may be presumed about the problem of the *pīṭhas*. Leaving aside minor indications, the legend which seeks to explain the origin of the *pīṭhas* is the well-known epico-purāṇic account of Dakṣa's sacrifice, interrupted by Śiva's wrath. The story seems to have developed out of certain allusions in the Brāhmaṇas referring to the peculiar misfortunes of Bhaga and Pūṣan. In the later Purāṇas and the Purāṇa-type Tantras, the image of Viṣṇu cutting off, part by part, Satī's corpse borne on Śiva's shoulder has been grafted on this legend. The severed parts of Satī's body fell on the earth and each formed a *pīṭha*, a cult having come to be crystallised on it. Dr. Sircar recalls in this connection the Buddhist legends about the Buddha's relics and the more distant Greek version of the Osiris myth. We see here, once again, that a cult, quite well localised geographically, develops on absolutely mythical conceptions.

Certain *pīṭhas* appear to be associated more especially with the breasts and the female organ of the Goddess, probably analogous to the conception of the phallic emblem of Śiva. Whatever that may be, the religious crystallisation seems to have taken place originally on the basis of a group of 4 *pīṭhas* at a time which, according to Dr. Sircar, may coincide with the appearance of the early Tantras. These 4 *pīṭhas* are supposed to represent the four cardinal points though, from the beginning, the region of Kāmarūpa (Assam) enjoyed a privileged position in the scheme. Gradually there appeared 7 *pīṭhas*, then 10, then 18 (a sanctified number), ultimately (through the intermediate numbers 42, 50 and 51) as many as 108 (an equally expected number). The *Pīṭhanirṇaya* is based on a list of 42, which was later enlarged, by the inclusion of the 10 *mahāvidyās* of the Mother Goddess, the counterpart of the 10 *avatāras* of the Viṣṇuite cycle.

In an appendix, Dr. Sircar discusses the evidence for determining the date of the celebrated encyclopaedic treatise *Tantrasāra* (first half of the 17th century). Another appendix, the scope of which is more general than novel, deals with the development of the Śakti cult from Vedic times going as far back as the Mohen-jo-daro motifs, the interpretation of which is, however, not quite decisive.

I may specially recommend this study of the *pīṭhas* as a model of accurate and penetrating investigation.

Paris, 1950 LOUIS RENOU

PREFACE TO THE SECOND EDITION

I am thankful to Messrs. Motilal Banarsidass for their kindness in taking up the reprinting of my work entitled *The Śākta Pīṭhas* which was not availâble in the market for some time. The book is now presented to the students of the religious life and historical geography of ancient and medieval India with some additional matter. It is hoped that the work will continue to prove useful to those for whom it is intended.

The book has been printed in the photolithographic process so that modifications in the text had to be indicated in the *Addenda et Corrigenda*. A large number of these became necessary for the political changes in the country such as the partition of the subcontinent and of certain provinces, districts, etc., as well as the creation of numerous administrative units of different categories resulting from the merger of the Native States, the reorganisation of the railways and the policy of reorganising the provinces on a linguistic basis followed after our independence. In such cases, we have sometimes avoided a change when it appeared to be minor or indicated it in an unorthodox way. Only in a few places of the book, changes were necessitated by new discoveries and further studies.

The index has been compiled by Dr. N. N. Bhattacharya, Senior Research Fellow at the Centre of Advanced Study in Ancient Indian History and Culture, Calcutta University, to whom my thanks are due.

645, New Alipore, Calcutta, D. C. SIRCAR
15th December, 1971.

PREFACE

First Edition

Tantric studies have not much progressed in India. The author of the present monograph originally approached the Tantra literature as a student of ancient and medieval Indian geography, although the subject under discussion in the following pages soon proved to be equally interesting from the viewpoint of the religious life of India. A Tantra text on the Śākta Pīthas, entitled *Pīṭhanirṇya* or *Mahāpīṭhanirūpaṇa*, has been edited here with notes and an attempt has been made in that connection to trace the history of the Pīṭha conception with reference not only to the Puranic legend in theoretical explanation of the origin of the Pīṭhas but also to the real basis of the conception itself. No less than six manuscripts and four published sources have been utilized in editing the *Pīṭha-nirṇaya* (*Mahāpīṭhanirūpaṇa*). A reconstructed text of the original work has been given in as Appendix, while a large number of relevant texts has been quoted either in the notes or in the Appendixes. The author has also discussed, however summarily, the location of several hundrdes of *tīrthas* or holy places, mentioned in various works as Pīṭhas. Much, unfortunately, still remains to be done in this direction. Any suggestion form the readers for the improvement of the work will be carefully considered and gratefully acknowledged.

The author is extremely thankful to Prof. H. C. Raychaudhuri and Dr. J. N. Banerjea of the Calcutta University, who have taken interest in the preparation of the monograph and have offered some valuable suggestions. His thanks are also due to Drs. R. C. Majumdar, I. B. Banerji and B. K. Ghosh for some help and suggestions. Mr. S. K. Saraswati has laid the author under a debt of gratitude by lending him a valuable manuscript (MS. G) of the *Pīṭhanirṇaya* from his own collection. As however, the manuscript was received after the monograph had been ready for the press, it has been utilized mainly in the notes on the text and in reconstructing the probable original text of the work for Appendix I—A.

Finally, the author thanks the authorities and managment of the Royal Asiatic Society of Bengal and the Baptist Mission Press, Calcutta.

D. C. Sircar

Department of
Ancient Indian History and Culture,
Calcutta University.
September 8, 1948.

CONTENTS

Subject *Page*

Foreword (Louis Renou) vii
The Pīṭhanirṇaya or Mahāpīṭhanirūpaṇa 3
Date of its Composition 4
An Ancient Legend 5
Its Development into the Dakṣa-yajña Story 5
Further Development of the Legend to explain the Origin of the Pīṭhas 6
Conception of the Yonikuṇḍa and Stanakuṇḍa associated with that of the Liṅga 7
Some Early Tīrthas associated with the Limbs of the Mother-goddess 8
The Tradition about Four Pīṭhas 11
The Tantric Schools of North-Western and Eastern India 15
Different Traditions regarding the Number of the Pīṭhas 17
Evidence of the Jñānārṇava and the Tantrasāra regarding the Number of the Pīṭhas 20
The Tradition about 108 Pīṭhas. 24
Freedom of the Writers on the Pīṭhas from any common Tradition 32
The List of the Pīṭhas in the Pīṭhanirṇaya (Mahāpīṭhanirupana) 35
Modification of the Pīṭhanirṇaya (Mahāpīṭhanirūpaṇa) in the Sivacarita 38
List of the Pīṭhas (Mahāpīṭhas) and Upapīṭhas in the Sivacarita .. 39
Materials utilized in the Present Edition of the Pīṭhanirṇaya (Mahāpīṭhanirūpaṇa) 41
Text of the Pīṭhanirṇaya (Mahāpīṭhanirūpaṇa) 42
Appendix I—A. Probable Original Text of the Pīṭhanirṇaya (Mahāpīṭhanirūpaṇa) Reconstructed on the basis of Manuscript G and the Annadāmaṅgala 59
B. Modified Text of the Pīṭhanirṇaya as found in Manuscript H 61
Appendix II — Puranic Text containing 108 Names of the Mother-goddess (Nāmāṣṭottaraśatam) 66
Appendix III— Evolution of the Dakṣayajña Story (Dakṣayajña-kathā-mūlam) 70
Appendix IV—Date of the Tantrasāra 74
Appendix V—An Index of Pīṭhas 80
Appemdix VI—Śiva and Śakti in the Orthodox Indian Pantheon .. 100

INTRODUCTION.

The Pīṭhanirṇaya or Mahāpīṭhanirūpaṇa.

There are three manuscripts of a very small work entitled *Pīṭhanirṇaya* or *Mahāpīṭhanirūpaṇa* (Nos. 196, 3400 and 5303) in the Government Collection of the library of the Royal Asiatic Society of Bengal. The work describes the fifty-one Pīṭhas (literally, altars or seats)[1] or places of pilgrimage, considered to be the favourite resorts of the mother-goddess who is variously known as Devī, Śakti Durgā, Pārvatī, Umā, Ambikā, Aparṇā, Kālī, Gaurī, etc., and is represented in Indian mythology as the wife of the great god Śiva.[2] The Pīṭhas are mentioned together with the names of particular forms of the Devī and of the accompanying Bhairava (form of Śiva) associated with each of them. It is admitted in the text that it forms a section of a Tantra work entitled *Tantracūḍāmaṇi*. Such works as the *Śabdakalpadruma* (1822–52) and the *Prāṇatoṣaṇī Tantra* (1820), which quote the same text of the descriptive list of fifty-one Pīṭhas, also ascribe it to the *Tantracūḍāmaṇi*. The Bengali poem *Annadāmaṅgala* (1752) by Bhāratacandra refers its section on the 'fifty-one' Pīṭhas, although it actually mentions only forty-two names of holy places and does not

---

[1] In early times altars (*pīṭhas*) appear to have been used as objects of aniconic worship. Sacred spots where particular Yogins or ascetics meditated and succeeded in attaining to *siddhi* or perfection are regarded as *Pīṭha* or *Siddhapīṭha*. The *Sarvānandataraṅgiṇī* refers to Mehāra, a Parganā in the Tippera District, as a Pīṭha-sthala, because Sarvānanda attained his Tantric *siddhi* there.

[2] The different names of the mother-goddess appear to have originally indicated different tribal deities who were afterwards identified with the wife of Śiva-Paśupati (Vedic Rudra), a pre-Aryan god, known to have been worshipped by the Mohenjodaro people. *Devī* means the 'goddess *par excellence*'. *Śakti* (force) and *Ādyā Śakti* (the primeval force) indicate the power underlying creation and the controlling energy responsible for the universal order, the first name being often applied to the energizing power of the different gods. The name *Sakti* is also applied to the female organ worshipped by the Śāktas (devotees of the mother-goddess) just as the Śaivas adore the Phallus of Śiva, i.e. Śiva in the form of the Phallus; cf. Apte, Sanskrit-English Dictionary, s.v.; also *yonistotra* quoted in *Des. Cat. Sans. MSS.*, R.A.S.B., VIII, p. 806:

भगरूपा जगन्माया (°न्माता) सृष्टिस्थितिलयान्विता ।
दशविद्यास्वरूपात्मा योनिर्मां पातु सर्वदा ॥ See *infra*, Appendix VI.

The names *Durgā* and *Pārvatī* emphasize their relation with inaccessible mountain regions (especially the Himālaya of which the Indian mother-goddess is conceived as a daughter) and suggest that these were originally names of deities worshipped by mountaineers (cf. Śiva's name *Giriśa* meaning a dweller of the mountains). The names *Umā* (cf. Ommo on the coins of Huviṣka) and *Ambikā* are derived from the Dravidian word *amma* (mother) in the sense of the universal mother. *Aparṇā* signifies the deity 'who is without her leaf-cloth', i.e. naked, nakedness being one of the striking characteristics of the Indian mother-goddess. She must have originally been worshipped by a tribe such as the Nagna-Śabara (the naked Śabaras) of the *Bṛihatsaṁhitā*, just as the Buddhist deity Parṇaśabarī was undoubtedly associated with the Parṇa-Śabaras (the leaf-clad Śabaras) of the same work. See *J.K.H.R.S.*, I, pp. 87-88. *Kālī* or the dark-complexioned deity may have been the goddess of some dark-skinned pre-Dravidian tribe; but the name may not be entirely unconnected with the conception of Kāla (time or death) with which Śiva is identified. *Gaurī* means the white-complexioned goddess and possibly points to her original worship among the Mongoloid xanthoderms of the Himalayan region. The name *Mahāmayā* apparently represents the mother-goddess as the spirit guiding the magician priests of primitive peoples. The name was later given a philosophical interpretation. Cf. other names like Yogamāyā. *Kātyāyanī*, although it may indicate a deified lady or a family or tribal goddess (Aryan ?), means 'a middle-aged widow in red clothes'. Cf. *Dākṣāyaṇī*, *Kauśikī*. She is also called the 'maiden', the 'angry' or 'fierce' one and 'death' (Kālanidrā).

follow the order in which the Pīṭhas are mentioned in the list of the *Pīṭhanirṇaya*, to the *Mantracūḍāmaṇi Tantra* which would appear to be a mistake for *Tantracūḍāmaṇi*.[1] The library of the Royal Asiatic Society of Bengal possesses a manuscript of the Tantra text entitled *Tantracūḍāmaṇi* (No. I, F3); but, although it gives a list of the Pīṭhas (p. 178) in connection with the later form of a Tantric ritual known as *Pīṭhanyāsa*, that has little to do with the text of the *Pīṭhanirṇaya*. As the *Pīṭhanirṇaya* or *Mahāpīṭhanirūpaṇa*, avowedly a part of the *Tantracūḍāmaṇi*, cannot be traced in the Tantra of this name in the Society's library, one has to suggest alternatively either that there are more than one Tantric text entitled *Tantracūḍāmaṇi* and the *Pīṭhanirṇaya* belonged to a different work of this name, or that the ascription of the *Pīṭhanirṇaya* to the *Tantracūḍāmaṇi*, although it is supported by various sources, is without any real foundation. It is, however, very probable that the author of the *Pīṭhanirṇaya* wanted to credit his small work with a stamp of authority by falsely claiming it to be a part of an earlier Tantra entitled *Tantracūḍāmaṇi* mentioned in the encyclopedia of Tantric knowledge known as the *Tantrasāra* (pp. 515, 948). This is possibly suggested by the uncertainty felt by some writers about the name of the source of the *Pīṭhanirṇaya*, variously given as the *Tantracūḍāmaṇi*, *Mantracūḍāmaṇi*, *Candracūḍāmaṇi*, *Bhāvacūḍāmaṇi* and *Pīṭhamālā* (*vide infra*, pp. 42, note 2; 58, note 10).

Date of its Composition.

The text of the *Pīṭhanirṇaya* or *Mahāpīṭhanirūpaṇa*, which is silent as to the date of its composition, seems to have been prepared in the late medieval period. The number of the recognized Pīṭhas given as fifty-one probably points to the seventeenth or the eighteenth century (*vide infra*, pp. 23-24). But the problem of its date is involved in a bigger question

---

[1] Cf. Vaṅgavāsī ed., p. 42: आमि कहि मन्त्रचूड़ामणितन्त्र मत । A few manuscripts of the work in question read *Bhāvacūḍāmaṇi* or *Candracūḍāmaṇi* in place of *Tantracūḍāmaṇi*. The *Rājamālā* (a Bengali chronicle of the kings of Tipperah), *Lahara* ascribed usually to the middle of the fifteenth century, quotes verse 18 of the *Pīṭhanirṇaya* (*Mahāpīṭhanirūpaṇa*) but refers it to the *Pīṭhamālā Tantra* which seems to be found in some manuscripts as the name of this small work or that of its source. No such manuscripts are, however, known to us. The *Rājamālā* says,

दक्षकन्या सती अङ्ग पतन येस्थाने ।
महापीठनिर्णय मुनि वलिछे पुराणे ॥
शिववाक्य पीठमाला तन्त्रेर प्रमाण ।
येइ राज्ये येइ अङ्ग सेइ पीठस्थान ॥
सेइ राज्ये एक देवी भैरव आर जन ।
दुइ नामे पीठस्थान करे निरूपण ॥
सतीर दक्षिण पद पड़े त्रिपुराते ।
त्रिपुरासुन्दरी ख्याति त्रिपुर भूमिते ॥
त्रिपुरेश नामे शिव त्रिपुरा राज्येते ।

It will be clear from our discussion on the text of the *Pīṭhanirṇaya* (*vide infra*) that the above passage of the *Rājamālā* could have been written only after the middle of the eighteenth century. It cannot be assigned to the fifteenth century as it follows interpolations in a work written not much earlier than the beginning of the eighteenth century.

Bhāratacandra's section on the Pīṭhas, styled *Pīṭhamālā*, may have given rise to the name of an imaginary *Pīṭhamālā Tantra*.

regarding the origin and evolution of the conception of the Pīṭhas with special reference to their recognized number in different works of various periods.

An Ancient Legend

There is a legend offering a mythological explanation of the origin of the Pīṭhas. The earlier versions have nothing, however, to do with the Pīṭhas. The germ of the legend can be traced in the *Ṛgveda* (X, 61, 5–7); but it received its final form in the latest *Purāṇas* and *Tantras* assignable to the late-medieval period. The Ṛgvedic tradition about the incestuous relation of a father with his daughter was elaborated in the *Brāhmaṇas* such as the *Śatapatha* (*Mādhyandina* version, I, vii, 4, 1–8; cf. II, i, 2, 9; *Kāṇva* version, II, vii, 2, 1–8; I, i, 2, 5-6) and *Aitareya* (III, 33-34); cf. also *Tāṇḍyamahābrāhmaṇa*, VIII, ii, 10-11.[1] According to the story found in these *Brāhmaṇas*, once Prajāpati, identified with *Yajña* or sacrifice, committed incest with his own daughter Dyaus or Ūṣas. Disgusted at this vile act of their father, the gods approached Rudra and requested him to pierce Prajāpati with his arrow. Rudra discharged an arrow at Prajāpati whereupon the latter's *retas* (germinal fluid) fell upon the ground. As Prajāpati represents sacrifice itself and as no part of his body could be thrown away without being utilized in the performance of sacrifice, the gods first took Prajāpati's *retas* to Bhaga who sits on the southern side of the sacrificial ground. Bhaga looked at the thing and at once his eyes were burned. The gods then took it to Pūṣan who, on tasting it, lost his teeth. The concluding part of the story is unnecessary for our purpose. But the first portion of the legend is found a little developed in the *Gopatha Brāhmaṇa* (II, 1), according to which Prajāpati, while performing a sacrifice, did not offer the requisite share of offerings to Rudra who thereupon 'seizing and piercing it (*Yajña* or *Yajñāṅga*) cut off a portion from it'. A look at it is said to have made Bhaga blind and Pūṣan toothless.

Its Development into the Dakṣa-yajña Story.

The same legend later (sometime before the rise of the Guptas in the fourth century A.D.) developed into the well-known story of the destruction of the sacrifice of Dakṣa-Prajāpati by the god Śiva, also called Rudra. The earliest form of the legend of *Dakṣa-yajña-nāśa* is probably to be traced in the *Mahābhārata* (XII, chapters 282-83; cf. *Brahma Purāṇa*, ch. 39) and a slightly modified form of the same story is found in many of the Purāṇas (*Matsya*, ch. 12; *Padma*, *Sṛṣṭikhaṇḍa*, ch. 5; *Kūrma*, I, ch. 15; *Brahmāṇḍa*, ch. 31, etc.) as well as in the *Kumārasambhava* (I, 21) of Kālidāsa who flourished in the fourth and fifth centuries and adorned the court of the Gupta Vikramādityas. According to this modified version of the legend, the mother-goddess, who was the wife of Śiva, was in the form of Satī one of the daughters of Dakṣa Prajāpati. Dakṣa was celebrating a great sacrifice for which neither Satī nor Śiva was invited. Satī, however, went to her father's sacrifice uninvited, but was greatly insulted by Dakṣa. As a result of this ill-treatment, Satī is said to have died by *yoga* or of a broken heart, or, as Kālidāsa says, she put herself into fire and perished. In the *Mahābhārata* version of the story, referred to above, the wife of Śiva is only responsible for pointing out, to her husband, Dakṣa's impertinence in disregarding the great god; but she is neither said to have been Dakṣa's

[1] See Appendix II.

daughter nor to have died at Dakṣa's house as a result of the latter's ill-treatment. It will be seen that the two strains of the legend as found in the *Brāhmaṇas*, viz. Prajāpati insulting his own daughter and disregarding Rudra-Śiva, have both been cleverly accommodated in the story of the Purāṇas. When the news of Satī's death reached her husband, Śiva is said to have become furious and hastened to the scene with his numerous attendants. The sacrifice of Prajāpati Dakṣa was completely destroyed. Śiva, according to some of the sources, decapitated Dakṣa who was afterwards restored to life and thenceforward acknowledged the superiority of Śiva to all gods. According to some subversions of the story, Dakṣa was punished by the demon Vīrabhadra, created for the purpose by Śiva. The hand of a sectarian devotee of Śiva, eager to glorify his tutelary deity, is quite clear in the above story. It also shows that Śiva was originally a non-Aryan deity who later secured a prominent position in the Brahmanical pantheon. That, however, the story of *Dakṣa-yajña-nāśa* evolved out of the old legend about Prajāpati found in the *Brāhmaṇas* is proved by the fact that the Puranic account (cf. *Bhāgavata*, IV, 5, 20-21; *Kālikā*, XVII, 42-49; etc.)[1] of the destruction of Dakṣa Prajāpati's sacrifice often refers to the blinding of Bhaga's eyes and the breaking of Pūṣan's (or, Sūrya's) teeth, incidents pointedly mentioned in the *Brāhmaṇas*. The sixteenth century Bengali poet Mukundarāma, in the *Dakṣa-yajña-bhaṅga* section of his *Caṇḍīmaṅgala* (Calcutta University ed., I, p. 48) speaks of the blindness of Bhaga and the toothlessness of Pūsan, both said to have been caused by Vīrabhadra on behalf of Śiva.[2]

Further Development of the Legend to explain the Origin of the Pīṭhas.

In still later times, probably about the earlier part of the medieval period,[3] a new legend was engrafted to the old story simply for the sake of explaining the origin of the Pīṭhas. According to certain later Purāṇas and Tantras (*Devībhāgavata*, VII, ch. 30; *Kālikā Purāṇa*, ch. 18; etc.), Śiva became inconsolable at the death of his beloved wife Satī, and, after the destruction of Dakṣa's sacrifice, he wandered over the earth in mad dance with Satī's dead body on his shoulder (or, head). The gods now became anxious to free Siva from his infatuation and made a conspiracy to deprive him of his wife's dead body. Thereupon Brahman, Viṣṇu and Śani entered the dead body by *yoga* and disposed of it gradually and

---

[1] Cf. विश्रान्तमेव तं यज्ञे प्रथमं पुरतो भगः ।***
तमागतमभिप्रेक्ष्य भर्गोऽपि श्मश्रुरोषितः ।
अङ्गुष्ठाग्रप्रहारेण तस्य नेत्रे जघान च ॥***
ततस्तस्य सूर्यस्य क्रोधेन वृषभध्वजः ।
दन्तान् करप्रहारेण पातयामास वक्त्रतः ॥ (कालिकापुराण)

For the evidence of the Bhāgavata, see Appendix II.

[2] भगेर लोचन करिला मोचन
पूषार भाङ्गिलाम दन्त । (चण्डीमङ्गल)

[3] The *Brahmavaivarta Purāṇa*, an old work known to Albīrūnī, contains interpolations of a date later than the Muslim occupation of eastern India where the Purāṇa was modified; cf. I, 10, 121 referring to the caste called Jolā (from *Julāhā*, weaver) said to have originated from Mleccha (Mahomedan) father and a girl of the Indian weaver caste. *Op. cit.*, IV, 43, 25, referring to Siddha-pīṭhas associated with Satī's limbs should similarly be assigned to a date not earlier than the 14th or 15th century. For the date of the *Kālikā Purāṇa*, see *infra*, p. 12, note 5.

bit by bit. The places where pieces of Satī's dead body fell are said to have become Pīṭhas, i.e. holy seats or resorts of the mother-goddess, in all of which she is represented to be constantly living in some form together with a Bhairava, i.e. a form of her husband Śiva. According to a modified version of this story, it was Vishṇu who, while following Śiva, cut Satī's dead body on Śiva's shoulder or head piece by piece by his arrows or his discus. The story of the association of particular limbs of the mother-goddess with the Śākta *tīrthas*, which may have some relation with the Tantric ritual called *Pīṭhanyāsa*,[1] belongs, as already pointed out, to the latest stage in the development of an ancient tale. But the story may have some connection with Buddhist legends regarding the worship of Buddha's corporeal relics and the construction of *Stūpas* in order to enshrine them (cf. *Select Inscriptions*, I, pp. 84, 102ff., 120, etc.) as well as with those concerning the various manifestations of Buddha in the Jambudvīpa (cf. the list of 56 countries in the *Candragarbhasūtra; I.C.*, VIII, pp. 34-35; *BEFEO*, V, p. 261f.). One cannot also fail to recall in this connection Plutarch's version of the Egyptian Osiris myth: Osiris's brother Set put Osiris in a wooden coffin which he nailed up and cast into the sea; the waves bore it to Syria where, long after, Osiris's sister and wife Isis found it and took the body to Egypt; there unfortunately Set 'found it and scattered the bones far and wide, whence came the innumerable relics of Osiris shown to the faithful of later days in the temples of Egypt' (*Camb Anc. Hist.*, I, p. 332). The mythological interpretation of the genesis of the Pīṭhas, however, has little bearing on the real origin and development of the Pīṭha conception.

Conception of the Yonikuṇḍa and Stanakuṇḍa associated with that of the Liṅga.

The idea of the Pīṭha, associated with certain limbs of the mother-goddess, seems to be essentially connected with that of the Liṅga or phallus. The worship of the *Liṅga* of the great god Śiva originated from the conception of the god as the father or procreator. But in the matter of the procreation of beings the *Yoni* (*pudendum muliebre*) of the mother-goddess should naturally be regarded as much important as the Liṅga of the father-god. Both the Father-god and the Mother-goddess were worshipped by the pre-Aryan peoples of India.[2] The objects discovered at Mohenjodaro show that Śiva and Śakti were worshipped not only in the human form but also in the symbolic form of the Liṅga and the Yoni the former representing procreation and virility and the latter motherhood and fertility (Marshall, *Mohenjodaro and Indus Civilization*, I, pp. 52ff.). The *Ṛgveda* (VII, 21, 5; X, 99, 3) speaks in a deprecatory manner of a class of people called *śiśna-deva* in which we have probably the earliest literary reference to the worshippers of the phallus. The actual worship of the *Yoni* of the Divine Mother is referred to in certain later Tantric texts such as the *Yonitantra* (cited *infra*). It is interesting to note that one of the popular names of

---

[1] Vide *Śabdakalpadruma*, s.v. *nyāsa*; cf. *aṅganyāsa* (touching limbs with the hand accompanied by appropriate *mantras*) and *ṣoḍhānyāsa* (six ways of touching the body with mystical *mantras*) from which the *pīṭhavinyāsa* seems to have later evolved. Originally certain limbs were mentioned in connection with a Tantric ritual in which the names of the Pīṭhas were afterwards introduced. In explaining *pīṭhanyāsa*, the *Vācaspatya* says पीठदेवतानाम् आधारशक्तिप्रकृत्यादीनां प्रणवादिनमोन्तेन हृदये न्यासभेदे तन्त्रसारः, etc. The association of the limbs of the *sādhaka* with certain localities may have given rise to the belief regarding the Pīṭhas arising from particular limbs of the mother-goddess.

[2] See *infra*, Appendix VI.

the mother-goddess is *Bhagavatī* (literally, a deity possessing the *bhaga*). As the word *bhaga* is a synonym of *Yoni*, it is possible to suggest (although it is not easy to prove it in the present state of our knowledge) that the expression *Bhagavatī* originally indicated the female deity who was thought to have given birth to all creatures, and that the epithet *Bhagavat*, applied to Śiva and other gods, is merely a masculine form afterwards coined on the basis of *Bhagavatī*. It should also be pointed out that hills or mountain-peaks roughly resembling a human phallus were regarded in ancient times as the *svayambhū* (natural) *Liṅga* of Śiva. There is reason to believe that tanks or pools of a particular shape were often conceived as the *Yoni* of the mother-goddess. A pair of hills or peaks of the shape and position of female breasts appear sometimes to have been likewise regarded as the *Stana* of the goddess; cf. Kālidāsa's description (*Raghuvaṃśa*, IV, 51)[1] of the Malaya and Dardura mountains in the Pāṇḍya country as the two breasts of the lady that is the southern quarter. Water coming out of the springs on such hills could be very naturally taken to be the milk of the mother-goddess. All the three conceptions, viz. those of the *Liṅga* of the father-god and the *Yoni* and *Stana* of the mother-goddess, are based on the bearing the three particular limbs have on the birth and growth of beings as well as on the resemblance that particular natural objects may have with certain human limbs. An idea of the importance the Indians of ancient times must have attached to a bath in the *Yoni-kuṇḍa* and to the drinking of the water of the *Stanakuṇḍa* may be formed from another ritual known as the *Hiraṇyágarbha-mahādāna*, which was conceived in imitation of the *Yonikuṇḍa* of the mother-goddess. A pious prince desiring merit and willing to perform the *mahādāna* is sometimes found to have made a *hiraṇya-garbha* or 'golden womb' which was a big pot made of gold and was three cubits in height. He then entered the pot, of which the priests performed the ceremonies of *garbhādhāna*, *puṃsavana* and *sīmantonnayana*, as they would do in the case of an ordinary pregnant woman. The prince was afterwards taken out of the 'golden womb' and the *jātakarman* and other necessary functions were performed by the priests as if the prince was a newly born child. Thereafter the prince declared, 'O the best of gods, previously I was given birth to by my mother and had only the qualities of an earthly creature; but now owing to my rebirth from your womb I have a celestial body' (cf. *Suc. Sāt.*, pp. 52–54). The celebration of the *Hiraṇyagarbha-mahādāna* was adapted from a ceremonial practice of the devotees of the mother-goddess by the worshippers of the male god Viṣṇu. Just like the concept of the *Liṅga*, that of the *Yoni* and *Stana* of the mother-goddess appears to be very old. The history of the socio-religious life in ancient India suggests that these conceptions, like many others, are due to non-Aryan influence on the culture of the Indo-Aryans.[2]

Some Early Tīrthas associated with the Limbs of the Mother-goddess.

It seems that the association of the *Yoni* and *Stana* of the mother-goddess with certain localities belongs to the earliest stage of the history of the Pīṭhas. The *Tīrtha-yātrā* section in the Vanaparvan of the *Mahābhārata*, which is probably earlier than the rise of the Guptas in the fourth century A.D., refers at least to three Śākta holy places associated with the *Yoni* and *Stana* of Śakti. These are the *Yonikuṇḍas* at the Bhīmāsthāna near the Pañchanada (Punjab) and on the hill or mountain-peak called Udyatparvata, and the *Stanakuṇḍa* on the peak known as Gaurīśikhara

1 स्तनाविव दिशस्तस्याः शैलौ मलयदर्दुरौ ।

2 See *infra*, Appendix VI.

(cf. *Mahābhārata*, III, 82, 83–85; III, 84, 93–95 and 151–53).[1] The name of the Gauriśikhara (literally, the peak of Gaurī, a form of the mother-goddess) probably connects the peak with the Himalayas.[2] The *Mahābhārata* seems to locate both the Gauriśikhara and the Udyatparvata in eastern India, the latter probably in the Gayā region. Their exact location is not beyond doubt, although it is tempting to identify the Gauriśikhara with the peak of that name placed by the *Pīṭhanirṇaya* in the Kāmarūpa country in the Gauhati region of Assam. The Bhīmāsthāna (literally, the resort of Bhīmā, a form of the mother-goddess) was situated on the Karamar not far from Shahbazgarhi in the Peshawar District of the North-Western Frontier Province. The *Mārkaṇḍeya Purāṇa* (ch. 91, vv. 45-46), an early Śākta work, speaks of the goddess Bhīmādevī of the Himācala (cf. also Appendix II, v. 22 *infra*). In the seventh century, this holy *tīrtha* belonging to the ancient country of Gandhāra (Rawalpindi-Peshawar region) was visited by the Chinese pilgrim Hiuen Tsang. According to the pilgrim, 'About 50 *li* (nearly 8 miles) to the north-east of Palusha was a great mountain which had a likeness of Maheśvara's spouse Bhīmādevī of dark blue stone. According to local accounts this was a natural image (*svayambhū mūrti*) of the goddess; it exhibited prodigies and was a great resort of devotees from all parts of India; to true believers, who after fasting seven days

---

1 (*a*) अथ पञ्चनदं गत्वा नियतो नियताशनः ।
पञ्चयज्ञानवाप्नोति क्रमशो येऽनुकीर्त्तिताः ॥
ततो गच्छेत राजेन्द्र भीमायाः स्थानमुत्तमम् ।
तत्र स्नात्वा तु योन्यां वै नरो भारतसत्तम ॥
देव्याः पुत्रो भवेद् राजन् रत्नकुण्डलविग्रहः ।
गवां शतसहस्रस्य फलं प्राप्नोति मानवः ॥
(*b*) उद्यन्तञ्च ततो गच्छेत् पर्वतं गीतनादितम् ।
सावित्र्यास्तु पदं तत्र दृश्यते भरतर्षभ ॥
तत्र सन्ध्यामुपासीत ब्राह्मणः संशितव्रतः ।
तेन ह्युपास्ता भवति सन्ध्या द्वादशवार्षिकी ॥
योनिद्वारञ्च तत्रैव विश्रुतं भरतर्षभ ।
तत्राभिगम्य मुच्यते पुरुषो योनिसङ्कटात् ॥
कृष्णशुक्लावुभौ पक्षौ गयायां यो वसेन्नरः ।
पुनात्यासप्तमं राजन् कुलं नास्त्यत्र संशयः ॥
(*c*) ततो गच्छेत धर्मज्ञ तीर्थसेवनतत्परः ।
शिखरं वै महादेव्या गौर्यास्त्रैलोक्यविश्रुतम् ॥
समारुह्य नरश्रेष्ठ स्तनकुण्डेषु संविशेत् ।
स्तनकुण्डमुपस्पृश्य वाजपेयफलं लभेत् ॥
तत्राभिषेकं कुर्वाणः पितृदेवार्चने रतः ।
हयमेधमवाप्नोति शक्रलोकञ्च गच्छति ॥

The same section of the *Mahābhārata* (III, ch. 83, verses 51, 58, 94, 99, 102, etc.) speaks of other places of pilgrimage, designated Mātṛ-tīrtha or Devī-tīrtha apparently named after the mother-goddess. It is unknown whether they were associated with any of the limbs of the goddess.

2 Cf. *Gaurī-guru* (father of Gaurī), an epithet of the Himālaya in *Raghu*, II, 26; *Kirāta*, V, 21; Badal pillar inscription, verse 5 (*Gauḍalekhamālā*, p. 27), etc.

prayed to her, the goddess sometimes showed herself and answered prayers. At the foot of the mountain was a temple to Maheśvaradeva (Śiva) in which the ash-smearing *Tirthikas* (Pāśupata Yogins) [1] performed much worship' (Watters, *On Yuan Chwang's Travels in India*, I, p. 221).[2] The account of

---

[1] In his description of Benares, Hiuen Tsang again refers to the devotees of Śiva some of whom 'cut off their hair, others made it into a top-knot; some went about naked and smeared themselves with ashes; they were persevering in austerities seeking release from mortal existence' (*loc. cit.*, II, p. 47). For the ash-smearing ascetics, see *Bṛhatsaṃhitā*, ch. 60, verse 19:

विष्णोर्भागवतान् मगांश्च सवितुः शम्भोः सभस्मद्विजान्
मातॄणामपि मातृमण्डलविदो विप्रान् विदुर्ब्रह्मणः ।
शाक्यान् सर्वहितस्य शान्तमनसो नग्नान् जिनानां विदु-
र्ये यं देवमुपाश्रिताः स्वविधिना तैस्तस्य कार्याः क्रियाः ॥

While annotating this verse, Albīrūnī (*op. cit.*, p. 121) refers to the devotees of Mahādeva (Śambhu-Śiva) as 'a class of saints, anchorites with long hair, who cover their skin with ashes, hang on their persons the bones of dead people, and swing in the pools'. They are the Śiva-bhāgavatas described by Patañjali in his commentary on Pāṇini, V, 2, 76, and were related to the Kāpālikas known from works like the *Pañcatantra* as characterized by carrying skulls of men in the form of garlands and eating and drinking from them. For this sect, cf. the *Mattavilāsaprahasana* attributed to Pallava Mahendravarman I (*c.* 600–35 A.D.), Bhavabhūti's *Mālatīmādhava* (eighth century), an Early Calukyā inscription, dated 639 A.D. (referring to the worship of the god Śiva Kāpāleśvara, i.e. lord of the wearers of skull-garlands, and to the maintenance of the Mahāvratins, i.e. observers of the great vow characteristic of the Kāpālikas or Kālāmukhas, who resided in the temple of the god), etc. See R. G. Bhandarkar, *Vaiṣṇavism, Śaivism*, etc. (Poona ed.), pp. 165ff.

Bhavabhūti's *Mālatīmādhava* speaks of a woman styled *yoginī*, who performed the *Kāpālikavrata* at the Śrīparvata and illustrates the *vrata* by the horrible activities of Aghoraghaṇṭa and his female disciple Kapālakuṇḍalā who are represented as coming from the Śrīparvata and staying near the *mahāśmaśāna* (at Padmāvatī in the Gwalior State) containing a temple of Cāmuṇḍā to whom they were going to offer the girl Mālatī in sacrifice. This eighth century authority not only testifies to the prevalence of human sacrifice before the mother-goddess but also to the interesting fact that the Kāpālikas were devoted to both Śiva and Śakti. The practices of the Kāpālikas are often called *Vīrācāra* and *Vāmācāra*.

'From the *Mattavilāsa-prahasana*, it becomes clear that, to a Kāpālika, the *Kapāla* is as essential as is a sacred thread to a Brāhmaṇa. If he loses it, he should provide himself with another in a stated time. He should cover his body with ashes and make himself hideous, and drink liquor from the skull of a human being..... One of the articles of faith is that the effect always resembles, to a certain extent, the cause; therefore from the practice of austerities in this life one cannot obtain bliss in another life, since austerities and bliss are of opposite nature. The Kāpālikas carried in addition to the *Kapāla* a cow's horn both for blowing during their worship and drinking from. The people of this faith associated freely with women Kāpālikas.' Cf. R. Gopalan, *History of the Pallavas*, pp. 94-95. The *Kūrma Purāṇa* (cf. I. 16, 117, etc.) distinguishes the Kāpālikas from the Pāśupatas as well as from the other Śaiva sects and says that 'the Pāśupatas hate those sects which are guided by the Tantras' (R. C. Hazra, *Puranic Rites*, p. 64; also *Ṣaṭtriṃśanmata* quoted at p. 201). Cf. the words *pākhaṇḍa* and *pākhaṇḍin* in the sense possibly of the Kāpālikas in the *Mālatīmādhava*, V, 24 and the *Mitākṣarā* on Yāj., III, 6. The *Rāj. tar.* (III, 267) refers to Śrīparvata as a centre of the Pāśupatas and also to their existence in Kashmir (I, 17; V, 404). The doctrines and practices of the Pāśupatas (distinguished from the Kāpālikas) as described in the *Kūrma Purāṇa* show that they were not extremists like the latter with whom they were sometimes identified. For the *Ātharvaśiras Upaniṣad* on the early doctrine of the Pāśupatas, see Bhandarkar, *Vaiṣṇavism, etc.*, pp. 158ff.

[2] While describing the Gandhāra country, Hiuen Tsang elsewhere (Watters, *op. cit.*, p. 215) says that at the distance of 50 *li* (about 8 miles) to the north-west of certain monasteries (including the Aśoka *stūpa* at Puṣkalāvatī, modern Mirziyarat-Charsadda area near Peshawar) there was a *stūpa* at the place where the Buddha converted the 'Mother of Demons' (the Buddhist goddess Hāritī) and that the people of the country worshipped this Demon-mother and prayed to her for offspring. The deity was apparently an aspect of the mother-goddess. The *stūpa* is now called Sāre Mākhe Ḍherī.

the foreign traveller points clearly to the importance and popularity of the ancient Bhīmā *tīrtha*. The existence of the temple of Śiva at the foot of Bhīmā's peak probably suggests that the association of a Bhairava with the Śākta Pīṭha is earlier than the seventh century. But it is not definitely known whether the Bhīmāsthāna, Udyatparvata and Gaurīśikhara were styled Pīṭhas in the technical Tantric sense of the term and whether they were counted among the recognized Pīṭhas in the days of Hiuen-Tsang.[1]

The Tradition about Four Pīṭhas.

Some of the early *Tantras* refer to four Pīṭhas. This *Catuṣpīṭha* conception may have been associated with a conception of the Sahajayāna school of the Buddhists, according to which one can rise to eternal bliss from sexual pleasure. A Sahajayāna text entitled *Catuṣpīṭhatantra* and its commentaries (one of which was copied in 1145 A.D.; cf. H. P. Sastri, *Cat. Palm-leaf and Selected Paper Manuscripts belonging to the Durbar Library, Nepal*, II, p. viii) speak of the four Pīṭhas as Ātmapīṭha, Parapīṭha, Yogapīṭha and Guhyapīṭha and deal with the various kinds of Vajrasattva's intercourse with the Yoginīs, such as Prajñāpāramitā and others. This philosophical concept of the *Catuṣpīṭha* was either the cause or the effect of the early recognition of four holy places as Pīṭhas.[2]

---

[1] See *infra*, Appendix VI. For the association of Śiva with the Pīṭhas, cf. *Devībhāgavata*, Bk. VII, ch. 30, verses 44–50:

अपश्यत्तां सतीं वह्नौ दह्यमानान्तु चित्कलाम् ।
स्कन्धेऽध्यारोपयामास हा सतीति वदन् मुहुः ॥
बभ्राम भ्रान्तचित्तः सन्नानादेशेषु शङ्करः ।
तदा ब्रह्मादयो देवाश्चिन्तामापुरनुत्तमाम् ॥
विष्णुस्तु त्वरया तत्र धनुरुद्यम्य मार्गणैः ।
चिच्छेदावयवान् सत्यास्तत्तत्स्थानेषु तेऽपतन् ॥
तत्तत्स्थानेषु तदासीन्नानामूर्त्तिधरो हरः ।
उवाच च ततो देवान् स्थानेष्वेतेषु ये शिवाम् ॥
भजन्ति परया भक्त्या तेषां किञ्चिन्न दुर्लभम् ।
नित्यं सन्निहिता यत्र निजाङ्गेषु पराम्बिका ॥
स्थानेष्वेतेषु ये मर्त्त्याः पुरश्चरणकर्मिणः ।
तेषां मन्त्राः प्रसिध्यन्ति मायाबीजं विशेषतः ॥
इत्युक्त्वा शङ्करस्तेषु स्थानेषु विरहातुरः ।
कालं निन्ये नृपश्रेष्ठ जपध्यानसमाधिभिः ॥

But the early association of Śakti and Śiva at Bhīmāsthāna does not prove that the story connecting certain *tīrthas* with Satī's limbs had already developed in the days of Hiuen Tsang. Cf. Banerjea, *Development of Hindu Iconography*, p. 92n.

[2] It is difficult to determine what relation the Catuṣpīṭha could have with the Catuṣpīṭha-parvata near Jajpur in Orissa and with other Sahajayāna conceptions of 'four', e.g. the Caturānanda. The *Caṇḍamahāroṣaṇatantra* (Sastri, *Cat.*, pp. ix-x) is said to have been uttered by Vajrasattva (Buddha) when he was staying in the female organ of Vajradhātvīśvarī. The first verse uttered is:

भावाभावविनिर्मुक्तश्चतुरानन्दतत्परः ।
निष्प्रपञ्चस्वरूपोऽहं सर्वसंकल्पवर्जितः ॥

Caturānanda, i.e. the pleasures of four kinds, has been explained as embracing, kissing, pressing the breast, and pricking with the nails (i.e. imprinting nail-marks). These are said to last as long as the *thunderbolt* is in union with the *lotus*.

In the opinion of some writers, the *Hevajra Tantra* of the Buddhists was composed shortly before 693 A.D.[1] But according to Buddhist tradition, Padmavajra, author of the *Hevajra Tantra*, was the preceptor of Anaṅgavajra, a son of king Gopāla[2] who founded the Pāla dynasty in Bengal about the middle of the eighth century A.D. If this tradition is to be accepted, the composition of the *Hevajra Tantra* may be assigned to the same century. This early work enumerates the following four holy regions as Pīṭhas: (1) Jālandhara, (2) Odiyāna (Uḍḍiyāna in the Swat valley),[3] (3) Pūrṇagiri and (4) Kāmarūpa[4] Exactly the same tradition is followed in the *Kālikā Purāṇa* (ch. 64, 43–45)[5] according to which the four Pīṭhas were: (1) Oḍra, seat of the goddess Kātyāyanī and god Jagannātha,[6] in the west, (2) Jālaśaila, seat of the goddess Caṇḍī and god Mahādeva in the north, (3) Pūrṇa or Pūrṇaśaila (Pūrṇagiri), seat of the goddess Pūrṇeśvarī and god Mahānātha, in the south, and (4) Kāmarūpa,

---

1 Cf. B. Bnattacharya, *Sādhanamālā* (G.O.S.), II, p. xliii.

2 *Op. cit.*, pp. l-li.

3 The suggestion that Oḍḍiyāna was situated in eastern India and is no other than Oḍra (Orissa) is unworthy of any serious consideration. Cf. Lévi, *Journ. As.*, 1915, pp. 105–10; P. C. Bagchi, *Studies in the Tantras*, I, pp. 37ff., 42. For some other unwarranted theories about the location of Uḍḍiyāna, see *I.H.Q.*, XI, pp. 142ff.; *J.As.R.S.*, V, pp. 14ff. For a discussion on the expressions *uḍḍiyānabandha*, *jālandharabandha*, etc., see *J.Or.Ac.*, II, pp. 55–68.

4 Cf. पीठं जालन्धरं ख्यातं ओड्डियानं तथैव च ।
पीठं पूर्णगिरिं चैव कामरूपन्तथैव च ॥

quoted by Bagchi (*op. cit.*, p. 38) from the seventh Paṭala of the *Hevajra Tantra*.

5 Cf. Vaṅgavāsī ed., p. 410:

ओड्राख्यं प्रथमं पीठं द्वितीयं जालशैलकम् ।
तृतीयं पूर्णपीठन्तु कामरूपं चतुर्थकम् ॥
ओड्रपीठं पश्चिमे तु तथैवोड्रेश्वरीं शिवाम् ।
कात्यायनीं जगन्नाथमोड्रेशञ्च प्रपूजयेत् ॥
उत्तरे पूजयेत् पीठं प्रशस्तं जालशैलकम् ।
जालेश्वरं महादेवं चण्डीं जालेश्वरीं तथा ॥
दीर्घिकाञ्चोग्रचण्डाञ्च तत्रैव परिपूजयेत् ॥
दक्षिणे पूर्णशैलन्तु तथा पूर्णेश्वरीं शिवाम् ।
पूर्णनाथं महानाथं सरोजामथ चण्डिकाम् ॥
पूजयेद्मन्तीं देवीं ग्राम्नामपि तथा शिवाम् ।
कामरूपं महापीठं तथा कामेश्वरीं शिवाम् ॥
नीलञ्च पर्वतश्रेष्ठं नाथं कामेश्वरं तथा ।
पूजयेद्द्वारि पूर्वे तु क्रमादेतांस्तु भैरव ॥

The *Kālikā Purāṇa*, quoted by Nānyadeva (c. 1097–1133 A.D.) in his *Bharatabhāṣya* and by Aparārka (c. 1115–40 A.D.) and Ballālasena (c. 1159–85 A.D.), seems to have been originally incorporated in the *Rudrayāmala Tantra*; cf. *Des. Cat. Sans. MSS., R.A.S.B.*, VIII, p. 70. This *Purāṇa* (really an Upa-Purāṇa) is earlier than 1000 A.D. according to Gode, *J.O.R.*, X, pp. 289ff.; *J.Or.Ac.*, II, p. 60. Cf. Hazra, *op. cit.*, p. 53; *infra*, p. 17, note 4. Some sections may, however, have been later added to the original *Purāṇa*.

6 Cf. the god Jagannātha in the Puri temple in Orissa (Oḍra). For the confusion of Oḍra and Oḍḍiyāna, see *infra*.

seat of the deities Kāmeśvarī and Kāmeśvara [1] in the east. That *Oḍra* in the list is a mistake for *Uḍḍiyāna* and that Jālaśaila is the same as Jālandhara are clear from another section of the same Purāṇa (ch. 18, 42–44 and 49–51) [2] representing the goddesses Kātyāyanī and Caṇḍī as the presiding deities respectively of Uḍḍiyāna and Jālandharagiri.[3] Other Buddhist works such as the *Sādhanamālā* (G.O.S., pp. 453, 455) give the four names as (1) Oḍiyāna or Uḍḍīyana, (2) Pūrṇagiri, (3) Kāmarūpa or Kāmākhyā, and (4) Śrīhaṭṭa or Sirihaṭṭa. Śrīhaṭṭa has been substituted in this list

---

[1] Cf. reference to Mahāgaurī (Kāmākhyā) and Kāmeśvara (on the Kāmakūṭa hill) in some early records of Assam; see *infra*. The identification of Mahāgaurī with Bhuvaneśī (*I.H.Q.*, XXIII, p. 324, *Kālikā P.*, 62, 127) on the top of the Kāmakhyā hill is rendered doubtful by her association with *Kāmeśvara*. The boundaries of Kāmarūpa are indicated by the *Yoginītantra* (Paṭala XI) quoted in *Ep. Ind.*, XII, p. 68:

नेपालस्य काञ्चनाद्रिं ब्रह्मपुत्रस्य सङ्गमम् ।
करतोयां समारभ्य यावद्दिक्करवासिनीम् ॥
उत्तरस्यां कञ्जगिरिः करतोया तु पश्चिमे ।
तीर्थश्रेष्ठा दिक्षु नदी पूर्वस्यां गिरिकन्यके ॥
दक्षिणे ब्रह्मपुत्रस्य लाक्षायाः सङ्गमावधिः ।
कामरूप इति ख्यातः सर्वशास्त्रेषु निश्चितः ॥

This Kāñcana or Kañja Mount is probably the Kunchenjinga. The Dikṣu, which may be associated with Dikkaravāsinī although the latter is located at Dikrang near Sadiya in north-eastern Assam, is the modern Dikhu falling in the Brahmaputra near Sibsagar. The confluence of the Lākṣā (Lakhyā) and the Brahmaputra is in the Mymensing District. The Karatoyā which now runs through North Bengal and falls in the Yamunā in the Pabna District, was the western boundary of Kāmarūpa also according to Chinese sources. A manuscript of the *Yoginī Tantra* (R.A.S.B., No. I. B. 29, p. 33) reads: नेपालस्य च काञ्चद्रिं । Some writers prefer the reading: उत्तरस्यां कुञ्जगिरिः । For Kāmarūpa's four divisions (*Pīṭhas*), viz. Kāma, Ratna, Bhadra or Suvarṇa and Saumāra, see Gait, *Hist. As.*, p. 11. Kāmarūpa is also called Kubjikā Pīṭha (*Kālikā P.*, 62, 58, etc.).

[2] Cf. Vaṅgavāsī ed., pp. 79-80:

देवीकूटे पादयुग्मं प्रथमं न्यपतत् क्षितौ ।
उड्डियाने चोरुयुग्मं क्षिताय जगतां ततः ॥
कामरूपे कामगिरौ न्यपतद् योनिमण्डलम् ।
तत्रैव न्यपतद् भूमौ पूर्वतो नाभिमण्डलम् ॥
जालन्धरे स्तनयुगं स्वर्णहारविभूषितम् ।
अंसग्रीवं पूर्णगिरौ कामरूपान्ततः शिरः ॥ * * *
देवीकूटे महादेवी महाभागेति गीयते ।
सतीपादयुगे लीना योगनिद्रा जगत्प्रभुः ॥
कात्यायनी चोड्डियाने कामाख्या कामरूपिणी (°रूपके) ।
पूर्णेश्वरी पूर्णगिरौ चण्डी जालन्धरे गिरौ ॥
पूर्वान्ते कामरूपस्य देवी दिक्करवासिनी ।
तथा ललितकान्तेति योगनिद्रा प्रगीयते ॥

For details of other Pīṭhas mentioned here, see *infra*, p. 17. For the same confusion between Oḍra (placed in north-western India) and Uḍḍiyāna in early literature, see *Mahābhārata*, II, 47, 19.

[3] The location of the Oḍra (Orissa) country in the western part of India has also to be noted. This points actually to Uḍḍiyāna in north-western India.

for Jālandhara which, however, seems to have been recognized as one of the four Pīṭhas even down to the late medieval period.[1] Abul Fazl's '*Ain-i-Akbarī*, composed about the end of the sixteenth century at the court of the Mughal emperor Akbar (1556–1605), contains an interesting description of the Pīṭha near Nagarkot together with the legend about the origin of the four Pīṭhas as known to the author. In this connection Abul Fazl says, 'Nagarkot is a city situated on a hill; its fort is called Kangrah. Near the town is the shrine of Mahāmāyā (a name of the Indian mother-goddess indicating "the goddess having great magical powers") which is considered as a manifestation of the divinity. Pilgrims from distant parts visit it and obtain their desires. Strange it is that in order that their prayers may be favourably heard, they cut out their tongues; with some it grows again on the spot, with others after one or two days. Although the medical faculty allow the possibility of growth in the tongue, yet in so short space of time it is sufficiently amazing. In the Hindu mythology Mahāmāyā is said to be the wife of Mahādeva, and the learned of this creed represent by this name the energizing power of the deity. It is said that on beholding the disrespect (shown to herself and her husband Śiva) she cut herself in pieces and her body fell in four places; her head and some of her limbs in the northern mountains of Kashmir near Kāmrāj and these relics are called Śāradā: other parts fell near Bījāpūr in the Deccan and are known as Tuljā (Turjā) Bhavānī. Such portions as reached the eastern quarter near Kāmarūpa are called Kāmākhyā, and the remnant that kept its place is celebrated as Jālandharī which is this particular spot. In the vicinity torch-like flames issue from the ground in some places, and others resemble the blaze of lamps. There is a concourse of pilgrims and various things are cast into the flames with the expectation of obtaining temporal blessings. Over them a domed temple has been erected and an astonishing crowd assembles therein. The vulgar impute to miraculous agency what is simply a mine of brimstone' (Jarrett's trans., II, pp. 312–14). The four Pīṭha-devīs recognized in the sixteenth century account are, therefore, (1) Śāradā at modern Sardi in northern Kashmir, (2) Tuljā Bhavānī in a locality in the medieval kingdom, the capital of which was at Bijapur in the southern part of the Bombay Presidency, (3) Kāmākhyā in Kāmarūpa, and (4) Jālandharī near Nagarkot in the Punjab. Abul Fazl has substituted Kashmir for Uḍḍiyāna. He refers to Jvālāmukhī and not to the neighbouring Jālandhara Pīṭha.[2] The Pīṭha that he

[1] For the tradition of the four Pīṭhas, cf. अथेदानीं प्रवक्ष्यामि अपार्थं पीठमुत्तमम्। पूर्णगिरिश्च प्रथममुड्डीयानं द्वितीयकम्॥ जालन्धरं तृतीयञ्च कामरूपं चतुर्थकम्। . . . . . मत्तेः सर्वशरीरं यत् पीठं पूर्णगिरिः स्मृतम्। तस्याः शिरश्च सुभगे उड्डीयानं प्रकीर्त्तितम्॥ स्तनौ जालन्धरं ज्ञेयं कामरूपं भगस्तथा॥ (*Samayācāra Tantra* quoted in the *Prāṇatoṣaṇī Tantra*, Vasumatī ed., p. 548); also पुण्यतीर्थं कुरुक्षेत्रे देवीपीठचतुष्टये। प्रयागे श्रीगिरौ काश्यां कालाकालं न शोधयेत्॥ (*Yāmala* quoted in the *Tantrasāra*, Vaṅgavāsī ed., p. 40). *Vide* the two *Pīṭhatattvanyāsas* mentioning the four Pīṭhas by name in the *Tantrasāra*, pp. 419-20, 451-52. The Pūrṇagiri Pīṭha is in these cases called *Uḍḍīśanāthātmaka*. For a tradition about five Pīṭhas accommodating the claim of both Jālandhara and Śrīhaṭṭa, cf. षट्चक्रं मेरुदण्डञ्च उड्डीयानं तथैव च। जालन्धरः कामरूपः पूर्णपीठः (°गिरिः) श्रीहट्टकः॥ quoted from the sixth Paṭala of the Tattvasāra in the *Prāṇatoṣaṇī Tantra*, pp. 39 and 40.

[2] For some foreign notices of Jvālāmukhī, see *Hobson-Jobson*, s.v. *Jowalla Mookhee*. In the third quarter of the fourteenth century, Shams-i-Shirāj 'Afīf (Elliot, *Hist. Ind.*, III, p. 318) mentions the idol Jvālāmukhī much worshipped by the

places in the Bijapur region may be the same as Pūrṇagiri mentioned in the other texts. The shrine of Bhavānī stands at Tuljapur to the south of Osmanabad in the Hyderabad State. Such was the celebrity of this goddess that, when Śivājī built the fort of Pratāpgarh near Javli, he set up there an image of his patron-deity Bhavānī as the Bhavānī of Tuljapur was beyond easy reach to him (J. N. Sarkar, *History of Aurangzib*, IV, p. 32). It is well known that the Thuggees (both Hindus and Muslims), many of whose organizations belonged to Western India and the Deccan, were followers of the goddess Bhavānī irrespective of their personal religious beliefs. This fact points also to the importance of the mother-goddess in the religious life of that part of India. The Śāradā-maṭha on the borders of Kashmir is mentioned in such other works as the *Śaktisaṅgama Tantra* (*I.C.*, VIII, pp. 38, 49). About 1030 A.D., Albīrūnī says (Sachau, *Alberuni's India*, I, p. 117), 'In inner Kashmir, about two or three days' journey from the capital in the direction towards the mountains of Bolor, there is a wooden idol called Śāradā, which is much venerated and frequented by pilgrims.' The temple of Śāradā is also mentioned in Kalhaṇa's *Rāj. tar.*, VIII, 2556, 2706. The ruins of Sardi, where the shrine of Śāradā stood, lie at the confluence of the Kishengaṅga and Kankatori rivers. The old shrine is substituted by the late Śāradā temple at Gusha (old Ghoṣa) which is now visited by pilgrims. See Stein, *Rāj. tar.* (trans.), II, pp. 279–89.

The Tantric Schools of North-Western and Eastern India.

Two things are apparent from the accounts of the four Pīṭhas. In the first place, Kāmarūpa has a prominent place in all the lists of four. This fact may suggest that the Kāmarūpa Pīṭha became unrivalled as a centre of Tantric culture by absorbing the popularity of the other Yoni *tīrthas* of ancient India at a fairly early date. The name of Kāmarūpa, with which that of the goddess Kāmākhyā (the original name probably being *Kāmā*, a shortened form of *Kāmarūpā*) [1] seems to be intimately associated, is mentioned in the Allahabad pillar inscription (middle of the fourth century A.D.) of Samudragupta. But the holy seat of the goddess near Gauhati in Assam does not appear to be mentioned in the *Tīrthayātrā* section of the Vanaparvan, even if the Stanakuṇḍa at Gauriśikhara is located in the neighbourhood. The Chinese pilgrim Hiuen Tsang who lived for some time at the court of the Kāmarūpa king Bhāskaravarman (*c.* 600–50 A.D.) in the seventh century, is also silent about the goddess Kāmākhyā. It is, therefore, not improbable that the presiding deity of Kāmarūpa did not quite attain to her pre-eminence in the days of Hiuen Tsang.[2] Worship of the mother-goddess was, however, widely prevalent among some of the primitive tribes of ancient Assam. The following note on the religious life of the Chutiyas of Assam throws interesting light on the subject: 'The religion of the Chutiyas was a curious one. They worshipped various forms of Kālī with the aid, not of Brāhmaṇas, but of their tribal priests or Deoris. The favourite form in which they worshipped this deity was that of Kesāi

---

infidels and situated on the road to Nagarkot and says, 'Some of the infidels have reported that Sulṭān Fīrūz went specially to see this idol and held a golden umbrella over its head.... Other infidels said that Sulṭān Muḥammad Shāh bin Tughlak Shāh held an umbrella over this same idol; but this also is a lie.'

[1] The name of the goddess is traced to the Austric words *Kāmoi* (demon), *Kāmoit* (devil), *Komin* (grave), *Kamet* (corpse in Khasi), *Kamru* (a god of the Santals), etc. Cf. B. Kakati in *Assam Tribune*, October 22, 1947.

[2] Kāmākhyā seems to be called Mahāgaurī in the records of Vanamāla (end of the 9th century) and Indrapāla (12th century), kings of Kāmarūpa. See *infra*, Appendix VI.

Khāti, "the eater of raw flesh", to whom human sacrifices were offered. After their subjugation by the Ahoms, the Deoris were permitted to continue their ghastly rites; but they were usually given, for the purpose, criminals who had been sentenced to capital punishment. Failing them, victims were taken from a particular clan, which in return was accorded certain privileges. The person selected was fed sumptuously, until he was in sufficiently plump condition to suit the supposed test of the goddess, and he was then decapitated at the Copper Temple at Sadiya, or at some other shrine of the tribe. Human sacrifices were also formerly offered by the Tipperas, Kachāriṣ, Koches, Jaintias and other Assam tribes' (E. Gait, *History of Assam*, 1926, p. 42; *J.A.S.B.*, 1898, p. 56).[1] It may be pointed out in this connection that the Chinese pilgrim noticed the influence of the Pāśupatas or Tīrthikas, with whom the Tantric devotees of Śakti and Śiva were associated, all over India—in Jālandhara, Ahicchatra (?), Malakūṭa (in the Far South), Mālava, Benares, Maheśvarapura (on the Narmadā), the land about eastern Makran, Bannu (?) and even Khotan (in Central Asia); cf. *loc. cit.*, I, 296, 331; II, 47, 229, 242, 251, 257, 262, 296, etc. Bhavabhūti's *Mālatīmādhava* not only speaks of a great centre of the Kāpālikas (cf. *supra*, p. 10, note 1), apparently devoted to the god Śiva Mallikārjuna, at Śrīparvata (Śrīśaila in the Karnool District, Madras Presidency), but also of their devotion to an image of the mother-goddess Cāmuṇḍā (another name of Tārā or Kālī according to the *Kālikā Purāṇa*, ch. 61, 85–91), entitled Karālā, in a temple at Padmāvatī (Padampawaya near Narwar in the Gwalior State).

Another point of interest in the account of the four Pīṭhas is the importance of the Gandhāra, Uḍḍiyāna, Jālandhara and Kashmir countries of north-western India as centres of Tantricism. Hiuen Tsang not only noticed the prevalence of Śakti worship in Gandhāra, but has also left an account of the popularity of Tantric practices among the people of Uḍḍiyāna. According to the pilgrim, 'The people (of Uḍḍiyāna) were pusillanimous and deceitful; they were fond of learning but not as a study, and they made the acquisition of magical formulae their occupation' (Watters, *op. cit.*, p. 225). Uḍḍiyāna's eminence in the Tantric world is also indicated by the recognized association of its name with the worship of the Buddhist deities Mārīcī, Kurukullā (identified with Kālī in some passages cited in the *Tantrasāra*), Lokeśvara and Ūrdhvapāda-Vajravārāhī (cf. *Sādhanamālā*, G.O.S., pp. 80, 83, 283ff., 361, 439). Indrabhūti, the Buddhist king of Uḍḍiyāna, was a celebrated Tantric teacher who composed the *Jñānasiddhi* and other works. He was the father of Padmasambhava, the famous teacher of the Yogācāra doctrine, who was responsible for the popularity of Buddhism in Tibet and established in that country the great Bsam-yas monastery in *c.* 787 A.D. with the help of a Bengali (?) Buddhist teacher named Śāntarakṣita or Śānti . The lady Lakṣīṃkarā, a sister of king

---

1 Cf. 'When the new temple of Kāmākhyā was opened, the occasion was celebrated by the immolation of no less than a hundred and forty men, whose heads were offered to the goddess on salvers made of copper. Similar sacrifices were offered to various aboriginal deities. According to the *Haft Iqlim*, there was in Kāmarūpa a class of persons called Bhogīs, who were voluntary victims of a goddess named Ai who dwelt in a cave; from the time when they announced that the goddess had called them, they were treated as privileged persons; they were allowed to do whatever they liked, and every woman was at their command; but when the annual festival came round, they were killed. Magic also held an important place in the estimation of the people, and in the '*Ain-i-Akbarī* they were accused, among other practices, of divination by the examination of a child cut out of the body of "a pregnant woman who has gone her full term of months"' (*History of Assam*, p. 58).

Indrabhūti, composed the Buddhist Tantra work entitled *Advayasiddhi*.[1] The rule of the Turkish Musalmans, that spread over north-western India from the tenth century, led to the gradual decline of the once flourishing Tantric culture in that part of India.

Different Traditions regarding the Number of Pīṭhas.

Although four Pīṭhas were associated roughly with the northern, southern, eastern and western regions of India,[2] writers on the subject are not unanimous as regards the exact number of the seats of the mother-goddess. The *Kālikā Purāṇa* account of the four Pīṭhas has been already noticed; but a different section of the same Purāṇa (ch. 18, verses 42–51) gives an account of seven Pīṭhas (including the four seats of the goddess described above), no less than three of which are located in Kāmarūpa. According to this section, the Pīṭhas are: (1) Devīkūṭa (i.e. Devīkoṭṭa, modern Bangarh in the Dinajpur District of Bengal) where Satī's two feet fell on the ground and where the Devī is Mahābhāgā; (2) Uḍḍiyāna where the two thighs fell and where the Devī is Kātyāyanī; (3) Kāmagiri in Kāmarūpa where the *pudendum muliebre* fell and the Devī is Kāmākhyā; (4) a locality on the eastern border of Kāmarūpa where the navel fell and where the Devī is Dikkaravāsinī; (5) Jālandhara where the two breasts fell and where the Devī is Caṇḍī; (6) Pūrṇagiri where the neck and shoulders fell and where the Devī is Pūrṇeśvarī; and (7) a locality on the borders of Kāmarūpa where the head fell and where the Devī is Lalitakāntā.[3] A Tantra work entitled *Rudrayāmala*, which seems to have been composed considerably earlier than 1052 A.D.,[4] mentions ten holy places as the 'principal' Pīṭhas. These ten Pīṭhas, which include the celebrated four discussed above are: (1) Kāmarūpa, (2) Jālandhara, (3) Pūrṇagiri, (4) Oḍḍiyāna (Uḍḍiyāna), (5) Vārāṇasī (Benares), (6) Jvalantī (probably Jvālāmukhī of later texts), (7) Māyāvatī (near Hardwar), (8) Madhupurī (Muttra), (9) Ayodhyā (near Fyzabad, U.P.), and (10) Kāñcī (Conjeeveram in the

---

[1] Cf. Bhattacharya, *op. cit.*, pp. li–liv. Bhattacharya gives the date of the foundation of the Bsam-yas monastery as 749 A.D. But the period of Padmasambhava's stay in Tibet is usually assigned to *circa* 780–95 A.D. by recent writers on the subject (F. W. Thomas, *Indianism and its Expansion*, p. 79).

[2] As the number 3 had a mystic significance with many ancient peoples of the world (cf. the Trimūrti, Triratna, Tribhuvana, etc., of the Indians, the Anu-Bel-Ea trinity of the Babylonians, and the Osiris-Isis-Horus triad of the Egyptians), there was also a tradition about three Pīṭhas; cf. *Ānandārṇava Tantra* quoted in *Des. Cat. Sans. MSS.*, R.A.S.B., VIII, p. 213:

विद्याख्यपञ्चयोपेतांस्त्रिपीठांस्त्रिदशान्तरे ।
कामरूपक-जालन्ध्र-पूर्णभूपुर(भूधर)संज्ञकान् ॥

[3] *Supra*, p. 13, note 2. A passage (probably adapted from the *Kālikā Purāṇa*) in the sixth Paṭala of the *Bṛhan-Nīlatantra* refers to the same five Pīṭhas:

देवीकोटे महाभागा उड्डीयाने च भैरवी ।
योनिमुद्रा कामरूपे महिषासुरमर्दिनी ॥
कात्यायनी कामभूमौ कामाख्या कामरूपिणी ।
जालन्धरे (पूर्णशैले) च पूर्णेशी पूर्णे शैले (जालन्धरे) च चण्डिका ॥
कामरूपे ततो देवी पूज्या दिक्करवासिनी ॥

The temple of Dikkaravāsinī is usually located at Dikrang near Sadiya. Lalitakāntā is now popularly associated with the hill-streams Sandhyā, Lalitā and Kāntā not far from Gauhati.

[4] The *Rudrayāmala* is mentioned in the *Brahmayāmala*, a manuscript of which was copied in 1052 A.D. (Bagchi, *op. cit.*, pp. 6-7). Cf. *supra*, p. 12, note 5.

Chingleput District, Madras Presidency).[1] The language of the *Rudrayāmala* suggests that its author had knowledge of some other Pīṭhas of lesser importance. A passage from this work quoted in the *Kulārṇava Tantra* (*Des. Cat. Sans. MSS.*, R.A.S.B., VIII, pp. 110-11) actually speaks of the following 18 Pīṭhas: (1) Uḍḍīyāna, (2) Devīdaikoṭha (Devīkoṭṭa), (3) Hiṅgulā, (4) Koṭimudrā, (5) Jālandhara, (6) Vārāṇasī, (7) Antarvedī, (8) Prayāga, (9) Mithilā, (10) Māgadha, (11) Mekhalā (Mekalā), (12) Aṅga, (13) Vaṅga, (14) Kaliṅga, (15) Siṃhala, (16) Strīrājya, (17) Rāḍhā and (18) Gauḍa. That, however, the list of even the *pradhāna* Pīṭhas were drawn arbitrarily without any basis of accepted tradition is clearly demonstrated by the discrepancy among similar lists of Pīṭhas found in different works. A passage of the *Jñānārṇava Tantra* (Ānandāśrama ed., Paṭala V, verses 66-67), which was composed considerably earlier than the middle of the sixteenth century,[2] enumerates eight important Pīṭhas in the following order: (1) Kāmarūpa, (2) Malaya, (3) Kaulagiri, (4) Kulāntaka, (5) Cauhāra (not mentioned in the *Jñānārṇava* list of 42 Pīṭhas and may be a result of misreading), (6) Jālandhara, (7) Uḍḍiyāna, and (8) Devakūṭa (Devīkoṭṭa).[3] As a matter of fact, there are only a few common names in the lists of the *Rudrayāmala* and the *Jñānārṇava*. Such is also the case with other lists of the Pīṭhas which usually contain only a number of common names.

There is a very small work entitled *Aṣṭādaśapīṭha* incorporated in Manuscript No. 5913 in the library of the Royal Asiatic Society of Bengal. This work, which is full of textual errors, is ascribed to Śaṅkarācārya (probably the same as Śaṅkara Āgamācārya, the Bengali author of the *Tārārahasya-vṛttikā*, an R.A.S.B. copy of which was made in Śaka 1583 = 1661 A.D.) and mentions eighteen Pīṭhas together with the Pīṭha-devīs. Although some of these names are apparently doubtful, it is interesting that the list of eighteen Pīṭhas includes: (1) Laṅkā—Śaṅkarī, (2) Ālāpura—Yugalā, (3) Śrīśaila—Bhramarāmbikā, (4) Kolhāpura—Mahālakṣmī, (5) Vārāṇasī—Viśālākṣī, and (6) Kāśmīra—Sarasvatī (Śāradā). The location of Bhramarāmbikā on the Śrīśaila and of Mahālakṣmī at Kolhapur in the southern part of the Bombay Presidency is specially interesting because Bhramarāmbā, still worshipped on the Śrīśaila, is not mentioned in the other texts, while Kolhapur reminds one of Kolvagiri, etc., and of Mahālakṣmī or Mahālakṣmīpura (cf. *I.C.*, VIII, p. 49). The interesting work on the eighteen

---

1 Vide *tārā-ṣoḍhā* in the *Rudrayāmala*, quoted in the *Tantrasāra*, Vaṅgavāsī ed., pp. 521-22:

मूलाधारे कामरूपं हृदि जालन्धरं तथा ।
ललाटे पूर्णगिर्याख्यम् ओड्डीयानं तदूर्द्ध्वके ॥
वाराणसीं भ्रुवोर्मध्ये ज्वलन्तीं लोचनत्रये ।
मायावतीं मुखवृत्ते कण्ठे मधुपुरीं ततः ॥
अयोध्यां नाभिदेशे च कट्यां काञ्चीं विनिर्दिशेत् ॥
इत्येतानि प्रधानानि पीठानि क्रमतो विदुः ।
ह्रस्वदीर्घस्वरैर्वर्गैर्नमोऽन्तैः क्रमतो न्यसेत् ॥

2 The *Jñānārṇava* is largely quoted by the Tantrācāryas Brahmānanda and Pūrṇānanda in the sixteenth century.

3 कामरूपं च मलयं ततः कौलगिरिं तथा ।
कुलान्तकं च चौहारं जालन्धरमतःपरम् ॥
उड्डीयानं देवकूटं पीठाष्टकमिदं क्रमात् ॥

Pīṭhas is said to have been written down by one Sambhunath Kar of Calcutta in Samvat 1863 = 1806 A.D. from the dictation of an Utkala Brāhmaṇa who was an inhabitant of Jahājapura (Jājpur) on the Vaitaraṇī.[1]

Another Tantra text entitled *Kubjikā Tantra*, usually supposed to be a fairly early work, enumerates the following Siddha-Pīṭhas: (1) Māyāvatī, (2) Madhupurī, (3) Kāśī, (4) Gorakṣakāriṇī or Gorakṣacāriṇī, (5) Hiṅgulā, (6) Jālandhara, (7) Jvālāmukhī, (8) Nāgarasambhava, (9) Rāmagiri, (10) Godāvarī, (11) Nepāla, (12) Karṇasūtra, (13) Mahākarṇa, (14) Ayodhyā, (15) Kurukṣetra, (16) Siṃhanāda or Siṃhala, (17) Maṇipura, (18) Hṛṣīkeśa, (19) Prayāga, (20) Badarī, (21) Ambikā, (22) Vardhamāna or Ardhanālaka, (23) Triveṇī (probably Muktaveṇī near Calcutta and not Yuktaveṇī at Prayāga which is separately mentioned), (24) Gaṅgā-sāgara-saṅgama, (25) Nārikela, (26) Virajā, (27) Uḍḍiyāna, (28) Kamalā, (29) Vimalā, (30) Māhiṣmatī, (31) Vārāhī, (32) Tripurā, (33) Vāgmatī, (34) Nīlavāhinī, (35) Govardhana, (36) Vindhyagiri, (37) Kāmarūpa, (38) Ghaṇṭākarṇa, (39) Hayagrīva or Akṣayagrīva, (40) Mādhava, (41) Kṣīragrāma, and (42) Vaidyanātha.[2]

महाकाल्यै नमः। अष्टादशपीठानि लिख्यन्ते।
लङ्कायां शङ्करी देवी कामाख्या काञ्चिकापुरी।
प्रद्युम्ने सिंग(ह)लद्वीपे चामुण्डा कुञ्चपट्टने (क्रौञ्च°?)॥
आल्लापुरे (एला°?) युगला देवी श्रीशैले भ्रमराम्बिका।
उज्जयिन्यां महाकाली माकरे (सह्याद्रौ?) एकवीरका॥
उत्कले विरजा देवी माणिक्यां(?) चक्रकोटिली(?)।
हयक्षेत्रे कामरूपी(?) प्रयागे माधवेश्वरी॥
ज्वालायां वैष्णवी देवी गया माङ्गल्यकोटिका(?)।
वाराणस्यां विशालाक्षी काश्मीरे तु सरस्वती॥
अष्टादशानि पीठानि योगिनां ध्याननिर्मितम्(?)।
तेषां पठनमात्रेण ज्वरदारिद्र्यनाशनम्॥

इति शङ्कराचार्यविरचितम् अष्टादशपीठं सम्पूर्णम्। इति श्रीशम्भुनाथकर (°करेण) उत्कलदेशस्य ब्राह्मण-जेलंपुरीकर-जहाजपुरीय-वैतरणीय-ब्राह्मणाच्छ्रुत्वा लिखितम्। संवत् १८६३ पौषकृष्णैकादश्याः शुक्रे लिखितं कलिकाताख्यपट्टने। शुभमस्तु सर्वजगताम्॥

[2] Cf. *Kubjikā Tantra* (Paṭala VII), Manuscript No. 3174 (R.A.S.B.); the same quoted in the *Prāṇatoṣaṇī Tantra* (Vasumatī ed., p. 234) and in the *Vācaspatya*, s.v. *pīṭha*.

मायावती मधुपुरी काशी गोरक्षकारिणी (v.l. °चारिणी)।
हिङ्गुला च महापीठं तथा जालन्धरं पुनः॥
ज्वालामुखी महापीठं पीठं नागरसम्भवम् (v.l. नगर°)।
रामगिरिर्महापीठं तथा गोदावरी प्रिये॥
नेपालं कर्णसूत्रञ्च महाकर्णं तथा प्रिये।
अयोध्या च कुरुक्षेत्रं सिंहलाख्यं (v.l. सिंहनादं) मनोरमम्॥
मणिपुरं हृषीकेशं प्रयागञ्च तपोवनम्।
बदरी च महापीठमम्बिका अर्द्धनालकम् (v.l. अम्बिकाम्वर्द्धमानकम्)॥
त्रिवेणी च महापीठं गङ्गासागरसङ्गमम्।
नारिकेलञ्च विरजा उड्डीयान महेश्वरि॥

This list, probably composed in eastern India, speaks rather independently of about forty-two Pīṭhas some of which seem to represent actually the names of deities. Reference to the Vindhyan region as a Pīṭha in this list no doubt points to the resort of the celebrated non-Aryan goddess Vindhyavāsinī (identified with the Indian mother-goddess) whose temple stands near modern Mirzapur in the United Provinces. The antiquity of the worship of this goddess is proved by the fact that, according to Vākpatirāja's *Gaüḍavaha,* king Yaśovarman (*c.* 730–53 A.D.) offered his homage to Devī Vindhyavāsinī in connection with his expedition for the conquest of the quarters. In the twelfth century, Kalhaṇa (*Rāj. tar.*, III, pp. 394–431) seems to refer to the same deity as Bhramaravāsinī [1] in connection with a sixth century Kashmirian king named Raṇāditya. The celebrated Śākta work entitled *Caṇḍī*, incorporated in the *Mārkaṇḍeya Purāṇa*, gives evidence to the cult of the goddess Vindhyavāsinī (cf. ch. 91, v. 37). That the resort of this early and important deity is not mentioned in all the different lists of Pīṭhas containing even names of lesser importance, indicates the absence of recognized traditions and the freedom an author may have exercised in this matter

Evidence of the Jñānārṇava and the Tantrasāra regarding the Number of Pīṭhas.

Eight Pīṭhas mentioned in the *Jñānārṇava Tantra* have been mentioned above. It is interesting to note that a different section of the same work definitely gives the recognized number of Pīṭhas as fifty only.[2] These fifty Pīṭhas are: (1) Kāmarūpa, (2) Vārāṇasī, (3) Nepāla, (4) Pauṇḍravardhana (Mahasthan in the Bogra District, North Bengal), (5) Kashmir, (6) Kānyakubja, (7) Purasthita (v.l. Purasthira), (8) Carasthita (v.l. Candrāsthira, Carasthira), (9) Pūrṇaśaila, (10) Arbuda, (11) Āmrātakeśvara, (12) Ekāmra (Bhuvaneśvar in Orissa), (13) Trisrotaḥ (the Tista river in north-eastern

कमला विमला चैव तथा माहिष्मती (v.l. माहेश्वरी) पुरी ।
वाराही त्रिपुरा चैव वाग्मती नीलवाहिनी ॥
गोवर्द्धनं विन्ध्यगिरिः कामरूपं कलौ युगे ।
घण्टाकर्णो हयग्रीवो (v.l. °हयग्रीवो) माधवश्च सुरेश्वरि ॥
चीरग्रामं वैद्यनाथं जानीयाद्वामलोचने ॥

This list can hardly be very early. But the idea (*Rājamālā*, I, ed. K. P. Sen, p. 124) that the *Kubjikā* speaks of 127 Pīṭhas is due to the wrong impression created by the *Prāṇatoṣaṇī* which quotes several lists from the *Bṛhan-Nīlatantra*, without reference to the source, in continuation of the *Kubjikā* list.

1 The name has, as the *Rāj. tar.* seems to imply, bearing on the condition of the Vindhyan forests infested with bees. The Indian mother-goddess is given the name Bhrāmarī in some texts (*Mārkaṇḍeya Purāṇa*, 91, 49; *Devībhāgavata*, X, 10, 13); cf. the name of Bhramarāmbā on the Śrīśaila. The *Pīṭhanirṇaya* locates this deity in northern Bengal and in the Nasik region of the Bombay Presidency. It is interesting to note that certain forms of the mother-goddess in western Asia, such as Nanaia and Artemes, had the bee for their symbol. The Indian mother-goddess riding a lion reminds one of the Cappadocian Ma who stands on a lioness or panther. Like Śiva, Ma's consort Teshub also rides on a bull and has the three-pronged thunder-bolt (cf. *triśūla*) as his distinctive weapon. See Raychaudhuri, *D. R. Bhand. Volume*, pp. 301–03. The goddess Vindhyavāsinī is possibly called Śūlinī in the *Tantrasāra*, p. 193. The *Gaüḍavaha* (verses 285–347) identifies Vindhyavāsinī with Kālī or Pārvatī, associates her with the Kols and Śabaras, and refers to human sacrifices offered to her. For the goddess, fond of wine and flesh and worshipped by the Śabaras, Pulindas and Barbaras, see *Hariv.*, II, iii, 7-8.

2 Cf. the expressions *pañcāśat-pīṭha-sañcaya* (v.l. *pañcāśat-sthāna°*) and *pañcāśat-pīṭha-vinyāsa* in the *Jñānārṇava* (Ānandāśrama ed., Paṭala XIV, verse 112); quotation from the same work in the *Tantrasāra*, p. 427n.; *Tantracūḍāmaṇi* (MS. No. I, F 3 in the library of the R.A.S.B.), p. 515.

India), (14) Kāmakoṭṭa (v.l. °koṭa), (15) Kailāsa, (16) Bhṛgu, (17) Kedāra, (18) Candrapura, (19) Śrīpīṭha (probably, Śrīhaṭṭa), (20) Oṅkāra, (21) Jālandhara, (22) Mālava (v.l. Mānava), (23) Kulānta (v.l. Kūpānta), (24) Devakoṭṭa, (25) Gokarṇa, (26) Māruteśvara, (27) Aṭṭahāsa, (28) Virajā, (29) Rājagṛha, (30) Kolvagiri (Kaulagiri), (31) Elāpura (Ellora), (32) Kāleśvara (v.l. Kāmeśvara), (33) Jayantikā (Jayantī), (34) Ujjayinī, (35) Kṣīrikā (Kṣīragrāma), (36) Hastināpura, (37) Uḍḍīśa (from Prakrit *Oḍḍavisa*, *Oḍḍaisa*> Sanskrit *Oḍraviṣaya*, i.e. Orissa), (38) Prayāga, (39) Vindhya, (40) Māyāpura, (41) Jaleśvara (in Orissa), (42) Malaya, (43) Śrīśaila, (44) Merugiri, (45) Mahendra, (46) Vāmana, (47) Hiraṇyapura, (48) Mahālakṣmī, (49) Uḍḍiyāna, (50) Chāyāchatrapura.[1] It is doubtful whether all the

---

[1] The same passage is also found in the manuscript of the *Tantracūḍāmaṇi* (pp. 515-16) in the R.A.S.B. library and in Brahmānanda's *Śāktānandataraṅgiṇī*, ch. 15 (referring to the *Gāndharva Tantra*).

कामरूपं महापीठं पीठं वाराणसीं तथा ।
नेपालञ्च तथा पीठं तथा वै पौण्ड्रवर्द्धनम् ॥
काश्मीरञ्च महापीठं कान्यकुब्जमतः परम् ।
पुरस्थितं (v.l. °स्थिरं) तथा पीठं चरस्थितमथापरम्
(v.l. चरस्थिर°, चन्द्रास्थिर°) ॥
पूर्णशैलं महापीठमर्बुदञ्च ततः परम् ।
आम्रातकेश्वरं पीठमेकाम्रञ्च ततःपरम् ॥
(v.l. दारुकेशं महापीठम् एकाम्रञ्च तथा शिवे ।)
त्रिस्रोतः पीठमनघं कामकोट्ट (v.l. °टि°) मतःपरम् ।
कैलासं भृगुपीठञ्च (v.l. °नगरं) केदारं चन्द्रपुरकम् ॥
(v.l. कैलासभृगुकेदारं पीठं चन्द्रपुरं ततः ॥)
श्रीपीठञ्च (श्रीहट्टञ्च ?) तथोङ्कारं जालन्धरमतः परम् ।
मालवञ्च (v.l. मानवञ्च) तथा पीठं कुलान्तं (v.l. कूपान्तं)
देवकोट्टकम् (v.l. देवी°, °कोटकम्, °कोटरम्) ।
(v.l. कैलासं भूतनगरं केदारं पीठमुत्तमम् ।
श्रीपीठञ्च कुलान्तञ्च देवमातृकमेव च ॥)
गोकर्णञ्च महापीठं मारुतेश्वरमेव च ।
अट्टहासञ्च विरजं राजगृहमथापरम् (v.l. महापथम्) ॥
पीठं कोल्वगिरिं प्रोक्तमेलापुरमथापरम् ।
कालेश्वरं (v.l. कामेश्वरं) महापीठं महापीठं (v.l. प्रणवाख्यं) जयन्तिकाम् ।
पीठमुज्जयिनीञ्चैव विचित्रं क्षीरिकाभिधम् ।
हस्तिनापुरपीठञ्च (v.l. पुरकं पीठम्) उड्डीशञ्च प्रयागकम् ॥
विन्ध्यञ्चैव (v.l. षष्ठीशञ्च, कान्यकुब्जं) महापीठं मायापुरजलेश्वरौ ।
मलयञ्च महापीठं श्रीशैलं मेरुकं गिरिम् ॥
महेन्द्रं वामनञ्चैव (v.l. माहेन्द्रं वारुण°) हिरण्यपुरमेव च (v.l. हिरण्यं) ।
महालक्ष्मीमयं (v.l. °पुर) पीठमुड्डीयानमतः परम् ॥
छायाछत्रपुरं पीठं तथैव परमेश्वरि ।
पञ्चाशत्पीठविन्यासं मातृकावन्न्यसेत् सदा ॥

places mentioned were Śākta *tīrthas*. In some cases there seems to be an attempt to trace Śākta influence in not only Śaiva but also Vaiṣṇava holy

---

The same passage is found in the fifth Paṭala of the *Bṛhan-Nīlatantra* in a modified and corrupt form (cf. *infra*, p. 37, note 1 for the emendations):

कामरूपं प्रियं वाराणसौ नैपालमेव च ।
पौण्ड्रं वर्द्धमपीठञ्च पावक्यं (पारस्यं) कान्यकुब्जकम् ।
पुष्पाद्रिमर्बुदश्चैव (पुण्या°) एकाम्रमाम्रकेश्वरम् (°वैकाम्रमाम्रातके°) ।
त्रैपुरं कामकोटञ्च तथा गुप्तपुरं (भृगु°) वरम् ॥
कैलासं पीठकेदार(°रं) शुभचन्द्रपुरं तथा ।
श्रीपुरं च तथा काल्याः (कन्या°) पुरं जालन्धरं तथा ॥
मानवं (मालवं) विल्वपीठञ्च देवीकोटं तथैव च ।
गोकर्णं मारुतेशञ्च तथाट्टहासमेव च ॥
अमुकानामगोत्रञ्च (विरजापुरक्षेत्रञ्च) एलापुरमतिप्रियम् ।
महापथपुरञ्चैव ओङ्कारपुरमेव च ॥
जयदञ्च जयपुरम् उज्जयिनीपुरं तथा ।
हरिद्रापीठकञ्चैव प्रिय(यं)चौरपुरं प्रियम् ॥
गजाह्वयपुरञ्चैव उड्डीनपुरमेव (उड्डीश°) च ।
प्रयागञ्च तथा षष्ठीपुरमेव शिवप्रदम् ॥
मायापुरमतिश्रेष्ठं पुरञ्च परमेश्वरम् (शमने° ?) ।
श्रीशैलमेरुपीठञ्च हिमालयमहागिरिम् ॥
महेन्द्रपुरपीठञ्च तथा बलिपुरं प्रियम् ।
हिरण्यपुरपीठञ्च महालक्ष्मीपुरं तथा ॥
चण्डीपुरमतिश्रेष्ठं (चण्ड°?) तथा छायापुरं (छायाछत्रपुरं) प्रिये ॥

To give the above passage an appearance of an original composition, it is preceded in the *Bṛhan-Nīlatantra* by the following verses which mention certain Pīṭhas in the alphabetical order:

अमरेशपुरञ्चैवासुरान्तकपुरं तथा ।
अम्बिकापीठमत्यन्तमनन्तपुरमेव च ॥
अनिरुद्धपुरं वेत्सि तथादितिपुरं परम् ।
अणिमादिपुरञ्चैव अश्वमेधपुरं परम् ॥
अन्नपूर्णामहापीठमम्बुजाख्यपुरन्तथा ।
आदिपीठानन्दपीठौ आमोदावादिस्वकरौ ॥
आम्रासिद्धिपुरञ्चैव यथाद्यान्तपुरं सुखम् ।
अकम्पादित्यपीठौ च आद्यादिनाथपीठकौ ॥
इष्टनाम(°नाभ°)पुरञ्चैव इन्दिरापुरमेव च ।
इलोदयगिरिश्चैव इलान्तेन्दुपुरे प्रिये ॥
इन्द्राणीन्द्रीश्वरश्चैव इन्द्रानन्दपुरन्तथा ।
पुरमिन्दुवती नाम तवेन्दुविजयं पुरम् ॥
ईश्वरेश्वरयोगी च ईशानेन्दीश्वरीपुरम् ।
ईशान्येशपुरं देवि कथितं पीठमुत्तमम् ॥

Some of the names mentioned appear to have been fabricated by the author and to have had no real existence.

places. This attempt may possibly be attributed to eastern India. The above list has been quoted and utilized in a *Pīṭhanyāsa* section of the *Tantrasāra* by the Bengali Tantric teacher Kṛṣṇānanda Āgamavāgīśa in the seventeenth century.[1] Curiously enough the *Tantrasāra*, in spite of its clear recognition of the number of Pīṭhas to be fifty only in accordance with the *Jñānārṇava Tantra*, actually makes fifty-one Pīṭhas out of the fifty enumerated above. This has been done strangely by splitting the name of one of the fifty Pīṭhas, viz. Merugiri (No. 44) into two names, viz. Meru Pīṭha and Giri Pīṭha,[2] in the formal *nyāsa* associating certain limbs with the Pīṭhas.[3] The anomaly was probably the result of a modification of the text of the *Tantrasāra* by later hands. What is, however, more interesting is that the *Pīṭhanirṇaya* or *Mahāpīṭhanirūpaṇa*, which has been quoted in the *Prāṇatoṣaṇī Tantra* by Rāmatoṣaṇa Vidyālaṅkāra, who was seventh in descent from the compiler of the *Tantrasāra*, in 1820 adheres exactly to this modified number of the Pīṭhas, viz. fifty-one, although the list itself is independent of the earlier lists of Pīṭhas. As this work is not quoted in the *Tantrasāra* or any other earlier Tantra dealing with the Pīṭhas, it seems that the *Pīṭhanirṇaya* was composed or became popular in eastern India shortly after the compilation of the *Tantrasāra* by Kṛṣṇānanda Āgamavāgīśa (seventeenth century) but before that of the *Prāṇatoṣaṇī Tantra* by Rāmatoṣaṇa in 1820. As the work was utilized by Bhāratacandra in his *Annadāmaṅgala* (1752), it must have been composed earlier than the middle of the

---

[1] For a detailed discussion on the date of the *Tantrasāra*, see Appendix IV.

[2] Cf. *Tantrasāra*, p. 426: लं लं लं मेरुपीठाय नमः ककुदि; वं वं वं गिरिपीठाय नमो वामस्कन्धे।

[3] Cf. *loc. cit.*; also the Rudrayāmala passage quoted above. The *Tantrasāra* associates the following limbs with the following Pīṭhas: (1) कामरूप—limb not mentioned; according to the *Rudrayāmala* मूलाधार (region of the organ of generation); (2) वाराणसी—मुखवृत्त; (3) नेपाल—दक्षचक्षुः (दक्ष = right); (4) पौण्ड्रवर्द्धन—वामचक्षुः; (5) काश्मीर—दक्षकर्ण; (6) कान्यकुब्ज—वामकर्ण; (7) पुरस्थित—दक्षिणनस् (नस् = nostril); (8) चरस्थित—वामनस्; (9) पूर्णशैल—दक्षगण्ड; (10) अर्बुद—वामगण्ड; (11) आम्रातकेश्वर—ओष्ठ; (12) एकाम्र—अधर; (13) त्रिस्रोतः—ऊर्द्धदन्त; (14) कामकोट्ट—अधोदन्त; (15) कैलास—ब्रह्मरन्ध्र; (16) भृगु—मुख; (17) केदार—दक्षबाहुमूल; (18) चन्द्रपुर—दक्षकूर्पर; (19) श्री—दक्षमणिबन्ध; (20) ओङ्कार—दक्षिणाङ्गुलिमूल; (21) जालन्धर—दक्षाङ्गुल्यग्र; (22) मालव (मानव)—वामबाहुमूल; (23) कुलान्तक (कूपान्तक)—वामकूर्पर; (24) देवीकोट्ट—वाममणिबन्ध; (25) गोकर्ण—वामाङ्गुलिमूल; (26) मारुतेश्वर—वामाङ्गुल्यग्र; (27) अट्टहास—दक्षपादमूल; (28) विरज—दक्षजानु; (29) राजगृह—दक्षगुल्फ; (30) कोल्लगिरि—दक्षपादाङ्गुलिमूल; (31) एलापुर—दक्षाङ्गुल्यग्र; (32) कामेश्वर (कालेश्वर)—वामपादमूल; (33) जयन्ती—वामजानु; (34) उज्जयिनी—वामगुल्फ; (35) चौरिका—वामपादाङ्गुलिमूल; (36) हस्तिनापुर—वामपादाङ्गुल्यग्र; (37) उड्डीश—दक्षिणपार्श्व; (38) प्रयाग—वामपार्श्व; (39) विन्ध्य—पृष्ठ; (40) मायापुर—नाभि; (41) जलेश्वर—उदर; (42) मलय—हृत्; (43) श्रीशैल—दक्षस्कन्ध; (44) मेरु—ककुत्; (45) गिरि—वामस्कन्ध; (46) महेन्द्र—हृदादिदक्षकर; (47) वामन—हृदादिवामकर; (48) हिरण्यपुर—हृदादिदक्षपाद; (49) महालक्ष्मीपुर—हृदादिवामपाद; (50) उड्डीयान—हृदाद्युदर; (51) छायाछत्रपुर—हृदादिमुख। It should be noted that the association of a Pīṭha with a limb in the *nyāsa* was suggested differently by different writers.

eighteenth century. The composition of the *Pīṭhanirṇaya* or *Mahāpīṭha-nirūpaṇa* may therefore be assigned to the closing years of the seventeenth century or more probably to the early years of the eighteenth (*c.* 1690–1720). The reference to Kālīghāṭa, whose popularity seems to be associated with the foundation of Calcutta (1690) and whose mention in earlier works is rare,[1] possibly supports this date. The important feature of this work, as it is usually accepted in Bengal, is that its list of Pīṭhas together with the names of the Devī and the Bhairava, includes a number of places in the rural areas of Bengal. The language is in some cases greatly influenced by Bengali. The history of the literature on the Pīṭhas no doubt points unmistakably to the great contribution Bengal must have made to the Tantric literature and culture in the medieval period. The greatest centre of Tantricism seems to have originally been in north-western India. Before the medieval period, the Tantric school of north-eastern India rose to eminence and became a great rival of the north-western school. With the gradual decline of Tantric culture in the north-west as a result of foreign occupation, Bengal seems to have come to the forefront as the abode of great leaders of Tantric thought.

The Tradition about 108 Pīṭhas.

The uncertainty about the recognized number of the Pīṭhas in the medieval period is also demonstrated by another fact. The number 108 had some importance in India to the sectarian worshippers who often attempted to endow their respective deities with 108 names.[2] In the list of such 108 names of a particular deity, names or epithets of various other deities were appropriated, the underlying idea being that the latter are only different manifestations of the former. The love of system and concord, which is a feature of the Indian mind, inspired theologians to harmonize Brahman, Viṣṇu and Śiva in the compound form of the Trimūrti, Viṣṇu and Śiva in that of Hari-Hara, and Śiva and Śakti in that of Ardha-nār-īśvara. The theory of the ten Avatāras of Viṣṇu was likewise the result of an attempt at harmonization of different religious sects worshipping different cult-deities.[3] Even in recent times, the Bāuls of Bengal, both Muslim and

---

[1] There is no mention of Kalighat as a Pīṭha in the *Caṇḍīmaṅgala* (16th century) by Mukundarāma of the Burdwan District. But Vipradāsa's *Manasāmaṅgala* (1495 A.D.) mentions Kālikā of Kalighat, Sarvamaṅgalā of Citpur (now included in Calcutta) and Betāi-Caṇḍī of Betor (near Sibpur in the Howrah District). Even if this reference is not an interpolation, it does not prove that Kalighat was regarded as an important *tīrtha* in the fifteenth century. The sixteenth century author Vaṃśīdāsa of Mymensing does not regard Kalighat as a Pīṭha. See *infra*, p. 33 and note 3.

[2] Cf. the list of various names of Śiva in the Sanatkumāra-saṁhitā section (ch. 31) of the *Śiva Purāṇa* and in the Kedārakhaṇḍa subsection of the Māheśvarakhaṇḍa section of the *Skanda Purāṇa*. For a list of the different names of Brahman, see *Padma Purāṇa*, Sṛṣṭikhaṇḍa, ch. 34; *Skanda Purāṇa*, Prabhāsakhaṇḍa, ch. 107. The idea seems to have originated from the Śatarudrīya section of the *Yajurveda* (Taittirīya Saṃhitā, IV, 5, 1; Vājasaneyī Saṃhitā, ch. 16). A Bengali text entitled *Śrīkṛṣṇa-śatanāma* (literally, the 100 names of Lord Kṛṣṇa) is very popular in Bengal and is daily recited by many pious people. There are also later lists of the 1,000 names of some gods, notably Viṣṇu. See *Des. Cat.*, R.A.S B., VIII, pp. 173, 500, 812, 815, 820ff., 842, etc. For two lists of the *sahasranāma* of Viṣṇu and Śiva, see *Mahābhārata*, XIII, chs. 149 and 17. For the importance of the numbers 108 and 1008, see *Tantrasāra*, pp. 48, 116, 131, 157, 538, 652, 733, 761, 781, 825-26, 903, 905, 918, 920, 973, etc., and 83, 157, 906-07, 928, etc. The importance of the number 108 is clearly demonstrated by the fact that even today the revered names of many religious teachers are mentioned as prefixed by the word *Śrī* for no less than 108 times, although in actual practice *Śrī* for 108 times is indicated by the expression '*śrī* 108'.

[3] See Sircar, 'Sectarian Difference among the Early Vaiṣṇavas' in *Bhār. Vid.*, VIII, pp. 109–11.

Hindu, have been declaring in their songs the absolute identity of Rāma and Rahim, of Christ (Beng. *Khṛṣṭa*) and Kṛṣṇa (vulgo *Kṛṣṭa*), of Śiva and 'Alī, and of Durgā and Fatima. A section of the devotees of the mother-goddess is known to have endowed their cult-deity with 108 names attempting thereby to identify her with various goddesses and with the female forms (Śaktis or energizing powers) of many gods worshipped in different parts of India. An early list of this nature can be traced in the *Mahābhārata* (VI, ch. 23); but a complete list of the 108 names of the mother-goddess with the specification of her association with particular holy places is probably to be found for the first time in the *Matsya Purāṇa*, ch. 13, the particular section, however, being assignable to the early medieval period.[1] The same text has been quoted in the description of the various manifestations of Bhadrakarṇikā (a form of the mother-goddess) in the Revākhaṇḍa subsection of the Āvantyakhaṇḍa in the *Skanda Purāṇa* (which in its present form is not earlier than the twelfth century) [2] as well as in the enumeration of the different names of the goddess Sāvitrī, the wife of Brahman, in the Sṛṣṭikhaṇḍa section (ch. 17) of the *Padma Purāṇa*. The same text is also quoted in the *Devībhāgavata* (VII, ch. 30) which, unlike the *Matsya*, *Skanda* and *Padma Purāṇas*, refers to the holy places, associated in this work with the different manifestations of the mother-goddess and of her consort, as Pīṭhas without, however, mentioning the particular limbs of the goddess and the particular Bhairavas, although it says that the list contains the names of some Pīṭhas in addition to those that 'sprang from' the limbs of Satī.[3]

---

[1] Ch. 13 of the *Matsya Purāṇa* refers to Vṛndāvana as the resort of Rādhā and to Puruṣottama. There is no genuine evidence to show that Rādhā was recognized as a divinity earlier than the post-Gupta period and that Puruṣottama (Purī) attained to any eminence before the days of Anantavarman Coḍagaṅga (1078–1147 A.D.) who laid the foundation of the great temple of Jagannātha at Purī. Cf. also reference to Māṇḍavyapura (Mandor in the Jodhpur State), Vaidyanātha, etc., which do not appear to be early, although the *Matsya Purāṇa* in some form must have existed in earlier times.

[2] Cf. references to Rāmānuja (Viṣṇukhaṇḍa, ch. 21) who flourished in the age of the Choḷa King Adhirājendra (c. 1070 A.D.) and the Hoysala Viṣṇuvardhana (c. 1106–41 A.D.), to the Gurjara-Pratīhāra King Bhoja I (c. 836–85 A.D.) and to King Āma of Kanauj who was either the same as Āma (c. 753–65 A.D.), son of Yaśovarman (c. 730–53 A.D.) or as Āma-Nāgabhaṭa II (c. 805–33 A.D.), grandfather of Bhoja I. *Vide* Prabhāsakhaṇḍa-Vastrāpathamāhātmya, ch. 1ff.; Brahmakhaṇḍa-Dharmāraṇya-khaṇḍa, ch. 36ff. These, however, do not prove that the *Skanda Purāṇa* did not exist in any form in earlier times. In the first-half of the 11th century, Albīrūnī had information about the 18 *Purāṇas* including the *Skanda* (Sachau, *loc. cit.*, pp. 130-31). For a Bengal manuscript of this *Purāṇa* 'written in Gupta hand, to which as early a date as the middle of the seventh century can be assigned on palaeographical grounds', see *JRAS*, 1903, p. 193; Smith *EHI*, 1924, p. 23.

[3] A later list of 108 Pīṭhas is found in the *Prāṇatoṣaṇī Tantra*, p. 236 (cf. *Vācaspatya*, s.v. *pīṭha*). The verses appear to have been quoted from the *Bṛhan-Nīlatantra* (Paṭala V) which was known to the Prāṇatoṣaṇī (cf. p. 2). As there are several lists in it, the *Bṛhan-Nīla*, itself a late-medieval work, probably also drew from some slightly earlier sources. If it is the same as the *Mahā-Nīlatantra*, it must be regarded as earlier than c. 1550 A.D. when Brahmānanda mentioned it in his *Tārārahasya* (Paṭala I). But this date is doubtful, as the *Bṛhan-Nīla* quotes one list of 52 Pīṭhas.

[पीठानां परमं पीठं कामरूपं महाफलम् ।]

* * * * * * *

पीठप्रसङ्गाद्देवेशि पीठानि शृणु भैरवि ।

* * * * * * *

पुष्करञ्च गयाक्षेत्रं अक्षयाख्यवटस्तथा (v.l. अक्षयाद्य°) ।
वराहपर्वतश्चैव तीर्थञ्चामरकण्टकम् (v.l. शिवञ्चा°) ॥

This interesting list of the 108 names of the mother-goddess and those of as many holy places in different parts of India includes the following names:

नर्मदा यमुना पिङ्गा गङ्गाद्वारं तथा प्रिये ;
गङ्गासागरसङ्गश्च कुशावर्त्तश्च विल्वकम् ॥
श्रीनीलपर्वतश्चैव कलम्बकुब्जके (v.l. °कुब्जिके) तथा ।
भृगुतुङ्गश्च (v.l. °भृङ्गश्च) केदारं सर्वप्रियमहालयम् (v.l.° चलम्) ॥
ललिता च सुगन्धा च शाकम्भरीपुरं प्रियम् ।
कर्णतीर्थं महागङ्गा लग्निकाश्रम (नग्निका° ?) एव (v.l. °मेव) च ॥
कुमाराख्यप्रभासौ च तथा धन्या सरस्वती ।
आवन्त्याश्रममिष्टं (v.l. अगस्त्या°) मे कण्वाश्रममतः (v.l. कन्या°, काण्वा°) परम् ॥
कौशिकीसरयूशोणज्योतिःसरपुरःसरम् ।
कामोदकं (v.l. कालोदकं) प्रियं श्रीमत् प्रियमुत्तरमानसम् ॥
मातङ्गवापी सप्तार्चिर्महाविष्णुपदं (v.l. °र्मन्यद्विष्णु°) महत् ।
वैद्यनाथं महातीर्थं प्रियः कालञ्जरो गिरिः ॥
रामोच्छेदं गर्गोच्छेदं हरोच्छेदं महानलम् ।
(v.l. वामो° ; रामोद्भेदं गङ्गोद्भेदं हरोद्भेदं महावनम् ।)
भद्रेश्वरं महातीर्थं लक्ष्मणोच्छेदमेव (v.l. लक्ष्मणोद्भेद°) च ॥
जानीहि प्रियश्रेष्ठा (v.l. °सृष्टा) च कावेरी कपिलोदका ।
सोमेश्वरं शुक्लतीर्थं कृष्णवेण्या (v.l. °वेण्वा°) प्रभेदकः ॥
पाटला च महाबोधिर्नगतीर्थं मदन्तिका (v.l. °न्तिके) ।
पुण्यं रामेश्वरं देवि तथा मेघवनं हरेः ॥
ऐलं रमणकश्चैव (v.l. ऐलेयकवनश्चैव) गोवर्द्धनमजप्रियम् ।
हरिश्चन्द्रं पुरश्चन्द्रं पृथूदकमये प्रियम् (v.l. °मथ प्रिये ; श्रियम्) ॥
इन्द्रनीलं महानादं तथैव प्रियमैलकम् ।
पद्माधरं (v.l. पद्मासर°) पद्मवटी वटी(ट)पर्वतिका तथा ॥
गङ्गाविल्वं प्रसङ्गश्च (v.l. °विल्वश्च प्रा°) प्रियनादवटं तथा (v.l. °टस्तथा) ।
गङ्गावामाचलश्चैव (v.l. गङ्गारामा°) तथैव ऋणमोचनम् ॥
गौतमेश्वरतीर्थञ्च वशिष्ठतीर्थमेव च ।
हारीतञ्च (v.l. °तकं) तथा देवि ब्रह्मावर्त्तं शिवप्रियम् (v.l. °प्रदम्) ॥
कुशावर्त्तमतिश्रेष्ठं हंसतीर्थं तथैव च ।
पिण्डारकवनं (v.l. °वकरणं) ख्यातं हरिद्वारं तथैव च ॥
तथैव बदरीतीर्थं रामतीर्थं (v.l. °वाम°) तथैव च ।
जयन्तं विजयन्तं च सर्वकल्याणदं प्रिये ॥
विजया सारदातीर्थं भद्रकालेश्वरं तथा ।
अश्वतीर्थं सुविख्यातं तथा वेदशिरः प्रियम् (v.l. वेदशिराप्रियः ; देवि शिवप्रियम्) ॥
ओघवती नदी चैव तीर्थमश्वप्रदं (v.l. °स्य पदं) तथा ।
छागलिङ्गं मातृगणं करवीरपुरं तथा ॥

(1) Viśālākṣī—Vārāṇasī, (2) Liṅgadhāriṇī—Naimiṣa, (3) Lalitā—Prayāga, (4) Kāmākṣī, Kāmukā or Kāmukī—Gandhamādana, (5) Kumudā—Mānasa, (6) Viśvakāyā or Viśvakāmā—Ambara, (7) Gomatī—Gomanta, (8) Kāmacāriṇī—Mandara, (9) Madotkaṭā—Caitraratha, (10) Jayantī—Hastināpura, (11) Gaurī—Kānyakubja, (12) Rambhā—the Malaya or Amala mountain, (13) Kīrtimatī—Ekāmra, (14) Viśvā or Vilvā—Viśveśvara, (15) Pūruhūtā—Puṣkara, (16) Mārgadāyinī—Kedāra, (17) Nandā or Mandā—the Himalayas, (18) Bhadrakarṇikā or Bhadrakālikā—Gokarṇa, (19) Bhavānī—Sthāṇvīśvara or Sthāneśvara, (20) Vilvapatrikā—Vilvaka or Vilvala, (21) Mādhavī—Śrīśaila, (22) Bhadrā or Bhadreśvarī—Bhadra, Bhadreśvara or Madreśvara, (23) Jayā—Varāhaśaila, (24) Kamalā—Kamalālaya, (25) Rudrāṇī or Kalyāṇī—Rudrakoṭi, (26) Kālī—Kālañjara, (27) Kapilā—Mahāliṅga, (28) Mukuṭeśvarī or Maṅgaleśvarī—Koṭa, Markoṭa, Mākoṭa or Karkoṭa, (29) Mahādevī—Śālagrāma or Śāligrāma, (30) Jalapriyā—Śivaliṅga, (31) Kumārī—Māyāpurī, (32) Lalitā—Santāna, (33) Utpalā or Utpalākṣī—Sahasrākṣa, (34) Mahotpalā—Sahasrākṣa or Hiraṇyākṣa, (35) Maṅgalā—the Gaṅgā or Gayā, (36) Vimalā—Puruṣottama, (37) Amoghākṣī—Vipāśā, (38) Pāṭalā—Puṇḍravardhana or Puṇyavardhana, (39) Nārāyaṇī—Supārśva, (40) Bhadrasundarī or Rudrasundarī—Trikūṭa, (41) Vipulā—Vipula, (42) Kalyāṇī—Mānasācala or Malayācala, (43) Koṭavī—Koṭitīrtha, (44) Sugandhā—Mādhavavana or Madhavīvana, (45) Trisandhyā—Godāśrama, Godāvarī or Kubjāmraka, (46) Ratipriyā or Haripriyā—Gaṅgādvāra, (47) Śivānandā, Śubhānandā, Sunandā or Sabhānandā—Śivakuṇḍa, Śivakuñja or Śivacaṇḍa, (48) Nandinī—the bank of the Devikā, (49) Rukmiṇī—Dvāravatī, (50) Rādhā—Vṛndāvana, (51) Devakī—Mathurā, (52) Parameśvarī—Pātāla, (53) Sītā—Citrakūṭa, (54) Vindhyavāsinī—the Vindhyas, (55) Ekavīrā—the Sahyādri (Western Ghats), (56) Candrikā—Hariścandra or Harmacandra, (57) Ramaṇā—Rāmatīrtha, (58) Mṛgāvatī—the Yamunā, (59) Mahālakṣmī—Karavīra, (60) Umā or Rūpā—Vināyaka, (61) Arogā or Ārogyā—Vaidyanātha, (62) Maheśvarī—Mahākāla, (63) Abhayā—the Uṣṇatīrthas, or Puṣpatīrtha, (64) Amṛtā, Nitambā or Mṛgī—the Vindhyan cave, (65) Māṇḍavī or Māṇḍukī—Māṇḍavya or Māṇḍava, (66) Svāhā—Māheśvarapura or Māheśvarīpura, (67) Pracaṇḍā—Chāgalāṇḍa, Chagalaṇḍa, Chāgaliṅga or Vegala, (68) Caṇḍikā—Amarakaṇṭaka, Makarandaka or Marakaṅkaṭa, (69) Varārohā—Someśvara, (70) Puṣkarāvatī—Prabhāsa, (71) Devamātā—Sarasvatī, (72) Mātā, Pārā or Pāvā—the shore of the sea or the bank of the Pārā, (73) Mahābhāgā or Mahāpadmā—Mahālaya, (74) Piṅgaleśvarī—the Payoṣṇī, (75) Siṃhikā—Kṛitaśauca, (76) Yaśaskarī, Śaṅkarī or Atiśaṅkarī—Kārttikeya, (77) Lolā—Utpalāvartaka,

---

सप्तगोदावरं तीर्थं लिङ्गाख्यं सर्वमोक्षनम् (v.l. सर्वधर्मफलप्रदम्) ।
[अयोध्या मथुरा माया दुर्गा द्वारवती (v.l. द्वारा°) हरेः ॥
विद्यापुरमवन्ती च काञ्चौ मङ्गलकोट्टकम् (v.l. °कोटरम्; °कुट्टकम्; नकुलकोटरम्; मकुलकोटरम्) ॥
कालीघट्टं गुप्ततीर्थं सिद्धाख्यं (v.l. लिङ्गाख्यं) सर्वमोक्षनम् ॥]
किरीटमुत्तरे (v.l. °रा°) तीर्थं दक्षिणे (v.l. °णा°) तीर्थमुत्तमम् ।
विशालतीर्थं काल्याश्च वनं वृन्दावनं तथा ॥
ज्वालामुखी त्रिकूला च महातीर्थं गणेश्वरम् ।
जानीहि सर्वसिद्धीनां (v.l. °तीर्थानां; °सिद्धानां) क्षेत्रस्थानानि सुन्दरि ॥

The text is not free from defects. Names like Aila, Kuśāvarta, etc., have been duplicated.

(78) Subhadrā—Śoṇasaṅgama or Sindhusaṅgama, (79) Mātā Lakṣmī or Umā Lakṣmī—Siddhapura, Siddhavana or Siddhavaṭa, (80) Aṅganā, Anaṅgā or Taraṅgā—Bharatāśrama, (81) Viśvamukhī—Jālandhara, (82) Tārā—the Kiṣkindhya hill, (83) Puṣṭi—Devadāruvana, (84) Medhā—Kāśmīra, (85) Bhīmā—the Himalayas, (86) Puṣṭi or Tuṣṭi—Vastreśvara or Viśveśvara, (87) Śuddhi or Śuddhā—Kapālamocana, (88) Mātā—Kāyāvarohaṇa, (89) Dhvani or Dharā—Śaṅkhoddhāra, (90) Dhṛti—Piṇḍāraka, (91) Kālā or Kalā—the Candrabhāgā, (92) Śivakāriṇī, Śivadhāriṇī, Siddhidāyinī or Śaktidhāriṇī—Acchoda, (93) Amṛtā—the Beṇā, (94) Urvaśī—Badarī, (95) Oṣadhi or Auṣadhi—Uttarakuru, (96) Kuśodakā—Kuśadvīpa, (97) Manmathā—Hemakūṭa, (98) Satyavādinī—Mukuṭa or Kumuda, (99) Vandanīyā or Vandinikā—Aśvattha, (100) Nidhi—in the home of Vaiśravaṇa, (101) Gāyatrī in grammar, (102) Pārvatī in the company of Śiva, (103) Indrāṇī in the world of gods, (104) Sarasvatī in the mouths of Brahman, (105) Prabhā (light) in the solar orb, (106) Vaiṣṇavī among the Divine Mothers,[1] (107) Arundhatī among chaste women, (108) Tillottamā among beautiful girls, (109) Brahmakalā in the hearts of men, and (110) Śakti (strength) in the living beings.[2] It will be seen that the names are actually more

---

[1] They are usually regarded as seven or eight in number.

Cf. ब्राह्मी माहेश्वरी चैव कौमारी वैष्णवी तथा ।
माहेन्द्री चैव वाराही चामुण्डा सप्त मातरः ॥ or
ब्राह्मी माहेश्वरी चण्डी वाराही वैष्णवी तथा ।
कौमारी चैव चामुण्डा चर्चिकेत्यष्ट मातरः ॥

(Apte, *Sanskrit-English Dictionary*, s.v. *mātṛ*). In place of Cāmuṇḍā of the first list, the *Mārkaṇḍeya Purāṇa* (ch. 88) gives Nārasiṃhī. These seven names are found in the list of the eight *nāyikās* or *yoginīs* to be worshipped along with the form of the mother-goddess called Kauṣiki-Caṇḍikā in the *Kālikā Purāṇa*, ch. 61, 84:

ब्रह्माणी प्रथमा प्रोक्ता ततो माहेश्वरी मता ।
कौमारी चैव वाराही वैष्णवी पञ्चमी तथा ॥
नारसिंही तथैवैन्द्री शिवदूती तथाष्टमी ॥

For Śivadūtī, cf. *Mārkaṇḍeya Purāṇa*, *loc. cit.*

In place of Carcikā of the second list, the *Tantrasāra* (pp. 314, 320) reads Caṇḍikā or Mahālakṣmī. It is not known if they are associated with the eight Bhairavas:

असिताङ्गो रुरुश्चण्डः क्रोधश्चोन्मत्तभैरवः ।
कपाली भीषणश्चैव संहारश्चाष्टभैरवाः ॥ (*ibid.*, pp. 332f.)

For a list of sixteen Mothers, see *Prāṇatoṣaṇī Tantra*, p. 146.

[2] See the text of the list edited in Appendix I. The *Bṛhan-Nīla* (Paṭala V) and *Prāṇatoṣaṇī* (pp. 237-38) *Tantras* supply a later list of similar nature.

Cf. पुष्करे कमलाक्षी च गयायाञ्च गयेश्वरी ।
अक्षया अक्षयवटेऽमरेशेऽमरकण्टके (v.l. अक्षयाक्षयवटकेमरेशामर°) ॥
वराहपर्वते च त्वं वाराही धरणीप्रिया ।
नर्मदा (v.l. दुर्मदा) नर्मदायाञ्च कालिन्दी यमुनाजले ।
शिवामृता च गङ्गायामम्बा देहलिकाश्रमे (v.l. ते°) ।
कुमारधामे कौमारी प्रभासे सुरपूजिता ॥
काश्याञ्चैवान्नपूर्णा च द्राविडे च सरस्वती ।
महाविद्या महामेधा अगस्त्याश्रमके तथा ॥

than 108 in number, but that a number of the holy places are only imaginary. The fact that even in an attempt to find out 108 aotual *tīrthas* that

---

कौशीतकिप्रियं नाम कौशिकामृत(v.l. घृत°)कौशिके ।
शारदा सरयूतीरे शोणे च कनकेश्वरी ॥
स्वप्रकाशा यदा (v.l. सदा) देवी ज्योतिर्मय्यब्धिसंगमे ।
(v.l. स्वप्रकाशवशादेवि ज्योतिर्मती ह्यसङ्गमे ।)
श्रीनामा (v.l. श्रीरङ्गं) श्रीगिरौ चैव काली कालोदके तथा ॥
महोदरी महातीर्थे नीला (v.l. महादेवी महाबुद्धिर्नी°) चोत्तरमानसे ।
मातङ्गी स्वार्मातङ्गे (v.l. मातङ्गिनी मतङ्गे ; स्वाम्मतङ्गे) च गुप्तार्चिर्विष्णुपादके
(v.l. °प्रादुके) ॥
स्वर्गदा स्वर्गमार्गे च गोदावर्यां गवेश्वरी ।
विमुक्तिश्चैव गोमत्यां विपाशायां (v.l. विप्रमा वा) महाबला ॥
शतद्रवां (शतद्रौ ; v.l. शतद्वां ; शतप्रभा) शतरूपा च चन्द्रभागा च तत्र वै ।
ऐरावत्याश्च (इरा°) ईर्नाम सिद्धिदा सिद्धितीरके ॥
दक्षपक्षनदे चैव दक्षिणा त्वं प्रकीर्तिता ।
चौरसे (v.l. चौजसे ; चौजिसे) वीर्यदा च त्वं सङ्गमा तीर्थसङ्गमे ॥
बाहुदायामनन्ता (v.l. °सन्ता) त्वं कुरुक्षेत्रे रणेक्षणा (v.l. °ऽवक्षेक्षणा; व[रू?]
पेक्षणा) ।
तपस्विनी पुण्यतमा भारती भरताश्रमे ।
सुकथा नैमिषारण्ये पाण्डौ च पाण्डुरानना (v.l. °वानना) ।
विशालायां (v.l. दिशाल्याश्च) विशालाक्षी मुण्डपृष्ठे शिवात्मिका ॥
श्रद्धा कनखले तीर्थे शुद्धबुद्धिर्मुनीश्वरे ।
सुवेशा सुमना गौरी मानसे च सरोवरे ॥
नन्दापुरे महानन्दा ललिता ललितापुरे ।
ब्रह्माणी ब्रह्मशिरसि महापातकनाशिनी ॥
पूर्णिमा चेन्दुमत्याश्च (v.l. चेन्दुमत्याद्यैः) सिद्धयन्ती (v.l. सिन्धोरति°)
प्रिया सदा ।
जाह्नवीसङ्गमे तृप्तिः (v.l. दृप्तिः) स्वधा त्वं पितृतुष्टिदा ॥
पुण्या त्वं वेणवत्याश्च (v.l. बाहुसितायाश्च) प्रपायां पापनाशिनी ।
शंखसंहारिणी (v.l. °संहरणे) चैव घोररूपा महोदरी ॥
स्वर्गोच्छेदे (v.l. स्वर्गाह्नदे) महाराचिः प्रबला च महावने ।
भद्रा च भद्रकाली च भद्रेश्वरीश्वरप्रिया ॥
भद्रेश्वरे रमा विष्णुप्रिया विष्णुपदे तथा ।
दारुणा नर्मदोच्छेदे (v.l. °ह्नदे) कावेर्यां कपिलेश्वरी ॥
भेदिनी कृष्णवेणायां संभेदे शुभवासिनी ।
श्रद्धा च शुक्रतीर्थे च प्रभासे चेश्वरी तथा ॥
(शुद्धा च शुक्लतीर्थे च प्रभा रामेश्वरे तथा ॥)
महाबोधौ महाबुद्धिः पाटले पाटलेश्वरी ।
सुरसा (v.l. सुबला) नागतीर्थे च नागेशी नागवन्दिता ॥

could be associated with Śakti rather arbitrarily the author does not refer to Kāmarūpa and Uḍḍiyāna may point to the author's aversion for these

---

मदन्ते च मदन्ती च प्रमदा च मदन्तिका ।

मेघस्वना मेघवने (v.l. °वासे ; मेघस्वना मेषवने ; मेघवला) विद्युत्
सौदामिनीच्छटा ॥

रामेश्वरे महासिद्धिर्वीरा (v.l. महाबुद्धि° ; °धीरा) चेलापुरे सती ।

प्रिया रमणके (v.l. प्रिये ; पियालमार्गके) दुर्गा सुवेशा सुरसुन्दरी ॥

कात्यायनी महादेवी गोवर्द्धने तथाम्बिका (v.l. °खिलात्मिका; °नेऽम्बिका तथा) ।

शुभेश्वरी हरिश्चन्द्रे पुरश्चन्द्रे पुरेश्वरी ॥

पृथूदके महावेगा मैनाकेऽखिलवर्द्धिनी ।

इन्द्रनीले महाकान्ती (v.l. °कान्ता) रत्नवेशा सुशोभना ॥

माहेश्वरी महानादे महातेजा महाबले (°वने ; v.l. °बला) ।

पम्पासरसि सारङ्गा (v.l. पम्पासरसि; शारङ्गा) पञ्चवट्यां (v.l. °कन्यां) तपस्विनी ॥

वटीपर्वटिकायाञ्च (वटपर्वतिका° ; v.l. वटीशी°) पञ्चवर्गा (v.l. सर्ववर्णे)
सुरङ्गिनी ।

सङ्गमे विन्ध्यगङ्गायां (v.l. °गङ्गाख्या) विन्ध्ये (v.l. विन्ध्य°) श्रीविन्ध्यवासिनी ॥

महानन्दा नन्दतटे (v.l. °वटे) गङ्गावामाचले (v.l. वाटाचले) शिवा ।

आर्यावर्त्ते महार्या त्वं विमुक्तिर्ऋणमोचने ॥

अट्टहासे च चामुण्डा तन्त्रे श्रीगौतमेश्वरी (v.l. तन्त्रेशी) ।

वेदमयी ब्रह्मविद्या वशिष्ठे (v.l. वाशिष्ठे) त्वमरुन्धती ॥

हारीते हरिणाक्षी च ब्रह्मावर्त्ते व्रजेश्वरी (v.l. व्रते°) ।

गायत्री चैव सावित्री कुशावर्त्ते कुशप्रिया ॥

हंसेश्वरी महातीर्थे परहंसेश्वरेश्वरी (v.l. परहंसेश्वरीति च) ।

पिण्डारकवने (v.l. पिण्डावकरणे) धन्या सुरसा सुखदायिनी ॥

नारायणी वैष्णवी च गङ्गाद्वारे विमुक्तिदा ।

श्रीविद्या बदरीतीर्थे रामतीर्थे (v.l. वाम°) महाधृतिः ॥

जयन्ती च जयन्ते त्वं विजयन्तेऽपराजिता ।

विजया च महाशुद्धिः शारदायाञ्च शारदा ॥

सुभद्रे भद्रदा भव्या भद्रकालेश्वरे तथा ।

महाभद्रा (v.l. महाभद्री) भद्रकाली (v.l. महाकाली) हरतीर्थे (v.l. हय°)
गवीश्वरी ॥

वेददा वेदमाता च वेदेशा (v.l. विदेशे) वेदमस्तके ।

ओघवत्यां (v.l. युवत्याञ्च) महाविद्या महानद्यां महोदया ॥

चण्डा च त्रिपदे (v.l. चात्रपदे) चैव छागलिङ्गे बलिप्रिया ।

मातृदर्शे (v.l. °देशे) जगन्माता करवीरपुरे सती ॥

मालिनी (v.l. मालवे) रङ्गिनी वामा परमा परमेश्वरी ।

सप्तगोदावरे तीर्थे देवर्षिरखिलेश्वरी (देवी श्रीर°; v.l. देवर्षीव°; देवर्षीशा°) ॥

अयोध्यायां भवानी च जयदा जयमङ्गला ।

माधवी मथुरायाञ्च देवकी यादवेश्वरी ॥

out-and-out Tantric *tīrthas*. It cannot possibly be held that the text was composed before Uḍḍiyāna and Kāmarūpa attained to eminence.

वृन्दावने गोपेश्वरी (v.l. गोपीश्वरी) राधा रासवृन्दावने रसे (v.l. रमा) ।
कात्यायनी महामाया भद्रकाली कलावती ॥
चन्द्रमाला महाशान्तिर्महायोगिन्यधीश्वरी (v.l. महायोगा म°) ।
व्रजेश्वरी यशोदेति व्रजश्रीगोकुलेश्वरी ॥

काश्यां कनककाञ्ची स्यारवन्त्यामतिपावनी (v.l. स्याद°) ।
विद्या विद्यापुरे चैव विमला नीलपर्वते ॥
रामेश्वरी सेतुबन्धे (v.l. राजेशी श्वेतगङ्गेशी) विमला पुरुषोत्तमे ।
विरजा याजपुर्यां च (v.l. नागपुर्यां च) भद्रेऽपि (v.l. भद्राश्वे ; भद्रेशी)
भद्रकर्णिका ॥

तमोलिप्ते तमोघ्नी च स्वाहा सागरसङ्गमे ।
कुलश्रीर्वंशवृद्धिश्च (v.l.° वंश°) माधवी माधवप्रिया ॥
मङ्गला मङ्गले कोटे राढे मङ्गलचण्डिका ।
ज्वालामुखी शिवापीठे मन्दरे (v.l. मन्दारे) भुवनेश्वरी ॥
कालीघट्टे (v.l. °घाटे) गुह्यकाली किरीटे च महेश्वरी ।
किरीटेश्वरी महादेवी लिङ्गाख्ये लिङ्गवासिनी ॥

*   *   *   *   *

अमरेशमहापीठे कुशतुङ्गारसंज्ञकः (v.l. ईशदुङ्कार°) ।
तत्र दुर्गाद्वयं नाम चण्डिका च महेश्वरी ॥
प्रभासे सोमनाथोऽसौ (v.l. °नाथादौ) देवी च पुष्करेक्षणा ।
देवदेवाधिपः शम्भुर्नैमिषे च महेश्वरः ॥
तत्र प्रज्ञा च देवी च शिवानी लिङ्गधारिणी ।
पुष्करे च राजगन्धिः पुरहूता महेश्वरी ॥
श्रीपर्वते प्रियं नाम (v.l. श्रिया नाम्ना) शङ्करस्त्रिपुरान्तकः ।
मायावी शङ्करी (v.l. माया विषङ्करी) तत्र भक्तानामखिलार्थदा ॥
जप्येश्वरे महास्थाने शङ्करी च त्रिशूलिनी ।
त्रिशूली (v.l. त्रिशूल:) शङ्करस्तत्र सर्वपापविमोचकः ॥
आम्रातकपुरे (v.l.° तकेश्वरे) सूक्ष्मः सूक्ष्माख्या परमेश्वरी ।
(महाकाले महाकालो महाकाली महेश्वरी ॥
मध्ये शिवस्य [v.l. शिवश्च] सर्वत्र सर्वाणी परमेश्वरी ।
केदारेश्वर ईशानो देवी सन्मार्गदायिनी ॥
भैरवे भैरवः शम्भुर्भैरवी परमेश्वरी ।)
गर्गच्चेत्रे (v.l. गण°) मङ्गलाख्या शिवोऽयं प्रपितामहः ॥
कुरुक्षेत्रे शिवः स्थाणुः शिवा स्थाणुप्रिया परा ।
दृष्टनाभे स्वयम्भूश्च देवी स्वायम्भुवा मता ॥
उग्रः कनखले प्रोक्तः शिवोग्रे (शिवोग्रा ; v.l. शिवोग्रः) शिववल्लभा ।
विमलेश्वरे विश्वशम्भुर्विश्वा (v.l. °विश्वस्तु ; °रिष्टा) विश्वप्रिया सदा ॥

Freedom of the Writers on the Pīṭhas from any Common Tradition.

We have seen that the lists of the Pīṭhas and those of the Devīs and Bhairavas connected with each of them are variously prepared by different authors and have a great deal of discrepancy among them. There was apparently little influence on these writers of something like a recognized tradition about the number of the Pīṭhas, the names of the deities worshipped at them, and their association with particular limbs of the mother-goddess. Names of the *tīrtha*, Devī and Bhairava were often fabricated by the writers and the association of a *tīrtha* with one of Satī's limbs was also determined usually by their individual imagination. The fact that in many cases entire countries are mentioned as Pīṭhas suggests that the writers had only vague ideas about some of the *tīrthas* and often took resort to imagination. That medieval writers on the subject of the Pīṭhas took the greatest liberty in these respects is clearly demonstrated by the sixteenth century Bengali

---

अट्टहासे महानन्दो महानन्दा महेश्वरी ।
महान्तको महेन्द्रे च पार्वती च महान्तका ॥
भीमेश्वरो भीमपीठे शिवा भीमेश्वरी तथा ।
वस्त्रपादे (वस्त्रापथे ?) भवनाम भवानी भुवनेश्वरी ॥
अद्रिकूटे महायोगी रुद्राणी परमेश्वरी ।
अविमुक्ते महादेवो विशालाक्षी शिवा परा ॥
महालये (v.l. महामाये) हरो रुद्रो महाभागा शिवा तथा ।
महाचलस्य गोकर्णे शिवभद्रा (v.l. शिवा ज्ञेया) च चण्डिका ॥
भद्रकर्णे महादेवो भद्रा च कर्णिका तथा (च भद्रकर्णिका) ।
सुपर्णाख्ये (v.l. सुवर्णाख्ये) सहस्राक्ष उत्पला परमेश्वरी ॥
स्थाणुसंज्ञे शिवस्था श्रीश्वरस्था (स्थाणुसंज्ञः शिवः स्थाण्वीश्वरस्थः; v.l. स्थाणुसंज्ञे
शिवस्था श्रीश्वरः स्वामीश्वरा; शिवः स्थाणुरीशस्था) श्रीधरा शिवा ।
कमलालये (v.l. कलालये) महास्थाने (v.l. °स्थाने) कमलाक्षो महेश्वरः ॥
कमलाक्षी महेशानि सकलार्थप्रदायिनी ।
छगलण्डे (v.l. छागला तु) कपर्दी च प्रसरा (v.l. प्रसभा) च महेश्वरी ॥
ऊर्द्धरेता वरेण्ये (v.l. त्वरण्डे ; स्वरण्ये) च सन्ध्याख्या परमेश्वरी ।
माकोटाख्ये (माकोटाख्ये; v.l. साकोटे च) महाकोटः शिवा च मुण्डकेश्वरी ॥
(मण्डलेश्वरपीठे च शङ्करः शाण्डवी शिवा ॥)
(कालञ्जरे नीलकण्ठो हर [हरः] काली शिवा मता ।
स्थलेश्वरे (v.l. °श्वरो) स्थलीनाम्ना स्थलाख्या परमेश्वरी ॥)
मण्डलेश्वरपीठे (v.l. मातुले°) च करवीराचलेश्वरः (v.l. °रार्घ्यप्रेश्वरा) ।
श्रीमद्व्याघ्रपुरे साक्षाद्धरनामा सभापतिः ॥

*   *   *   *

अस्मिन् महोत्तमे स्थाने शिवगङ्गाख्यमद्भुतम् ।
तडागमस्ति तत्तीरे दक्षिणे नृत्यतीश्वरः ॥

*   *   *   *

[अष्टोत्तरसहस्रन्तु अपिकृद्धामुदान्वितः ।]

poet Mukundarāma in the *Dakṣa-yajña-bhaṅga* section of his *Caṇḍīmaṅgala*. According to an interpolated passage found in some manuscripts of this work, the following nine places are the Pīṭhas where Satī's limbs fell: (1) Ghāṭaśilā (between the Kharagpur and Tatanagar Railway Stations on the B.N.R.) where Satī's left foot fell and where the Devī is Rukmiṇī (apparently the Sanskritized form of the name of the aboriginal deity Raṅkiṇī whose worship is widely prevalent in the Burdwan Division of Bengal and the adjoining region of the west),[1] (2) Yājapura (in Orissa) where the right foot fell and where the Devī is Virajā, (3) Rājabolahāṭa (near Serampur in the Hooghly District) where the left hand fell and where the Devī is Viśālalocanī, (4) Bālidāṅgā (near Dhaniakhali in the Hooghly District) where the right hand fell and where the Devī is Rājeśvarī, (5) Kṣīragrāma (near Katwa in the Burdwan District) where the back fell and where the Devī is Yogādyā, (6) Nagarakoṭa where the head fell and where the Devī is Jvālāmukhī, (7) Hiṅglāja (in Baluchistan) where the navel fell,[2] (8) Kāmākhyā where the central part of Satī's body fell and where the Devī is Ķāmarūpa-Kāmākhyā, and (9) Vārāṇasī where the chest fell and where the Devī is Viśālākṣī.[3] Needless to say that the unimportant

---

[1] For human sacrifices in the Raṅkiṇī temple at Burdwan, see an instance cited in the newspapers in January, 1837, and quoted by B. N. Banerji in *Saṃvādpatre Sekāler Kathā*, Vol. II, pp. 532–34.

[2] Owing to defect in the text, the name of the Devī at Hiṅglāja cannot be determined.

[3] Cf. Calcutta University ed., pp. 49-50:

चक्र कीटरूप धरि   शरीरे प्रवेश करि
ग्रन्थे ग्रन्थे काटिते लागिल।
वामचरण शिला   पड़िल ये घाटशिला
तार नाम रुक्मिणी हइल॥
दक्षिण चरणवरे   पड़िल ये याजपुरे
तार नाम हइल विरजा।
देवता सकल मेलि   सिद्धपीठ तारे बलि
सुरपति तार करे पूजा॥
चक्रे सव्य हात काटे   पड़े राजबोलहाटे
विशाललोचनी महेश्वरी।
सतीर दक्षिण हाथ   वालिडाङ्गाय हैल पात
राजेश्वरी बलि नाम धरि॥
तबे सदाशिव धाय   महापरिश्रम पाय
क्षीरग्रामे करिला विश्राम।
ताहे पृष्ठदेश पड़े   देवेर आनन्द बाढ़े
योगाद्या हइल तार नाम॥
तबे प्रभु धूर्जटि   गेलेन नगरकोटे
दिवसेक रहिला पिनाकी।
मस्तक काटे चक्रकीट   सेइ महा सिद्धपीठ
तार नाम हैल ज्वालामुखी॥

rural *deva-sthānas* in Rāḍha, such as Rājabolahāṭa and Bāliḍāṅgā, received the status of Pīṭha in the hands of Mukundarāma merely because the poet was originally an inhabitant of the village of Dāmunyā in the Burdwan District. The *Pīṭhanirṇaya* (in its accepted form), likewise, includes in the list of Pīṭhas Chittagong, Tipperah, Nalahati, Vakresvara, Kiritakona, Jessore, Kalighat, etc., which are late and unimportant *deva-sthānas* in Bengal,

---

तबे त देवेर राज उत्तरिला हिंगुलाज
नाभिस्थल पड़िल तथाय ।
देवकरे तन्त्रमान (?) सेइ महासिद्धस्थान
जपिले पातक नाश पाय ॥
ईशाने ईशान याय उत्तरिला कामिख्याय
तथा हैल देवीप्रियस्थान ।
मध्य चक्र काटे कोठ सेइ महासिद्धपीठ
कामरूप कामाख्या तार नाम ॥
तबे त कैलासवासी उत्तरिला वाराणसी
वक्षःस्थल पड़िल ताहाते ।
विशालाक्षी रूप हैल सर्व देव पूजा कैल
उठे शिव शूल करि हाते ॥
प्रभु शूल शून्य देखि सेहेते सकल आँखि
अस्थिखण्ड पाइल शूलआगे ।
कारण पदान्यवलि सेइ अस्थि कण्ठे धरि
ध्यान करि वसिलेन योगे ॥

It is very interesting to note that the name of Kālīghāṭa near Calcutta is not found in this list prepared in South-west Bengal possibly a little later than the composition of the *Caṇḍīmaṅgala*. The popularity of Kālīghāṭa is probably later than the foundation of Calcutta by Job Charnock in 1690. Cf. *supra*, p. 24, note 1. Certain editions of Vaṃśīdāsa's *Manasāmaṅgala*, said to be composed in 1570 A.D., has:

एतेक शुनिया हरि वज्रकीट हइया ।
खण्ड खण्ड करि काटे चक्र प्रवेशिया ॥
सतीर माथार केश पड़िलेक यथा ।
काशी नामे तीर्थ हैल पूजये देवता ॥
चक्षुगुला खसिया ये पड़िल येखाने ।
उग्रतारा नाम तीर्थ विख्यात भुवने ॥
मुखह'ते जिह्वा पड़िल येथा थाकि ।
देवेर दुर्लभ तीर्थ नाम ज्वालामुखी ॥
नाभि काटिया विष्णु पाड़िल येखाने ।
नाभिगया नाम ताहा विख्यात भुवने ॥
दुइ चक्र चाके मात्र केह नाहि छाड़े ।
नीलाचल गिरि गिया योनिमुद्रा पड़े ॥
कामाख्या नाम तार चारिवेदे गाइ ।

Note the non-mention of Kalighat and the differences of this account from the other. Mahal Kalkattā in Sarkār Satgāon is, however, mentioned in the '*Ain-i-Akbarī* as paying in 1582, together with two other Mauzas, a land revenue of Rs.23,905 (*J.A.S.B.*, 1873, p. 217).

but omits such important old names as Uḍḍiyāna and Pūrṇagiri. The absence of such celebrated deities as Vindhyavāsinī is also striking. Some obscure names, e.g. Maṇiveda, Ratnāvalī, etc., do not appear in the earlier lists. Another feature of the list is that it (in its usually accepted form) not only regards the Devī's *hāra* (necklace), *kuṇḍala* (ear-ring) *kirīṭa* (crown) and *nūpura* (anklet) as so many of her limbs but, strangely enough, even includes in the same category her *manas* (mind). The author's knowledge of Sanskrit was probably poor, while the copyists and modifiers of the work could hardly claim any knowledge of the language. As a result of this, different versions of the text before us are full of discrepancies and mistakes often of an extremely baffling nature. In some manuscripts of the work the text is found in an exceptionally modified form. It will be interesting to compare the probable original text of the *Pīṭhanirṇaya* (reconstructed on the basis of Manuscript G and the *Annadāmaṅgala*) with the late modification in Manuscript H both quoted in Appendix I (A and B).

The List of Pīṭhas in the Pīṭhanirṇaya (Mahāpīṭhanirūpaṇa).

Reserving for the foot-notes on the text discussion on the discrepancies as regards the names of the Pīṭhas, the Pīṭha-devatās (forms of the Devī), the Kṣetrādhīśas (Bhairavas) and the Devī's *aṅga-pratyaṅga* (limbs including ornaments, etc.), the descriptive list supplied by the *Pīṭhanirṇaya* (*Mahāpīṭhanirūpaṇa*) may be offered in a tabular form.

Number	*Pīṭha*	*Aṅga-pratyaṅga*	*Devī*	*Bhairava*
1.	Hiṅgulā Hiṅgulāṭa	Brahmarandhra	Koṭṭarī Koṭṭavī Koṭṭarīśā	Bhīmalocana
2.	Karavīra Śarkarāra	Trinetra	Mahiṣamardinī	Krodhīśa Krodheśa
3.	Sugandhā	Nāsikā	Sunandā Sugandhā	Tryambaka
4.	Kāśmīra	Kaṇṭha	Mahāmāyā	Trisandhyeś-vara Trinetreśvara
5.	Jvālāmukhī	Jihvā	Siddhidā Ambikā	Unmatta
6.	Jālandhara	Stana	Tripuramālinī Tripuranāśinī	Bhīṣaṇa Īśāna
7.	Vaidyanātha	Hṛdaya	Jayadurgā	Vaidyanātha
8.	Nepāla	Jānu	Mahāmāyā	Kapālī
9.	Mānasa Mālava	Dakṣiṇa-hasta	Dākṣāyaṇī	Hara Hari Amara
10.	Virajākṣetra in Utkala	Nābhi	Vimalā Vijayā	Jagannātha Jaya
11.	Gaṇḍakī Gaṇḍaka	Gaṇḍa	Gaṇḍakī Caṇḍī	Cakrapāni Jagannātha
12.	Bahulā Bāhulā	Vāma-bāhu	Bahulā Bāhulā	Bhīruka Tīvraka
13.	Ujjayinī Ujānī Ujjanī Urjanī Urjayinī	Kūrpara	Maṅgalā Maṅgalacaṇḍī	Kapilāmbara Kapileśvara

Number	*Pīṭha*	*Aṅga-pratyaṅga*	*Devī*	*Bhairava*
14.	Caṭṭala (Candraśekhara)	Dakṣiṇa-bāhu	Bhavānī	Candraśekhara
15.	Tripurā	Dakṣiṇa-pāda	Tripurā Tripurasundarī	Nala Tripureśa Tripurākṣa
16.	Trisrotā (Sans. *Trisrotas*) Tirotā	Vāma-pāda	Bhrāmarī Amarī	Īśvara Ambara Amara
17.	Kāmagiri in Kāmarūpa (Ten Pīṭhas were originally located here)	Mahāmudrā (Yoni)	Kāmākhyā	Umānanda Śivānanda Rāmānanda Rāvānanda
18.	Yugādyā (Kṣīragrāma)	Dakṣiṇa-pādāṅ- guṣṭha	Yugādyā (Yogādyā)	Kṣīrakhaṇḍa Kṣīrakaṇṭha
19.	Kālīpīṭha Kālapīṭha (Kalighat)	Dakṣiṇa-pādāṅ- guli	Kālī	Nakuleśa Nakulīśa Nalīśa
20.	Prayāga	Hast-āṅguli	Lalitā	Bhava
21.	Jayantī Jayantā	Vāma-jaṅghā	Jayantī	Kramadīśvara
22.	Kirīṭa Kirīṭakoṇā	Kirīṭa	Bhuvaneśī Vimalā	Siddhirūpa Saṃvarta
23.	Maṇikarṇikā at Vārāṇasī	Kuṇḍala	Viśālākṣī	Kāla
24.	Kanyāśrama (see p. 37, note 1)	Pṛṣṭha Dṛṣṭi	Sarvāṇī	Nimiṣa
25.	Kurukṣetra	[Dakṣiṇa]-gulpha	Sāvitrī	Sthāṇu Snāyu
26.	Maṇiveda Maṇivedika Mānavedaka	Maṇibandha	Gāyatrī	Sarvānanda
27.	Śrīśaila Śrīhaṭṭa	Grīvā	Mahālakṣmī Mahāmāyā	Saṃvarānanda Samarānanda Sarvānanda
28.	Kāñcī	Kaṅkāla	Devagarbhā	Ruru
29.	Kālamādhava	Nitamba	Kālī	Asitāṅga
30.	Narmadā Śoṇa Śaila	Nitamba	Śoṇā Narmadā	Bhadrasena
31.	Rāmagiri Rājagiri Rāmākiṇī	Stana Nāsā Nalā	Śivānī	Caṇḍa
32.	Vṛndāvana (Umāvana) Keśajāla	Keśa	Umā Kātyāyanī	Bhūteśa Kṛṣṇanātha
33.	Śuci Anala	Ūrdhva-danta	Nārāyaṇī	Saṃhāra Saṃkrūra
34.	Pañcasāgara	Adhodanta	Vārāhī	Mahārudra
35.	Karatoyātaṭa	Vāma-karṇa Talpa Gulpha	Aparṇā	Vāmana Vāmeśa

Number	Pīṭha	Aṅga-pratyaṅga	Devī	Bhairava
36.	Śrīparvata	Dakṣiṇa-karṇa Talpa [Dakṣiṇa]-gulpha	Sundarī	Sundarānanda Sunandānanda
37.	Vibhāsa	Vāma-gulpha	Bhīmarūpā Kapālinī	Kapālī Sarvānanda
38.	Prabhāsa	Udara Adhara	Candrabhāgā	Vakratuṇḍa
39.	Bhairavaparvata Bhīruparvata	Ūrdhvoṣṭha Oṣṭha Tuṇḍa	Avantī	Lambakarṇa Namrakarṇa
40.	Janasthāna Jala-sthala	Civuka	Bhrāmarī	Vikṛta Vikṛtākṣa
41.	Godāvarītīra	[Vāma]-gaṇḍa	Viśveśī Rākiṇī	Viśveśa Daṇḍapāṇi Vatsanābha
42.	Ratnāvalī Ratnavatī	Dakṣiṇa-skandha	Kumārī Śivā	Śiva Kumāra
43.	Mithilā	Vāma-skandha	Umā Mahādevī	Mahodara

(The following Pīṭhas were omitted in the original text which located ten Pīṭhas in Kāmarūpa.)

Number	Pīṭha	Aṅga-pratyaṅga	Devī	Bhairava
44.	Nalāhāṭi	Nalā	Kālī	Yogīśa Yogeśa
45.	Kālīghāṭa (Kālīpīṭha)	Muṇḍa	Jayadurgā	Krodhīśa Krodheśa
46.	Vakreśvara	Manas	Mahiṣamardinī	Vakranātha
47.	Yaśora	Pāṇi	Yaśoreśvarī	Caṇḍa Caṇḍeśa
48.	Aṭṭahāsa	Oṣṭha	Phullarā	Viśveśa
49.	Nandipura	Hāra	Nandinī	Nandikeśvara
50.	Laṅkā	Nūpura	Indrākṣī	Rākṣaseśvara Nandikeśvara
51.	Virāṭa	Padāṅguli	Ambikā	Amṛta Amṛtākṣa[1]

[1] For Manibandha, a name created out of a confused text, and for Magadha and Karṇāṭa, interpolated by later modifiers of the text who could not make out 51 names from the text before them, see foot-notes on the text. Bhāratacandra omitted the last eight names together with Vārāṇasī and Kanyāśrama but recognized the ficticious Manibandha, while our G text omits only the last eight names and thus makes the number of Pīṭhas 52 (with Vārāṇasī and Kanyāśrama and with the extra nine Pīṭhas located at Kāmarūpa). It seems that the original text made a reference either to Kanyāśrama or to Vārāṇasī. The fifth Paṭala of the late *Bṛhan-Nīlatantra* contains no less than five lists of Pīṭhas. Four out of them together with another from the sixth Paṭala of the same Tantra have already been quoted (see *above*, pp. 21, note 1; 25, note 3; 28, note 2). A list like the following one quoted from the *Bṛhan-Nīla* may be regarded as the source of the belief, prevalent in some parts of Bengal, that the number of Pīṭhas is fifty-two (cf. our G text enumerating fifty-two Pīṭhas owing to confusion).

कामेशा कामरूपे त्वं पूर्णा काश्यां विशुद्धिदा
नेपाले पुष्पदा पुण्या सुवेशा पौण्ड्रवर्धने ॥

Modification of the Pīṭhanirṇaya (Mahāpīṭhanirūpaṇa) in the Śivacarita.

An attempt was made to utilize and improve upon the text of the *Pīṭhanirṇaya* (*Mahāpīṭhanirūpaṇa*) by the author of the *Śivacarita* which

---

धर्मबुद्धिः सुधा चैव सुखदा पापमोचनी ।
पारस्थे परमानन्दा ब्रह्माणी कान्यकुब्जके ॥
पुण्याद्री च महापुण्या पूर्णा यज्ञफलेश्वरी ।
कात्यायन्यर्बुदे देवि धनदा शिववल्लभा ॥
एका चैकाम्रके देशे सुरूपेशामकेश्वरे ।
त्रिपुरे सुन्दरी दिव्यरूपाखिलमनोहरा ॥
कामकोटे महापीठे प्रमदा मदनालसा ।
कामेश्वरी रतिश्चैव भृगुपुर्यां ब्रह्मेश्वरी ॥
ब्रह्मेशा च तपोलक्ष्मीः कैलासे भुवनेश्वरी ।
केदारे वरदा चैवाम्बता चन्द्रपुरे सिता ॥
कलावती प्रभेशा च श्रीपुरे श्रीरमा प्रिया ।
कुमारी ब्रह्मचर्या च कन्या च कन्यकापुरे ॥
जालन्धरे महापीठे नागर्याग्निमुखी शुभा ।
ज्वालामुखी लोलजिह्वा सुवेशा च सुरङ्गिणी ॥
मालवे च महाविद्या विल्वपीठे च रूपिणी ।
रूपवती महादेवी देवीकोटेऽखिलेश्वरी ॥
गोकर्णे प्रियपीठे त्वं रुद्राणी सर्वमङ्गला ।
पवने हरपीठे च गन्धश्रीश्च सुगन्धिका ॥
अट्टहासे महापीठे भीमकाली च कालिका ।
विरजे मुक्तिहेतुश्च नमःस्वस्तिस्वधामयी ॥
जयश्रीराजलक्ष्मीश्च सुवेशा राजपर्वते ।
एलापुरे महासम्पत् माहेश्वरी महापथे ॥
गायत्री ब्रह्मरूपा च तत्पदोङ्कारपीठके ।
जया जयपुरे देवी जयदा जयमङ्गला ॥
विजया मङ्गला गौरी उज्जयन्यां सदाशिवा ।
गौरीश्वरी महादेवी हरिद्रापीठके शिवा ॥
क्षीरपीठे युगाद्या च क्षीराख्या नियमप्रभा ।
राजेश्वरी महालक्ष्मीर्हस्तिनापुरवासिनी ॥
कमला विमला भक्ती रौद्री च नीलपर्वते ।
योगेश्वरी त्रिवेणी च त्रिस्रोता ब्रह्मरूपिणी ॥
सिन्धुस्थली कामधेनु षष्ठी षष्ठीपुरे प्रिये ।
माया मायापुरे देवी सुरभी सौरभेश्वरी ॥
विलासिनी महानन्दा प्रियचन्दनपर्वते ।
महाव्रजेश्वरी श्रेष्ठा श्मनेश्वरपीठके ॥
भवानी भवभक्ता च श्रीशैले शिववल्लभा ।
देवता या स्वर्गलक्ष्मीः कनकामरपर्वते ॥

has been analyzed by N. N. Vasu in the *Viśvakoṣa*, s.v. *pīṭha*. This work supplies a list of 51 Mahā-Pīṭhas (great Pīṭhas) and another of 26 Upa-Pīṭhas (Pīṭhas of lesser importance). Although the word *upapīṭha* is traced in such works as the *Sādhanamālā* (p. 479), no early lists of the less important Pīṭhas are known to us. The *Śivacarita* closely follows the text of the *Pīṭhanirṇaya* in regard to 41 (actually 42, but the name Maṇibandha is due to textual confusion) out of the 51 great Pīṭhas, the remaining 10 names as given in the latter not being found in that work. It is interesting to note in this connection that Bhāratacandra, who mentions 42 Pīṭhas (including Manibandha) by name and locates 10 Pīṭhas at one of them to make the number 51, closely follows in his *Annadāmaṅgala* the readings of the *Śivacarita* in spite of his avowed indebtedness to the *Mantracūḍāmaṇi* (for *Tantracūḍāmaṇi*) *Tantra*. These facts suggests that the original text of the *Pīṭhanirṇaya* actually but partially followed the *Kubjikā Tantra* in offering only the names of 42 Pīṭhas, while the number of the Pīṭhas was made 51 by locating the ten Mahāvidyās (manifestations of Śakti conceived in imitation of the Daśāvatāra of Viṣṇu) at Kāmarūpa. If such was the case, it is tempting to suggest that some verses containing the names of certain obscure Pīṭhas especially in the concluding part of the *Pīṭhanirṇaya* text (cf. verses 48–55) were added to the original text at a later date. They may have been inspired and influenced by the *Śivacarita*. The above suggestion seems to be strongly supported by the fact that verses 48–55 of our *Pīṭhanirṇaya* text containing the names of Nalāhāṭī, Kālīghāṭa, Vakreśvara, Yaśora, Aṭṭahāsa, Nandipura, Laṅkā and Virāṭadeśa (including the variants Karṇāṭa and Magadha) are conspicuous by their absence from some manuscripts of the *Pīṭhanirṇaya*; cf. our G text.

The evidence of the *Annadāmaṅgala* has been quoted in the foot-notes on the text of the *Pīṭhanirṇaya*, while the descriptive list of the *Śivacarita* is offered below in a tabular form.

List of the Pīṭhas (Mahāpīṭhas) and Upapīṭhas in the Śivacharita.

A—*Mahāpīṭhas*

Number	*Pīṭha*	*Aṅga-pratyaṅga*	*Devī*	*Bhairava*
1.	Hiṅgulā	Brahmarandhra	Koṭṭarī	Bhīmalocana
2.	Śarkara	Trinetra	Mahiṣamardinī	Krodhīśa
3.	Tārā	Netrāṃśa-tārā	Tāriṇī	Unmatta

उमा गौरी सती सत्या पार्वती हिमपर्वते ।
इन्द्रेश्वरी सुराराध्या माहेन्द्रे जगदीश्वरी ॥
चक्षा भोगेश्वरी नित्या श्रीमद्द्विपुरे शिवा ।
सुवर्णा कनका रामा हिरण्यपुरपीठके ॥
महालक्ष्मीर्महेशानी महालक्ष्मीपुरेऽम्बिका ।
चण्डपुरे प्रचण्डा च चण्डा चण्डवती शिवा ॥
वङ्गे मेघस्वना चैव मायाख्येश्वरी (काया° ?) तथा ।
कालीघट्टे महापीठे काली कालात्मिका तथा ॥
लिङ्गाख्ये भैरवी विद्या विजया जाह्नवीतटे ।
इति ते कथितं दिव्यं पीठक्रममुदाहृतम् ॥

It is to be noted that the six lists of Pīṭhas found in the *Bṛhan-Nīlatantra* do not agree fully with one another and are not free from mistakes.

Number	*Pīṭha*	*Aṅga-pratyaṅga*	*Devī*	*Bhairava*
4.	Karatoyātaṭa	Vāma-karṇa	Aparṇā	Vāmeśa
5.	Śrīparvata	Dakṣiṇa-karṇa	Sundarī	Sundarānanda
6.	Sugandhā	Nāsikā	Sunandā	Tryambaka
7.	Vakranātha	Manas	Pāpaharā	Vakranātha
8.	Godāvarī	Vāma-gaṇḍa	Viśvamātṛkā	Viśveśa
9.	Gaṇḍakī	Dakṣiṇa-gaṇḍa	Gaṇḍakī	Cakrapāṇi
10.	Anala	Ūrdhva-danta	Nārāyaṇī	Saṃkrūra
11.	Pañcasāgara	Adho-danta	Vārāhī	Mahārudra
12.	Jvālāmukhī	Jihvā	Ambikā	Vaṭakeśvara Unmatta
13.	Kāśmīra	Kaṇṭha	Mahāmāyā	Trisandhya
14.	Śrīhaṭṭa	Grīvā	Mahālakṣmī	Sarvānanda
15.	Bhairavaparvata	Oṣṭha	Avantī	Namrakarṇa
16.	Prabhāsa	Adhara	Candrabhāgā	Vakratuṇḍa
17.	Prabhāsakhaṇḍa	Marma	Siddheśvarī	Siddheśvara
18.	Janasthāna	Civuka	Bhrāmarī	Vikṛtākṣa
19.	Prayāga	Dvi-hast-āṅguli	Kamalā	Veṇīmādhava
20.	Mānasa-sarovara	Dakṣiṇa-hastārdha (Vāma-hasta)	Dākṣāyaṇī	Hara
21.	Caṭṭagrāma	Dakṣiṇa-hastārdha	Bhavānī	Candraśekhara
22.	Mithilā	Vāma-skandha	Mahādevī	Mahodara
23.	Ratnāvalī	Dakṣiṇa-skandha	Śivā	Śiva Kumāra
24.	Maṇibandha	Vāma-maṇibandha	Gāyatrī	Śaṅkara Sarvāṇa
25.	Maṇiveda	Dakṣiṇa-maṇibandha	Sāvitrī	Sthāṇu
26.	Ujānī	Vāma-kaphoni	Maṅgalacaṇḍī	Kapilāmbara
27.	Raṇakhaṇḍa	Dakṣiṇa-kaphoni	Bahulākṣī	Mahākāla
28.	Bahulā	Vāma-bāhu	Bahulā	Bhīruka
29.	Vakreśvara	Dakṣiṇa-bāhu	Vakreśvarī	Vakreśvara
30.	Jālandhara	Vāma-stana	Tripuramālinī	Bhīṣaṇa
31.	Rāmagiri	Dakṣiṇa-stana	Śivānī	Caṇḍa
32.	Vaivasvata	Pṛṣṭha	Tripuṭā	Śamanakarman Nimiṣa
33.	Vaidyanātha	Hṛdaya	Navadurgā Jayadurgā	Vaidyanātha
34.	Utkala	Nābhi	Vijayā	Jaya
35.	Haridvāra	Jaṭhara	Bhairavī	Vakra
36.	Kŏkāmukha	Kŏk (Sans. *Kukṣi*)	Kŏkeśvarī	Kŏkeśvara
37.	Kāñcī	Kaṅkāla	Vedagarbhā	Ruru
38.	Kālamādhava	Vāma-nitamba	Kālī	Asitāṅga
39.	Narmadā	Dakṣiṇa-nitamba	Śoṇākṣī	Bhadrasena
40.	Kāmarūpa	Mahāmudrā (Yoni)	Kāmākhyā Nīlapārvatī	Rāvānanda Umānanda
41.	Mālava	Vāma-jānu	Śubhacaṇḍī	Tāmra
42.	Trisrotā (Sans. *Trisrotas*)	Dakṣiṇa-jānu	Caṇḍikā	Sadānanda
43.	Jayantī	Vāma-jaṅghā	Jayantī	Kramadīśvara
44.	Nepāla	Dakṣiṇa-jaṅghā	Mahāmāyā Navadurgā	Kapālī

Number	*Pīṭha*	*Aṅga-pratyaṅga*	*Devī*	*Bhairava*
45.	Trihuta (Sans. *Tīrabhukti*)	Vāma-pāda	Amarī	Amara
46.	Tripurā	Dakṣiṇa-pāda	Tripurā	Nala
47.	Kṣīragrāma	Dakṣiṇa-pād-āṅguṣṭha	Yogādyā	Kṣīrakhaṇḍa
48.	Kālīghāṭa	Dakṣiṇa-pād-āṅguli	Kālikā	Nakuleśa
49.	Vibhāsa	Vāma-gulpha	Bhīmarūpā	Kapālī
50.	Kurukṣetra	Dakṣiṇa-gulpha	Saṃvarī Vimalā	Saṃvarta
51.	Vindhyaśekhara	Vāma-pād-āṅguli	Vindhyavāsinī	Puṇyabhājana

B—*Upapīṭhas*

1.	Kirīṭakoṇā	Kirīṭa	Bhuvaneśī	Kirīṭin
2.	Keśajāla	Keśa	Umā	Bhūteśa
3.	Vārāṇasī	Kuṇḍala	Viśālākṣī Annapūrṇā	Kālabhairava Viśveśvara
4.	Uttarā	Vāma-gaṇḍ-āṃśa	Uttariṇī	Utsādana
5.	Nalasthāna	Dakṣiṇa-gaṇḍ-āṃśa	Bhrāmarī	Virūpākṣa
6.	Aṭṭahāsa	Oṣṭhāṃśa	Phullarā	Viśvanātha
7.	Saṃhāra	Dantāṃśa	Śūreśī	Śūreśa
8.	Nīlācala	Ucchiṣṭa	Vimalā	Jagannātha
9.	Ayodhyā	Kaṇṭha-hāra	Annapūrṇā	Harihara
10.	Nandipura	Hār-āṃśa	Nandinī	Nandīśvara
11.	Śrīśaila	Grīv-āṃśa	Sarveśvarī	Carcitānanda
12.	Kālīpīṭha	Śiroṃśa	Caṇḍeśvarī	Caṇḍeśvara
13.	Cakradvīpa	Astra	Cakradhāriṇī	Śūlapāṇi
14.	Yaśora	Pāṇi	Yaśoreśvarī	Pracaṇḍa
15.	Satīcala	Karāṃśa	Sunandā	Sunanda
16.	Vṛndāvana	Skandhāṃśa	Kumārī	Kumāra
17.	Gaurīśekhara	Vasā	Yugādyā	Bhīma
18.	Nalahāṭī	Śirānālī	Śephālikā	Yogīśa
19.	Sarvaśaila	Kakṣāṃśa	Viśvamātā	Daṇḍapāṇi
20.	Śoṇa	Nitambāṃśa	Bhadrā	Bhadreśvara
21.	Trisrotā (cf. p. 40, No. 42)	Pādāṃśa	Pārvatī	Īśvara
22.	Laṅkā	Nūpura	Indrākṣī	Rākṣaseśvara
23.	Kaṭaka	Carmāṃśa	Kaṭakeśvarī	Vāmadeva
24.	Puṇḍra	Loma	Sarvākṣiṇī	Sarva
25.	Tailaṅga	Lomakhaṇḍa	Caṇḍadāyikā	Caṇḍeśa
26.	Śvetabandha	Bhagnāṃśa	Jayā	Mahābhīma[1]

Materials utilized in the Present Edition of the Pīṭhanirṇaya (Mahāpīṭhanirūpaṇa).

The subjoined text of the *Pīṭhanirṇaya* (*Mahāpīṭhanirūpaṇa*) is based upon the following sources.

A—Manuscript No. 196, entitled *Pīṭhanirṇaya* (and probably also *Mahāpīṭhalakṣaṇa*), in the Government Collection of the Royal Asiatic Society of Bengal.

[1] I have failed to secure and examine any copy of the *S'ivacarita*.

B—Manuscript No. 3400, entitled *Mahāpīṭhanirūpaṇa*, in the Government Collection of the Royal Asiatic Society of Bengal.

C—Manuscript No. 5303, entitled *Mahāpīṭhanirūpaṇa*, in the Government Collection of the Royal Asiatic Society of Bengal.

D—Text entitled *Mahāpīṭhanirūpaṇa*, quoted from the *Tantracūḍāmaṇi* in the *Prāṇatoṣaṇī Tantra*, Vasumatī ed., pp. 234ff.

E—Text entitled *Pīṭhanirṇaya*, quoted from the *Tantracūḍāmaṇi* in the *Śabdakalpadruma*, s.v. *pīṭha*.

F—Text quoted in the *Vācaspatya* by Tārānātha Tarkavācaspati, s.v. *pīṭha*.

G—Manuscript entitled *Pīṭhanirṇaya*, in the Collection of Mr. S. K. Saraswati of the Calcutta University. This manuscript, collected from Rajshahi, was copied about the second quarter of the eighteenth century.

H—Manuscript No. 10863, entitled *Pīṭhanirṇaya*, in the Indian Museum Collection of the Royal Asiatic Society of Bengal. As the text found in this manuscript has wide variations it has been quoted in Appendix I—B. Cf. this text with that of the *Śivacarita*.

I—Manuscript No. 402 (Sanskrit), entitled *Pīṭhanirṇaya*, in the Collection of the Vaṅgīya Sāhitya Pariṣat, Calcutta; copied on the 14th Bhādra, Śaka 1760 (1838 A.D.) and B.S. 1245.

AM—The Bengali version of the *Pīṭhanirṇaya* (*Mahāpīṭhanirūpaṇa*) in the Pīṭhamālā section of the *Annadāmaṅgala* by Bhāratacandra, Vaṅgavāsī ed., pp. 43–47.

Text of the Pīṭhanirṇaya or Mahāpīṭhanirūpaṇa.

पीठनिर्णयः (महापीठनिरूपणम्)[1]

[Sections within square brackets are due to later modifications of the text. They have either to be omitted or to be corrected according to indications given in the foot-notes. Vide Appendix I.]

ईश्वर उवाच ।[2]

मातः परात्परे देवि सर्वज्ञानमयीश्वरि ।
कथ्यतां मे सर्वपीठशक्तिभैरवदेवताः[3] ॥ १ ॥

---

[1] The section is styled पीठनिर्णयः in AEGHI; but महापीठनिरूपणं in BCD. The expression महापीठलक्षणं also occurs in A.

[2] A—अथ महापीठलक्षणं ॥ श्रीईश्वर उवाच ॥ B—श्रीगुरवे नमः ॥ श्रीईश्वर उवाच ॥ CD—तन्त्रचूडामणौ (चन्द्रचूडामणौ in C) महापीठनिरूपणं यथा । ईश्वर उवाच । E—ईश्वर उवाच । G—श्रीहरिः । ईश्वर उवाच । H—ॐ नमो भगवत्यै ॥ उक्तं भावचूडामणौ । अथ पीठनिर्णयः । I—ॐ नमः शिवाय । ईश्वर उवाच । Reference to the *Tantracūḍāmaṇi* is found in the colophon of ABEI.

[3] BCDE—शक्तिभैरव°

देव्युवाच ।[1]

शृणु वत्स प्रवक्ष्यामि दंयाल भक्तवत्सल ।

याभिर्विना न सिध्यन्ति जपसाधनसत्क्रियाः[2] ॥ २ ॥

पञ्चाशदेकपीठानि एवं भैरवदेवताः[3] ।

अङ्गप्रत्यङ्गपातेन विष्णुचक्रक्षतेन च[4] ।

ममाद्यवपुषो[5] देव हिताय त्वयि कथ्यते ॥ ३ ॥

ब्रह्मरन्ध्रं हिङ्गुलायां[6] भैरवो भीमलोचनः ।

कोट्टरी[7] सा महादेव त्रिगुणा या दिगम्बरी ॥ ४ ॥

---

1 A—श्रीपार्वत्युवाच; G—श्रीदेव्युवाच ।

2 ABDEI—°तत्क्रियाः; G—मन्त्रसाधनतत्क्रियाः; I—यासां विना ।

3 A—एकपञ्चाशतं पीठं शक्तिभैरवदेवताः; BCD—एकपञ्चाशतं पीठं शक्तिभैरवदेवताः; F—एकपञ्चाशच्च पीठाः शक्तिभैरवदेवताः । I—पञ्चाशदेकपीठञ्च ।

AM— तथाय सतीर देह गिया चक्रपाणि ।
काटिलेन चक्रधारे करि खानि खानि ॥
येखाने येखाने अङ्ग पड़िल सतीर ।
महापीठ सेइ स्थान पूजित विधिर ॥
करिया एकान्न खण्ड काटिला केशव ।
विधाता पूजिला भव हइला भैरव ॥

Although AM refers to 51 Pīṭhas, it actually speaks of 42 and omits Vārāṇasī, Kanyāśrama, Nalāhāṭī, Kālīpīṭha or Karṇāṭa, Vakreśvara, Aṭṭahāsa, Yaśora (Jessore), Virāṭadeśa, Nandipura and Laṅkā. This is because AM locates ten Pīṭhas (associated with the ten fingers of Satī's hands) at Prayāga. AM's readings in most cases tally with those of the *Śivacarita*. Our G text omits all the extra names excepting Vārāṇasī and Kanyāśrama, while AM's original suggested Maṇibandha instead. The original text seems to have had 42 names (with 10 Pīṭhas located in Kāmarūpa) including either Vārāṇasī or Kanyāśrama.

4 च is omitted in AC. G—हरिचक्र° ।

5 A—ममान्यवपुयो; B—[ममा]द्यवपुषा; CDE—ममान्यवपुषो; F—ममास्य वपषो: G—ममास्य वपुषो देव हिताया:मररक्षसाम्; I—सामान्यवपुषो देव हिताय देवरक्षसाम् ।

6 I—हिङ्गुलाटे ।

7 AGI—कोट्टवी सा महादेवी; B—क[ट्टरी] सा महादेवी त्रिगुणा च; C—कोट्टरीशा महादेवी; D—कोट्टरी सा महादेव; E—कोट्टरी सा महामाया; F—कोट्टरीशा महादेव ।

AM— हिङ्गुलाय ब्रह्मरन्ध्र फेलिल केशव ।
देवता कोट्टवी भीमलोचन भैरव ॥

The words *Koṭarī*, *Koṭavī* and *Koṭṭavī* are found in Sanskrit lexicons in the sense of 'a naked woman'; cf. *digambarī* (naked) as an epithet of the Indian mother-goddess. Hiṅgulā is modern Hinglaj (lat. 25° N., long. 65° E.) in Baluchistan. The goddess is locally known as Bībī Nānī, probably the same as Nana known from the Kuṣāṇa coins. Nana was the great mother-goddess worshipped in wide regions of Western and Central Asia.

करवीरे[1] त्रिनेत्रं मे देवी महिषमर्दिनी ।
क्रोधीशो[2] भैरवस्तत्र
सुगन्धायाश्च नासिका[3] ॥ ५ ॥
देवस्त्र्यम्बकनामा च सुनन्दा तत्र देवता ॥ ६ ॥
काश्मीरे कण्ठदेशश्च[4] त्रिसन्ध्येश्वरभैरवः ।
महामाया भगवती गुणातीता वरप्रदा ॥ ७ ॥
ज्वालामुख्यां तथा जिह्वा[5] देव उन्मत्तभैरवः ।
अम्बिका सिद्धिदा नाम्नी (देवी)[6]
स्तनं[7] जालन्धरे मम ॥ ८ ॥

---

[1] D (v.l.) EGI—शर्करारे ।

AM— शर्करारे तिन चक्षु त्रिगुणभैरव (वैभव) ।
महिषमर्दिनी देवी क्रोधीश भैरव ॥

Karavīra or Karavīrapura is often identified with Śarkarāra which is supposed to be no other than modern Sukkur, the chief city of the District of that name in Sind. According to the *Kālikā Purāṇa* (chs. 38-39), Karavīrapura was the capital of the Brahmāvarta country (Eastern Punjab) and was situated near the river Dṛṣadvatī; but the city is usually identified with Kolhapur (locally called Karvir) in the Bombay Presidency.

[2] ABI—क्रोधेशो ।

[3] GI—सुगन्धा नासिका मम ; I—सुगन्धा तत्र देवता ;

E—क्रोधीशो भैरवस्तत्र सर्वसिद्धिप्रदायकः ॥
सुगन्धायां नासिका मे देवस्त्र्यम्बकभैरवः ।
सुन्दरी सा महादेवी सुनन्दा तत्र देवता ॥

The elaboration of the text in E seems to be a later modification of the original.

AM— सुगन्धाय नासिका पड़िल चक्रहता ।
त्र्यम्बक भैरव ताहे सुनन्दा देवता ॥

The Pīṭha is located at Shikārpur (about 13 miles to the north of Barisal in the Buckergungé District) on the Sondha (Sugandhā). The temple of Tryambakeśvara stands at Ponābāliā-Sāmrāil (about 3 miles to the south of Jhālakāṭi) on the same stream.

[4] B—कण्ठदेशं मे ; I—त्रिनेत्रेश्वरभैरवः ।

AM— काश्मीरेते कण्ठ देवी महामाया ताय ।
त्रिसन्ध्य-ईश्वर नाम भैरव तथाय ॥

As there is no reference to the celebrated Śāradā (Sardi) and Amaranātha *tīrthas* of Kāshmīr, there seems to be a fantastic element in the description of this Pīṭha.

[5] A—महाजिह्वां देवशोन्मत्त° ; B—तथा जिह्वां ; CDEF—महाजिह्वा ; G—महाजिह्वा देवतो° ; I—महाजिह्वां देव उन्मत्तभैरव ।

[6] A—लक्ष्मीः ।

AM— ज्वालामुखे जिह्वा ताहे अग्नि अनुभव ।
देवीर अम्बिका नाम उन्मत्त भैरव ॥

This seems to suggest the reading अम्बिका सिद्धिदा देवी । Jvālāmukhī (lat. 31° N., long. 76° E.) lies in the Kangra District of the Punjab.

[7] F—स्तनौ ।

भीषणो भैरवस्तत्र देवी त्रिपुरमालिनी[1] ॥ ९ ॥

हार्दपीठं[2] वैद्यनाथे वैद्यनाथस्तु भैरवः ।

देवता जयदुर्गाख्या

नेपाले जानु मे शिव[3] ॥ १० ॥

कपाली भैरवः श्रीमान् महामाया च देवता ॥ ११ ॥

मानसे दक्षहस्तो[4] मे देवी दाक्षायणी हर (हरः) ।

[अमरो भैरवस्तत्र सर्वसिद्धिप्रदायकः] ॥ १२ ॥

[उत्कले नाभिदेशस्य[5] विरजाक्षेत्रमुच्यते] ।

विमला सा महादेवी जगन्नाथस्तु भैरवः ॥ १३ ॥

---

1 E—त्रिपुरमासिनी ; B—ईशानो भैरवस्तत्र देवी त्रिपुरनाशिनी ।

AM— जालन्धरे तांहार पड़िल एक स्तन ।
त्रिपुरमालिनी देवी भैरव भीषण ॥

Jālandhara (lat. 31° N., long. 75° E.) is the chief city of the Jullundur District of the East Punjab. But the Pīṭha is located near Jvālāmukhī.

2 ACF—हृद्यपीठं ; B—हृद्यं पीठं ; I—देवताख्या जयदुर्गा ।

AM— वैद्यनाथे हृदय भैरव वैद्यनाथ ।
देवी ताहे जयदुर्गा सर्वसिद्धि साथ ॥

Vaidyanātha is the same as Deoghar-Vaidyanathdham (lat. 86° E., long. 24° N.) in the Santal Parganas District of Bihar.

3 DE—जानुनी मम ।

AM— नेपाले दक्षिण जङ्घा कपाली भैरव ।
देवी ताय महामाया सदा महोत्सव ॥

The non-mention of Paśupatinātha, the most famous deity in Nepal, in this connection seems to expose the imaginary character of the description.

4 I—°हस्तं ; ABC—मालवे दक्षहस्तं ; F—मालवे ; G—दाक्षायणी हरिः ।

AM— चार चर्द्ध डानि हस्त मानसरोवरे ।
देवी दाक्षायणी हर भैरव विहरे ॥

AM suggests the reading हरः and the omission of the second half of the verse. The Mānasa lake (lat. 30° N., long. 81° E.), the source of the river Śatadru (Satlej), is in the Himalayas. Since Ujjayinī, a city in Mālava, is separately mentioned (v. 16), मानसे appears to be the reading intended. But nothing can be said definitely as Ujjayinī in this case may actually represent a village of Bengal. It is, however, to be noted that the celebrated god Mahākāla (Śiva) is not mentioned in connection either with Ujjayinī or with Mālava. Mālava is modern Malwa; but the name often indicated East Malwa of which the ancient capital was Vidiśā (modern Besnagar in the Gwalior State).

5 ABCF—नाभिदेशस्तु ; I—°देशश्च ।

G— विरजा चोत्कले ख्याता नाभिर्मे मम(जय ?) भैरवः ।
गण्डक्यां गण्डकी(गण्डकः?) चण्डी जगन्नाथस्तु भैरवः ॥

Although not free from mistake, this probably points to the original reading of verses 13-14. For elaboration of the earlier text as a later trait, cf. p. 44, note 3.

गण्डक्यां[1] गण्डपातश्च तत्र सिद्धिर्न संशयः ।
तत्र सा[2] गण्डकी चण्डी चक्रपाणिस्तु भैरवः ॥ १४ ॥]
बहुलायां वामबाहुर्बहुलाख्या च देवता ।
भीरुको भैरवस्तत्र[3] सर्वसिद्धिप्रदायकः ॥ १५ ॥
उज्जयिन्यां कूर्परश्च[4] माङ्गल्य-कपिलाम्बरः (मङ्गला कपिलाम्बरः) ॥
[भैरवः सिद्धिदः साक्षाद्देवी मङ्गलचण्डिका] ॥ १६ ॥

AM— उत्कले पड़िल नाभि मोच याचा सेवि ।
जय नामे भैरव विजया नामे देवी ॥

AM suggests the reading विजया सा महादेवी जयनामा तु भैरवः । or
विजया चोत्कले ख्याता नाभिर्मे जयभैरवः ॥

Virajā or Virajākṣetra is identical with modern Jājpur (lat. 20° N., long. 86° E.) in the Cuttack District of Orissa.

Cf. ततो वैतरणीं गच्छेत् सर्वपापप्रमोचनीम् ।
विरजं तीर्थमासाद्य विराजति यथा शशी ॥
(महाभारत ।३।८५।६)

The name of the Bhairava in the modified text is apparently borrowed from the god Jagannātha at Purī and probably hints at an attempt of claiming that deity to be a manifestation of Śiva.

1 B—गण्डकी गण्डपातश्च; E—गण्डपातश्च; I—गण्डक्यां गण्डकी चण्डी चक्रपाणिस्तु भैरवः ।

AM— गण्डकीते हानि गण्ड पड़े चक्रधाय ।
चक्रपाणि भैरव गण्डकी चण्डी ताय ॥

This suggests the reading गण्डक्यां दक्षगण्डश्च । The Gaṇḍakī (modern Gandak) is a tributary of the Ganges and meets the latter river near Bakhtyarpur in Bihar. The Pīṭha has been located at Śālagrāma at the source of the Gandak.

2 A—सा तत्र ।

3 I—बाहुलायां; तीवको भैरवो देवः; D—भैरवो देवः ।

AM— बाहुलाय वामबाहु फेलिला केशव ।
बाहुला चण्डिका तारे भीरुक भैरव ॥

AM suggests the reading बाहुलायां वामबाहुर्बाहुलाख्या । The Pīṭha is located at Ketugrāma near Katwa in the Burdwan District.

4 A—उज्जन्यां कर्परश्चैव; B—उजंन्यां कुर्परश्चापि; G—उर्ज्जयिन्यां कुर्परश्च माङ्गल्ये (मङ्गला ?); I—तर्ज्जन्यां च कार्पूरं माङ्गल्ये कपिलेश्वर ।

AM— उजानीते कफोनि मङ्गलचण्डी देवी ।
भैरव कपिलाम्बर शुभ यांरे सेवि ॥

AM seems to refer to Ujānī or Kogrām in the Burdwan District of Bengal, although Ujjayinī (modern Ujjain) in the early lists of Pīṭhas must be identified with the famous city in Avanti or West Mālava, now lying in the Gwalior State in Western India. Note that the name of the Bhairava is not Mahākāla who is known to have been the tutelary deity of Ujjayinī. The 12 *jyotirliṅgas* as enumerated in the *Śiva Purāṇa* (I, 38, 17–20) are Somanātha in Saurāṣṭra, Mallikārjuna on the Śrīśaila, Mahākāla at Ujjayinī, Oṅkāra at Amareśvara, Kedāra in the Himalayas, Bhīmaśaṅkara at Ḍākinī

चट्टले दक्षबाहुर्मे भैरवश्चन्द्रशेखरः ।
व्यक्तरूपा भगवती भवानी यत्र[1] देवता ।
विशेषतः कलियुगे वसामि चन्द्रशेखरे ॥ १७ ॥
त्रिपुरायां दक्षपादो देवी त्रिपुरसुन्दरी (देवता त्रिपुरा नलः)[2] ।
[भैरवस्त्रिपुरेशश्च[3] सर्वाभीष्टप्रदायकः[4]] ॥ १८ ॥
त्रिस्रोतायां वामपादो भ्रामरी भैरवेश्वरः[5] ॥ १९ ॥
योनिपीठं कामगिरौ[6] कामाख्या तत्र देवता ।
यत्रास्ते त्रिगुणातीता रक्तपाषाणरूपिणी[7] ॥ २० ॥

(at the source of the Bhīmā north-west of Poona), Viśveśvara at Vārāṇasī, Tryambaka on the bank of the Gautamī (Godāvarī) near Nasik, Vaidyanātha at Citābhūmi (Deoghar-Baidyanathdham in the Santal Parganas), Nāgeśa at Dārukāvana (Aundh ?), Rāmeśvara at Setubandha, and Ghṛṣṇeśa (Ghuśriṇeśa, Ghuśmeśa) at Śivālaya (Ellora near Daulatabad). The original reading of the passage may have been उज्जयिन्यां कूर्परश्च मङ्गल्या कपिलाम्बरः with the second line of the verse omitted. Cf. pp. 44, note 3 ; 45, note 5.

1 BDEFI—तत्र ।

AM— चट्टग्रामे डानिहस्त पड़े अनुभव ।
भवानी देवता चन्द्रशेखर भैरव ॥

The Pīṭha is located at the Sītākuṇḍa on the Chandranath hill in the Chittagong District of East Bengal.

2 D (v.l.) E—देवता त्रिपुरा मता ; G—देवता त्रिपुरा मलः ।

AM— दक्षिण चरणखानि पड़े त्रिपुराय ।
नल नामे भैरव त्रिपुरा देवी ताय ॥

The original reading was apparently त्रिपुरायां दक्षपादो देवता त्रिपुरा नलः with the second line of the verse omitted (cf. p. 46, note 4). The Pīṭha is located at Radhakishorepur (old Rāṅgāmāṭi or Udaypur) in the Tripurā (Hill Tipperah) State in Bengal. The city of Tripura or Tripurī, mentioned in early literature, has, however, to be identified with modern Tewar near Jubbulpur in the Central Province. The temple of the goddess at Radhakishorepur was built by king Dharmamāṇikya in Śaka 1423 (1501 A.D.).

3 A—°स्त्रिपुराश्च । See the *S'ivacarita*, AM, and the G text which speak of the Bhairava as Nala (cf. note 2 above).

4 E—°फलप्रदः ।

5 DEG—भैरवोऽम्बरः ; I—भैरवाम्बरः ।

AM— तिरोताय पड़े वामपद मनोहर ।
भ्रामरी देवता ताहे भैरव अमर ॥

AM suggests the reading तिरोतायां वामपादश्चामरी भैरवोऽमरः । It is interesting to note that the word *tirotā* stands for Sanskrit *strī* in the Assamese language. But AM here follows the *S'ivacarita* passage referring to *Trihuta* (Sans. *Tīrabhukti*), modern Tirhut or North Bihar. Trisrotā is of course the modern Tista, a tributary of the Brahmaputra or Yamunā. The Pīṭha is located at Sālbāri in the Jalpaiguri District.

6 G—कामरूपे ।

7 AG—व्यक्ता (I—व्यक्त°) पाषाण° ; G—°श्चिवानन्दोऽथ भैरवः ; तस्मान्नीलाचलो यत्र ; I—°मात्रात् उमानन्दाथ ; भस्माचलो भवेद्यत्र ।

AM— महामुद्रा कामरूपे रजोयोग याय ।
रामानन्द (v.l. रावा°) भैरव कामाख्या देवी ताय ।

यत्रास्ते माधवः साक्षादुमानन्दोऽथ भैरवः ।
सर्वदा विहरेद्देवी तत्र मुक्तिर्न संशयः ॥ २१ ॥
तत्र श्रीभैरवी देवी तत्र च क्षेत्रदेवता[1] ।
प्रचण्डचण्डिका तत्र मातङ्गी त्रिपुराम्बिका[2] ।
वगला कमला तत्र भुवनेशी सधूमिनी[3] ॥ २२ ॥

AM suggests the reading साक्षाद् रामानन्दोऽथ or साक्षाद् रावानन्दोऽथ । The Kāmarūpa Pīṭha has been located near Gauhati in Assam. The homage paid by certain early rulers of Assam to Kāmeśvara and Mahāgaurī (Kāmākhyā) seems to point to the old name of the Bhairava at the Kāmarūpa Pīṭha.

[1] ABCE—नक्षत्रदेवता ; D—न क्षेत्रदेवता ; GI—यत्र च भैरवी देवी यत्र नक्षत्रदेवता । Kāmagiri in Kāmarūpa is represented as the seat of the ten Mahāvidyās whose names are given as Bhairavī, Kāmākhyā (Kṣetradevatā), Pracaṇḍacaṇḍikā (i.e. Chinnamastā; cf. *Tantrasāra*, pp. 802ff.), Mātaṅgī, Tripurā, Ambikā, Vagalā, Bhuvaneśī (Bhuvaneśvarī) and Dhūminī (Dhūmāvatī). The usually recognized names of the Mahāvidyās (a late medieval Śākta adaptation of the Daśāvatāra conception) are however Kālī, Tārā, Ṣoḍaśī, Bhuvaneśvarī, Bhairavī, Chinnamastā, Dhūmāvatī, Vagalā, Mātaṅgī and Kamalā (the *Bṛhaddharma P.*, II, 6, 126, having Sundarī for Kamalā and Bagalāmukhī for Bagalā). Cf.

काली तारा महाविद्या षोडशी भुवनेश्वरी ।
भैरवी छिन्नमस्ता च विद्या धूमावती तथा ।
वगला सिद्धविद्या च मातङ्गी कमलात्मिका ॥

referred to the *Cāmuṇḍā Tantra* in the *Śabdakalpadruma*, s.v., and to the *Muṇḍamālā Tantra* (cf. *Des. Cat. Sans. MSS.*, R.A.S.B., VIII, p. 164) in the *Tantrasāra* (p. 14). Only some of the names are common to the two lists. That, however, there was no unanimity about the names of the ten Mahāvidyās is demonstrated by another list quoted from the *Mālinīvijaya* in the *Tantrasāra* (*loc. cit.*):

काली नीला महादुर्गा त्वरिता छिन्नमस्तका ।
वाग्वादिनी चान्नपूर्णा तथा प्रत्यङ्गिरा पुनः ॥
कामाख्यावासिनी वाला मातङ्गी शैलवासिनी ॥

This list agrees with that of the *Pīṭhanirṇaya* in recognizing Kāmākhyāvāsinī or Kāmākhyā as one of the ten Mahāvidyās. The name Pracaṇḍacaṇḍikā, recognized by the *Pīṭhanirṇaya*, is found in the following list of the ten Mahāvidyās quoted from the *Tantracintāmaṇi* in *Des. Cat. Sans. MSS.*, R.A.S.B., VIII, p. 388: (1) Śyāmā (Kālī), (2) Tārā, (3) Pracaṇḍacaṇḍikā, (4) Śrī (Kamalā), (5) Bhairavī, (6) Mahālakṣmī, (7) Mātaṅgī, (8) Bhuvaneśvarī, (9) Dhūmāvatī, and (10) Vagalā. An interesting list of the Mahāvidyās in the *Guhyātiguhya Tantra* (*Des. Cat.*, p. 206) identifies the manifestations of the mother-goddess with the ten Avatāras of Viṣṇu :

कृष्णमूर्त्तिः कालिका स्याद् राममूर्त्तिस्तु तारिणी ।
छिन्नमस्ता नृसिंहः स्याद् वामनी भुवनेश्वरी ॥
जामदग्न्यः सुन्दरी स्यान्मीनो धूमावती भवेत् ।
वाला(वगला ?) कूर्ममूर्त्तिः स्याद्बलभद्रश्च भैरवी ॥
महालक्ष्मीर्भवेद्बुद्धो दुर्गा स्यात् कल्किरूपिणी ।
स्वयं भगवती काली कृष्णस्तु भगवान् स्वयं ॥

Cf. Mahālakṣmī and Durgā for Kamalā and Mātaṅgī. The *Tantracintāmaṇi* (*ibid.*, p. 385) also says, कालिकाकृष्णयोस्ताराराममयोश्चैकरूपता । The *Muṇḍamālā* list of the Mahāvidyās quoted in the *Tantrasāra* is elsewhere (*ibid.*, p. 580) ascribed to the *Viśvasāra* or the *Cāmuṇḍā Tantra*.

[2] ABCF—त्रिपुरात्मिका ; G—यत्र मातङ्गी ; I—°चण्डिका देवी ।

[3] A—सुधामिनी ; F—सभूमिनी ; G—यत्र भुवनेशी सुधूमिनी ; I—यत्र ; सुधामिनी ।

एतानि परपीठानि[1] शंसन्ति वरभैरवाः[2] ।
[एवं तु[3] देवताः सर्वा एवं तु[4] दश भैरवाः[5] ॥ २३ ॥
सर्वत्र विरला चाहं[6] कामरूपे गृहे गृहे ।
गौरीशिखरमारुह्य पुनर्जन्म न विद्यते[7] ॥ २४ ॥
करतोयां समारभ्य[8] यावद्दिक्करवासिनीम्[9] ।
शतयोजनविस्तीर्णं[10] त्रिकोणं सर्वसिद्धिदम् ।
देवा मरणमिच्छन्ति[11] किं पुनर्मानवादयः[12] ॥ २५ ॥]
भूतधात्री (क्षीरग्रामे) महामाया (°देव) भैरवः क्षीरखण्डकः[13] ।
युगाद्या सा[14] महामाया दक्षाङ्गुष्ठं पदो मम ॥ २६ ॥

---

[1] ACDF—नव° ; EGI—वर° ।

[2] ADE—वरभैरव ; BF—नवभैरवाः ।

[3] A—ते ; DEGI—ता । The whole line is omitted in C.

[4] ADEGI—ते ।

[5] ABC read verse 28 after verse 23. F omits the second line of verse 23 as well as verses 24-25. I reads verse 28 between verses 23 and 24, and verse 25 between verses 27 and 29.

[6] B—देवी ; I—कामरूवे ।

[7] A reads verse 26 after verse 24.

[8] A—समारुह्य ; I—समासाद्य ।

[9] I—°वासिनी ; BDE—यावच्छिखरवासिनीम् । The seat of Dikkaravāsinī is located in the *Kālikā Purāṇa* in the eastern part of Kāmarūpa which is the Gauhāti region of Assam. See *supra*, pp. 13, note 1; 17, note 3.

[10] C—°विस्तारं ।

[11] A—°मिहन्ति ; I—मरणमिच्छन्ति ।

[12] G—पुनर्मानुषादयः । C adds here: इति कामरूपमाहात्म्यम् । It is probable that some of the verses in the description of the Kāmarūpa Pīṭha were a later addition. F reads verses 26-27 after verse 28.

[13] AFG—क्षीरकण्ठकः ; I—क्षीरखण्डज ।

AM— क्षीरग्रामे डानिपार अङ्गुष्ठवैभव ।
युगाद्या देवता क्षीरखण्डक भैरव ॥

AM suggests the reading

क्षीरग्रामे महादेव भैरवः क्षीरखण्डकः ।
युगाद्या सा महामाया दक्षाङ्गुष्ठं पदो मम ॥

The Pīṭha is located at Khīragrām near Katwa in the Burdwan District. Cf. note 14 *infra*. B has for verses 26-27:

भूतधात्री महामाया वामपदाङ्गुली मम ।
नकुलीशः कालीपीठे दक्षपदाङ्गुली मम ॥

[14] A—युगाद्या सा महामाया दक्षाङ्गुष्ठपदी ; F—युगाद्या सा महादेव दक्षाङ्गुष्ठः ; BCDE—युगाद्यायां महादेव ; G—युगाद्या सा महादेवी दक्षाङ्गुष्ठे ; I—महादेवी दक्षांगुष्ठपदे ।

The *Caṇḍīmaṅgala* mentions the goddess as Yogādyā and connects Kṣīragrāma with Satī's back. For the goddess Yogādyā at Kṣīragrāma, see also *Des. Cat. Vernacular MSS. in the collection of the R.A.S.B.*, IX (Bengali MSS.), pp. 317-18 (Nos. 318, 5372).

नकुलीशः कालीपीठे[1] दक्षपादाङ्गुली च मे[2] ।
[3][सर्वसिद्धिकरी देवी कालिका तत्र देवता] ॥ २७ ॥
अङ्गुलीवृन्दं[4] हस्तस्य प्रयागे ललिता भवः[5] ।
जयन्त्यां वामजङ्घा[6] च जयन्ती क्रमदीश्वरः ॥ २८ ॥
भुवनेशी सिद्धिरूपा (सिद्धरूपः) किरीटस्था[7] किरीटतः
(किरीटाख्ये किरीटकः) ।
[देवता विमला नाम्नी संवर्त्तो भैरवस्तथा] ॥ २९ ॥

---

1 ABDE—कालि°; G—नलीशः कालपीठे च ।

AM— कालीघाटे चारिटि अङ्गुलि डानि पार ।
नकुलेश भैरव कालिका देवी ताँर ॥

G explains कालपीठे as कालीघाटख्याते while AM suggests the reading नकुलेशः कालीघट्टे । Cf. verse 49 below (p. 56). The Pīṭha is located at Kālighāṭ in the southern suburb of Calcutta. Cf. the description of the Pīṭha in the *S'ivacarita* (p. 41 above). The original text seems to refer to Kālīpīṭha indicating 'the Pīṭha which is the resort of Kālī'. The name of the Pīṭhadevī was possibly not mentioned separately.

2 ABCDEG—°पादाङ्गुलीषु मे; I—°पादाङ्गुलीषु च ।

3 This line is omitted in ABCGI. It was interpolated to provide separate mention of the goddess at the Pīṭha.

4 A—अङ्गुलीच्छन्दं; B—अङ्गवङ्गे तु; F—अङ्गुल्यश्चैव; GI—अङ्गुलीषु च ।

AM— प्रयागेते दुहातेर अङ्गुली सरस ।
ताहाते भैरव दश महाविद्या दश ॥

It seems that the manuscript consulted by Bhāratacandra read verses 22-23 after verse 28 and, therefore, the ten Mahāvidyās, associated in the text with Kāmarūpa, were transferred to Prayāga. It was also easy to connect the ten Mahāvidyās with the ten fingers of Satī's hands that are said to have fallen at Prayāga (modern Allahabad). The *S'ivacarita* speaks of the Bhairava as Veṇīmādhava whose temple stands at the confluence of the Ganges and the Jumna.

5 I—भवेत्; ABC—भव ।

6 G—°जङ्घा मे; I—जयन्त्यां वामजङ्घायां;

AM— जयन्ताय वामजङ्घा फेलिल केशव ।
जयन्ती देवता क्रमदीश्वर भैरव ॥

The Pīṭha is located at Kalajor-Bāurbhog in the Sylhet District of East Pakistan. Gait says (*History of Assam*, p. 268), 'There is a spot in the Faljur Pargana where part of Satī's left leg is said to have fallen, and here human victims were immolated yearly on the ninth day (*mahānavamī*) of the Durgā Pūjā. Similar sacrifices were also offered on special occasions, such as the birth of a son in the royal family, or the fulfilment of some request made to the gods. Frequently the victims were self-chosen, in which case, for some time previous to the sacrifice, they enjoyed the privilege of doing whatever they pleased without let or hindrance. Sometimes, however, the supply of voluntary victims ran short, and then strangers were kidnapped for the purpose from foreign territory.'

7 AI—किरीटाख्या; B—किरीटस्था किरीटिनी; G—किरीटाख्ये किरीटकः ।

AM— किरीटकोणाय पड़े किरीट सुरूप ।
भुवनेशी देवता भैरव सिद्धरूप ॥

AM suggests the reading सिद्धिरूपः and the omission of the following line (cf. p. 47. note 2). The Pīṭha is located at Vaṭanagar near Lālbāg in the Murshidabad District.

[वाराणस्यां विशालाक्षी देवता कालभैरवः ।
मणिकर्णीति विख्याता कुण्डलं च मम श्रुतेः[1] ॥ ३० ॥
कन्याश्रमे च[2] पृष्ठं मे[3] निमिषो भैरवस्तथा] ।
सर्वाणी देवता तत्र[4]
कुरुक्षेत्रे च गुल्फतः[5] ॥ ३१ ॥
स्थाणुर्नाम्ना च सावित्री देवता
मणिवेदके[6] ।
मणिबन्धे[7] च गायत्री सर्वानन्दस्तु भैरवः ॥ ३२ ॥

---

[1] A—श्रुतेर्मम; G—मणिकर्णिकेति; I—श्रुतिः । E reads verse 29 after this verse. The reference is to Maṇikarṇikā at Benares in U.P. AM substitutes the fictitious Maṇibandha for Kanyāśrama or Vārāṇasī. Vārāṇasī, not found in the AM, may have been later inserted in the original text (cf. p. 43, note 3). *S'iva* omits Kanyāśrama and connects Satī's back with Vaivasvata.

[2] B—तु । The name of the Pīṭha reminds one of Kanyākubja or Kānyakubja (modern Kanoj) in the United Provinces. But Kanyāśrama was well known to Bengali Tantric writers who located it in Eastern India. In a discussion on the places which are not suitable for *dīkṣā* (Tantric initiation), the *Tantrasāra* (Vaṅgavāsī ed.. p. 41) quotes the verse

गयायां भास्करक्षेत्रे विरजे चन्द्रपर्वते ।
चट्टले च मतङ्गे च तथा कन्याश्रमेषु च ॥

with the following note: भास्करक्षेत्रं दक्षिणदेशे कोणार्क इति प्रसिद्धम् । विरजे विरजक्षेत्रे । चन्द्रपर्वते चन्द्रशेखरपर्वते । चट्टले चाटगाँ इति ख्याते । मतङ्गे मतङ्गदेशे । कन्याश्रमश्चन्द्रशेखर-गिरिसमीपवर्त्तिकुमार्याश्रमत्वेन कामरूपे प्रसिद्धः । The location of Kanyāśrama, in the passage, near the Candraśekhara hill and in Kāmarūpa suggests its identification with Kumārīkuṇḍa in the Chittagong District.

[3] AF—मे इष्टं; G—दृष्टिमं; I—पीठं मे निमेशो ।

[4] G—चात्र ।

[5] AM— कुरुक्षेत्रे डानि पार गुल्फ अनुभव ।
विमला ताहाते देवी संवर्त्त भैरव ॥

AM apparently reads the second line of verse 29 after verse 31.. The Bhairava Sthāṇu has to be associated with Sthāṇvīśvara (modern Thanesar) in the Karnal District of the Punjab.

[6] ABCDI—स्थाणू नाम्नी च सावित्री अश्वनाथस्तु भैरवः; F—मणिवेदिकदेशतः; G—स्थायुर्नाम्ना सावित्री देवता मानवेद्के ।

AM— मणिवेदे मणिवन्ध पड़िल तांहार ।
स्थाणु नामे भैरव सावित्री देवी तांर ॥

This is because of the textual confusion referred to in note 5 above.

[7] A—मणिरन्धे; BI—मणिरन्ध्रे; G—मुनिबन्धे ।

AM— मणिवन्धे वाममणिवन्ध अभिराम ।
सर्वानन्द भैरव गायत्री देवी नाम ॥

This is also due to the textual confusion referred to in note 5 above. Maṇibandha (i.e. wrist) cannot be regarded as the name of a place; cf. the confusion in the *S'ivacarita* (p. 40 above).

श्रीशैले (श्रीहट्टे) च मम ग्रीवा महालक्ष्मीस्तु[1] देवता ।

भैरवः सम्बरानन्दो[2] देशे देशे व्यवस्थितः ॥ ३३ ॥

काञ्चीदेशे च कङ्कालो[3] भैरवो रुरुनामकः ।

देवता देवगर्भाख्या[4]

नितम्बः कालमाधवे[5] ॥ ३४ ॥

भैरवश्चासिताङ्गश्च देवी काली सुसिद्धिदा[6] ।

दृष्ट्वा दृष्ट्वा[7] नमस्कृत्य[8] मन्त्रसिद्धिमवाप्नुयात् ॥ ३५ ॥

[9][कुजवारे भूततिथौ निशार्द्धे यस्तु साधकः ।

नत्वा प्रदक्षिणीकृत्य मन्त्रसिद्धिमवाप्नुयात् ॥ ३६ ॥]

---

1 G—महामाया ; I—महालक्ष्मी च ।

2 E—शम्बरानन्दो ; G—कचः स्थितः ।

AM— श्रीहट्ट पड़िल ग्रीवा महालक्ष्मी देवी ।

सर्वानन्द भैरव वैभव यांहा सेवि ॥

AM therefore suggests the readings श्रीहट्टे and सर्वानन्दश्च in places respectively of श्रीशैले and सम्बरानन्दो ; cf. *S'ivacarita* (p. 40, Nos. 5, 14). As Śrīparvata, probably identical with Śrīśaila, is separately mentioned in verse 41, the reference in this case may actually be to Śrīhaṭṭa (modern Sylhet) in East Pakistan. The Pīṭha is located at Gotatikar-Jainpur near Sylhet. The expression देशे देशे is not quite happy.

3 G—कङ्काली भैरवो रुरुनामतः ; I—काञ्चिदेशे च कङ्कालि भैरवो रुरुनामतः ।

4 A—वेदगर्भाख्या ।

AM— काञ्चीदेशे पड़िल काँकालि अभिराम ।

देवगर्भा देवता भैरव रुरु नाम ॥

Kāñcī, mentioned in the early lists, certainly stands for modern Conjeeveram in the Chingleput District of the Madras Presidency. The Pīṭha in this case, however, is usually located on the Kopāi near Bolpur in the Birbhum District of Bengal.

5 A—नितम्बं ; B—नितम्बं कालमागधे ; I—नितम्बकालिमाधवे ।

AM— नितम्बेर अर्द्ध कालमाधवे ताँहार ।

असिताङ्ग भैरव देवता काली तार ॥

6 E—च सुसिद्धिदा ; G—भैरवोऽत्रासिताङ्गश्च ।

7 A—दृष्टादृष्ट ; G—दृष्टादृष्टा ।

8 ABEGI—महादेव ।

9 This verse is omitted in CF and may be a later interpolation.

शोणाख्या[1] भद्रसेनस्तु नर्मदाख्ये[2] नितम्बकः ।
रामगिरौ[3] स्तनान्यश्च[4] शिवानी चण्डभैरवः ॥ ३७ ॥
[वृन्दावने केशजालमुमा[5] नाम्नी च[6] देवता] ।
[भूतेशो भैरवस्तत्र सर्वसिद्धिप्रदायकः] ॥ ३८ ॥
संहाराख्य[7] ऊर्द्धदन्तो[8] देवी (°ऽनले) नारायणी शुचौ ।
अधोदन्तो[9] महारुद्रो वाराही पञ्चसागरे ॥ ३९ ॥

---

1 AFG—शोणाख्ये; I—शैलाख्ये; B—शोणभद्रे भद्रसेनो ।

AM— नितम्बेर आर अर्द्ध पड़े नर्मदाय ।
भद्रसेन भैरव शोणाक्षी देवी ताय ॥

AM suggests the reading शोणाक्षी भद्रसेनस्तु । There is some doubt whether the Pīṭha has to be located on the Sone or on the Narmada.

2 BCD—नर्मदाख्या नितम्बके; F—नर्मदाख्या नितम्बकम्; G—नर्मदाख्ये नितम्बके; I—नम्बदाखे नितम्बके ।

3 B—राजगिरौ; G—रामाकिन्यां; I—रामगिर्य्यां । Rāmagiri is modern Ramtek near Nagpur in the Central Province. There is also a tradition identifying Rāmagir with the Chitrakūṭa in Bundelkhand.

4 AB—तथा नासा; CDF—तथा बाला; I—स्तुवान्यश्च ।

AM— आर स्तन पड़े ताँर रामगिरि स्थाने ।
शिवानी देवता चण्ड भैरव सेखाने ॥

Note that the nose of Satī is associated in verse 5 (p. 44 above) with Sugandhā.

5 B—°जालान्; CD—°जाल; EF—°जाले; G—उमानाम्नी केशजाले भूतेशः परभैरवः (with the second line of the verse omitted)

I— वृन्दावने केशजाले कृष्णनाथस्तु भैरवः ।
कात्यायनी तत्र देवी सर्वसिद्धिप्रदायिनी ॥

AM— केशजाल नाम स्थाने पड़े ताँर केश ।
उमा नामे देवी ताहे भैरव भूतेश ॥

It seems that the original reading was उमावने केशजालं भूतेशः परभैरवः ॥ Umāvana was a name of Devikoṭṭa; cf. style of v. 27 (*supra*, p. 50, notes 1 and 3). AM supports the reading in G. In the modified text there is reference to the fanciful Śākta claim on the celebrated Vaiṣṇava *tīrtha* near Mathurā (Muttra) in the United Provinces (cf. Kṛṣṇa referred to in the I text). Keśajāla was sometimes regarded as the name of the Pīṭha owing to confusion; cf. the case of Maṇibandha in verse 32. See the confusion in the *S'ivacarita.*

6 A—नाम्नीति ।

7 ABI—संहाराख्ये ।

AM— ऊर्द्ध दन्तपाँतिर अनले हइल धाम ।
संक्रूर भैरव देवी नारायणी नाम ॥

AM suggests the reading संक्रूराख्य ऊर्द्धदन्तोऽनले । The *S'ivacarita* regards *Saṃhāra* as the name of an Upapīṭha; cf. ABI.

8 ACFGI—ऊर्द्धदन्ते ।

9 ACFGI—अधोदन्ते ।

करतोयातटे तल्पं (कर्णे) वामे[1] वामनभैरवः ।

अपर्णा देवता यत्र ब्रह्मरूपाकरोद्भवा[2] ॥ ४० ॥

श्रीपर्वते दक्षगुल्फ(कर्ण)स्तत्र[3] श्रीसुन्दरी परा ।

सर्वसिद्धीश्वरी[4] सर्वा सुन्दरानन्दभैरवः[5] ॥ ४१ ॥

कपालिनी (कपाली च) भीमरूपा वामगुल्फो[6] विभाषके ।

[7] [भैरवश्च महादेव सर्वानन्दः शुभप्रदः] ॥ ४२ ॥

AM— पञ्चसागरेते पड़े अधोदन्तसार ।
महारुद्र भैरव वाराही देवी तांर ॥

Pañcasāgara seems to indicate the oceans, the traditional number of which was, however, four or seven. The reference may also be to the five *Kuṇḍas* near Hardwar.

1 B—तन्यात् बलि°; G—गुल्फं; I—तल्प ।

AM— करतोयातटे पड़े वामकर्ण तांर ।
वामेश भैरव देवी अपर्णा तांहार ॥

AM suggests the reading कर्णे वामे वामेशभैरवः । The Karatoyā is a sacred river of northern Bengal. The Pīṭha is located at Bhavānīpur in the Bogra District. G has a note reading भवानीपुरख्याते ।

2 A—°करोद्भवः; I—तत्र । The last word of the verse is not quite satisfactory.

3 ACI—गुल्फं; E—तल्प; FG—गुल्फं तत्र ।

AM— श्रीपर्वते डानि कर्ण फेलिलेन हरि ।
भैरव सुन्दरानन्द देवता सुन्दरी ॥

AM suggests the reading दक्षकर्णस् तत्र । Śrīparvata is the same as the Śrīśaila in the Nallamalur range to the south of the Krishna. But the non-mention of Mallikārjuna (Śiva) and of Devī Bhramarāmbā on the Śrīśaila shows that the description is probably fantastic. As two other places are associated with Satī's *gulpha* (verses 31 and 42), AM possibly suggests the correct reading of the verse.

4 ABGI—°सिद्धेश्वरी; E—°सिद्धिकरी ।

5 CDF—सुनन्दानन्द° ।

6 C—गुल्फ; DI—गुल्फे; B—गुल्फा; F—गुल्फविभागतः; G—कपालिनी क्रोधरूपा वामगुल्फे विभीषके ।

AM— विभाषेते वाम गुल्फ फेलिला केशव ।
भीमरूपा देवी ताहे कपाली भैरव ॥

AM suggests the reading कपाली च भीमरूपा and the omission of the second line of the verse (cf. p. 50, note 7). The Pīṭha is located near Tamluk in the Midnapur District.

7 This line is omitted in ABE and may be a later interpolation. Cf. p. 50, notes 3 and 7.

उदरञ्च (अधरञ्च) प्रभासे मे[1] चन्द्रभागा यशस्विनी ।

वक्रतुण्डो भैरव-

श्चोर्द्ध्वोष्ठो भैरवपर्वते[2] ॥ ४३ ॥

अवन्ती[3] च महादेवी लम्बकर्णस्तु भैरवः ॥ ४४ ॥

चिवुके[4] भ्रामरी देवी विकृताक्षो[5] जले स्थले (जनस्थाने)[6] ।

गण्डो गोदावरीतीरे विश्वेशी (विश्वेशो) विश्वमातृका[7] ॥ ४५ ॥

---

1 A—प्रभासमे; BCDE—प्रभासे; G—अधरञ्च प्रभासे मे चन्द्राभामा; I—अधरञ्च ।

AM— प्रभासे अधर देवी चन्द्रभागा ताहे ।

वक्रतुण्ड भैरव प्रत्यक्षरूप याहे ॥

AM suggests the reading अधरञ्च प्रभासे; of, verse 52 below. Prabhāsa or Somnath is a famous holy place in southern Kathiawar.

2 B—चोष्ठो भैरवपर्वते; A—ऊर्द्ध्वोष्ठं भौरुपर्वते; G—तुण्ड भैरवपर्वते; I—तुण्डो भैरव° ।

AM— भैरव पर्वते ओष्ठ पड़े चक्रघाय ।

लम्बकर्ण भैरव अवन्ती देवी ताय ॥

AM suggests the reading लम्बकर्णस्तु भैरवः । The Devī's name seems to refer the Pīṭha to West Malwa.

3 ABCDFI—अवन्त्यां ।

4 ABC—चिबुके ।

5 ABFG—विकृताख्या; I—विकृताख्य; C—किकुभाख्या; D—किक्षभाक्षो । Probably विकृताख्यो is intended.

6 AM— जनस्थाने चिवुक पड़िल अभिराम ।

विकृताक्ष भैरव भ्रामरी देवी नाम ॥

AM suggests the reading विकृताक्षो जनस्थाने । **Janasthāna,** celebrated in the *Rāmāyaṇa*, lay in tho upper Godavari valley in the present **Nasik region** cf the Bombay Presidency. CDF read after this verse: भैरवः सर्वसिद्धीशस्तत्र सिद्धिरनुत्तमा apparently because the reading विकृताख्या invited a name of the **Bhairava** at the Pīṭha.

7 I—गण्डे;

AM— गोदावरी तीरे पड़े वाम गण्डस्थानि ।

विश्वेश भैरव विश्वमातृका भवानी ॥

AM suggests the reading विश्वेशो विश्वमातृका which shows hat verse 46 is probably an interpolation. The reading विश्वेशो necessitated the fabrication of the name of the Bhairava at the Pīṭha. The two lines of verse 46 appear to have been inserted by two different hands. Cf. p. 56, note 8.

[दण्डपाणिर्भैरवस्तु[1] वामगण्डे तु[2] राकिणी ।
[3]भैरवो वत्सनाभस्तु तत्र सिद्धिर्न संशयः[4] ॥ ४६ ॥]
रत्नावल्यां (रत्नवत्यां) दक्षस्कन्धः कुमारी भैरवः शिवः[5] ।
मिथिलायामुमा देवी[6] वामस्कन्धो[7] महोदरः[8] ॥ ४७ ॥
[9] [नलाहाट्यां नलापातो योगीशो[10] भैरवस्तथा ।
तत्र सा कालिका देवी सर्वसिद्धिप्रदायिका[11] ॥ ४८ ॥
[12]कालीघाटे मुण्डपातः क्रोधीशो[13] भैरवस्तथा ।
देवता जयदुर्गाख्या नानाभोगप्रदायिनी ॥ ४९ ॥

---

[1] A—दक्षपाणि ; G—भैरवश्च वामगण्डे च । Rākiṇī is the same as Raṅkiṇī ; cf. *supra*, p. 33 and note 1.

[2] I—च । For the right cheek, see verse 14 (p. 46) above.

[3] D(v.l.)E read in place of this line: चमायौ भैरवो वत्स सर्वशैलाश्मकोपरि । The reference to Sarvaśaila (literally, all hills) is no doubt fanciful; cf. Pañcasāgara.

[4] B—वत्सनाभश्च तत्र सिद्धिमवाप्नुयात्; GI—वसामि भैरवो वत्स सर्वशैलाश्मगोमिथः (I—°गोविषः) ।

[5] G—रत्नवत्यां दक्षस्कन्धः कुमारो भैरवी शिवा । I—रत्नावल्यां दक्षिणस्कन्धः कुमारी भैरवी शिव ।

AM— रत्नावली स्थाने डानि स्कन्ध अभिराम ।
कुमार भैरव ताहे देवी शिवा नाम ॥

AM suggests the reading कुमारो भैरवी शिवा as in G. A city called Ratnavatī is mentioned in the *Kāvyamīmāṃsā* ; but probably Khanakul-Krishnanagar, on the river Ratnākara (Kānānadī) in the Hooghly District and famous for its temple of Ghaṇṭeśvara Śiva, is indicated. Cf. also the Pramodā *tīrtha* at the confluence of the Vāgmatī and the Ratnāvalī in Nepal.

[6] A—नाम्नी ; CFI—महादेवी ; G—मिथिलायां वामस्कन्धो महादेवी महोदरी ।

AM— मिथिलाय वामस्कन्ध देवी महादेवी ।
महोदर भैरव सर्वार्थं यारे सेवि ॥

AM supports the reading in G with महोदरः for महोदरी । Mithilā has been identified with Janakpur in the Nepalese Tarai.

[7] ABE—स्कन्दी : CFI—स्कन्धे ।

[8] D—महोदरे । I reads after this line भैरवो वत्सनाभस्तु तत्र सिद्धिर्न संशयः (*vide* verse 46).

[9] The following eight verses are not found in G (and the AM original) and were apparently interpolated.

[10] EI—योगेशो । The Pīṭha is located at Nalahati in the Birbhum District of West Bengal. The word *nalā* is a Bengali corruption of Sanskrit *nalaka* (any long bone).

[11] B—तत्र सिद्धिर्न संशयः ।

[12] Verse 49 is omitted in I. DEF have in place of this line: कर्णाटे चैव कर्णौ (v.l. कर्णं) मे अभीरु(v.l. लभीरु) र्नाम भैरवः । Cf. verse 27 (p. 50) above. This Kālī Pīṭha is located at Juranpur near Katwa in the Burdwan District. The Pīṭha was not mentioned in the original text.

[13] D (v.l.)—क्रोधेशो ; B—क्रोधश्च ।

वक्रेश्वरे मनःपातो वक्रनाथस्तु भैरवः । [1]
नदी पापहरा तत्र देवी महिषमर्दिनी ॥ ५० ॥
यशोरे पाणिपद्मञ्च देवता यशोरेश्वरी ।
चण्डश्च [2] भैरवो यत्र तत्र सिद्धिर्न संशयः [3] ॥ ५१ ॥
अट्टहासे चोष्ठपातो देवी सा फुल्लरा स्मृता ।
विश्वेशो [4] भैरवस्तत्र सर्वाभीष्टप्रदायकः ॥ ५२ ॥
हारपातो नन्दिपुरे भैरवो नन्दिकेश्वरः ।
नन्दिनी सा महादेवी तत्र सिद्धिमवाप्नुयात् [5] ॥ ५३ ॥
लङ्कायां नूपुरश्चैव भैरवो राक्षसेश्वरः । [6]
इन्द्राक्षी देवता तत्र इन्द्रेणोपासिता पुरा ॥ ५४ ॥
विराटदेशमध्ये तु [7] पादाङ्गुलिनिपातनम् ।
भैरवश्चामृताख्यश्च [8] देवी तत्राम्बिका स्मृता ॥ ५५ ॥ [9]]

---

1 I—मुण्डपातं । The Pīṭha, which had no mention in the original text, is located near Dubrajpur in the Birbhum District. The *Śivacarita* separately mentions Vakreśvara and Vakranātha, which, however, appear to be the same place.

2 A—चण्डस्तु; BF—चण्डश्च भैरवस्तत्र; I—चण्डेशो भैरवो देवस्तत्र ।

3 I—सिद्धिरवाप्नुयात्; BE—तत्र सिद्धिमवाप्नुयात्; CF—यत्र सिद्धिमवाप्नुयात् । The Yaśora Pīṭha is located at Īśvarīpur (about 25 miles from the Hasanabad Railway Station) in the Khulna District and not actually at Jessore.

4 C—विघ्नेशो । The Pīṭh , which was not mentioned in the original text, is located near Lābhpur in the Birbhum District.

5 BCDEFI—सिद्धिर्न संशयः । The Pīṭha is located near Sainthia in the Birbhum District.

6 I—नन्दिकेश्वरः । The name of the Bhairava suggests that this Laṅkā is identical with Ceylon, although the author may have had no knowledge of the Ceylonese *tīrthas*. Laṅkā (literally, an island) was not referred to in the original text.

7 A—विराट मध्यदेशे तु; I—°निपातनः । The ancient Virāṭa or Matsya country lay in the Jaipur-Alwar-Bharatpur region of Rajputana; but late medieval writers often placed a Virāṭa country in northern Bengal (cf. *I.C.*, VIII, pp. 53-54). This Pīṭha had no place in the original text.

8 AE—चामृताचश्च; I—भैरवोऽमृताख्यश्च ।

9 D (v.l.) EF add after this verse:

मगधे (v.l. मागधे) दक्षजङ्घा मे व्योमकेशस्तु भैरवः ।
सर्वानन्दमयी (v.l. °करी) देवी सर्वकाम(v.l. सर्वानन्द)फलप्रदा ॥

This verse was fabricated by one who could not find out all the 51 Pīṭhas owing to errors in the manuscripts consulted; cf. the case of Karṇāta (p. 56, note 12).

एतास्ते कथिताः पुत्र पीठनाथाधिदेवताः[1] ।
क्षेत्राधिपं[2] विना देव पूजयेत् पीठदेवताम्[3] ।
भैरवैर्ह्रियते सर्वं जपपूजादिसाधनम्[4] ॥ ५६ ॥
अज्ञात्वा भैरवं पीठे पीठशक्तिञ्च शङ्कर[5] ।
प्राणनाथ न सिध्येत्तु[6] कल्पकोटिजपादिभिः ॥ ५७ ॥
न देयं परशिष्याय[7] निन्दकाय दुरात्मने ।
शठाय क्रूरकार्याय[8] दत्वा मृत्युमवाप्नुयात् ।
दद्याच्छान्ताय[9] शिष्याय मन्त्री मन्त्रार्थसिद्धये ॥ ५८ ॥[10]

---

1 A—पीठनाथादि° ; G—एतत्ते कथितं वत्स पीठनाथादि° ; I—एतत्ते कथित ।

2 D—क्षेत्राधीशं ; G—क्षेत्राधीशं विना यस्तु ; I—क्षेत्राधीशं विना देवि ।

3 CDF—पूजयेच्चान्य° ।

4 G—जपपूजादिकं धनम् ; I—भैरवे हृदयः सर्वं ।

5 BCDE—पीठ ; A—भैरवपीठं ; G—पीठं पीठशक्ति ; I—अज्ञत्वा भैरवं पीठं ।

6 A—सिध्यन्ति ; B—सिद्धे तु ; CEG—सिध्येत ; I—सिद्धेत ।

7 A—°शिष्येभ्यो ; I—देया ।

8 B—क्रूरकर्माय ; EG—वञ्चकायेदं ; I—वञ्चकायेत्यं ।

9 A—दयात् शान्ताय शिष्टाय ;
EI—दद्यात् शान्ताय शिष्याय नैष्ठिकाय शुचौ प्रिये (I—धिरे) ।
साधकाय कुलीनाय मन्त्री मन्त्रार्थसिद्धये ॥

G supports the reading of E with शिष्याय शान्ताय for शान्ताय शिष्याय and शुचि for शुचौ Here is an attempt to make a complete verse in the *anuṣṭubh* out of a half verse. Similar cases are also noticed elsewhere in the text. Cf. pp. 44, note 3; 45, note 5, etc.

10 Colophon: A—इति तन्त्रचूडामणौ पार्वतीशिवसंवादे एकपञ्चाशद्विद्योत्पत्तौ पीठनिर्णयः समाप्तः ; B—इति तन्त्रचूडामणौ शिवपार्वतीसंवादे महापीठनिरूपणं समाप्तं ; C—goes on to quote some verses of the *Mahānīlatantra*; E—इति तन्त्रचूडामणौ शिवपार्वतीसंवादे एकपञ्चाशद् विद्योत्पत्तौ पीठनिर्णयः समाप्तः । G—इति चन्द्रचूडामणितन्त्रे (cf. p. 42, note 2 पार्वतीशिवसंवादे विद्योत्पत्तौ पीठनिर्णयः समाप्तः । श्रीदुर्गा । श्रीरमानाथशर्मणः पुस्तकमिदम् । H—इति श्रीभावचूडामणौ षट्कर्मसाधनविधौ पीठनिर्णयः पटलः । I—इति तन्त्रचूडामणौ विद्यत्पत्तौ (विद्यो°) पीठनिर्णयं समाप्तं ॥ ॐ नमः परमदेवतायै । शुभमस्तु शकाब्दाः १७।९० (१७९०) सन १२।४५ (१२४५) साल तारिख १४ भाद्रस्य श्रीकालीनाथदेवशर्मणः स्वाक्षरं पुस्तकञ्च ॥ श्रीश्रीविश्वेश्वराय नमः । श्रीश्रीदुर्गा ।

Cf. AM— एकमत ना हय पुराण मत यत ।
आमि कहि मन्त्रचूडामणि तन्त्र मत ॥

It has been noted above that the *Tripurā Rājamālā* says about a verse of our text: शिववाक्य पीठमाला तन्त्रेर प्रमाण । See p. 4, note 1. Note also that Bhāratacandra was aware of the differences of opinion about the Pīṭhas.

APPENDIX I

A

Probable Original Text of the Pīṭhanirṇaya (Mahāpīṭha-nirūpaṇa) Reconstructed on the Basis of Manuscript G and the Annadāmaṅgala.

ईश्वर उवाच ।

मातः परात्परे देवि सर्वज्ञानमयीश्वरि ।
कथ्यतां मे सर्वपीठशक्तिभैरवदेवताः ॥ १ ॥

देव्युवाच ।

शृणु वत्स प्रवक्ष्यामि दयाल भक्तवत्सल ।
याभिर्विना न सिध्यन्ति जपसाधनसत्क्रियाः ॥ २ ॥
पञ्चाशदेकपीठानि एवं भैरवदेवताः ।
अङ्गप्रत्यङ्गपातेन विष्णुचक्रक्षतेन च ॥ ३ ॥
ममाद्यवपुषो देव हिताय त्वयि कथ्यते ।
ब्रह्मरन्ध्रं हिङ्गुलायां [1] भैरवो भीमलोचनः ॥ ४ ॥
कोट्टरी सा महादेवी त्रिगुणा या दिगम्बरी ।
शर्करारे [2] त्रिनेत्रं मे देवी महिषमर्दिनी ॥ ५ ।
क्रोधीशो भैरवस्तत्र
सुगन्धायाश्च [3] नासिका ।
देवस्त्र्यम्बकनामा च सुनन्दा तत्र देवता ॥ ६ ॥
काश्मीरे [4] कण्ठदेशश्च त्रिसन्ध्येश्वरभैरवः ।
महामाया भगवती गुणातीता वरप्रदा ॥ ७ ॥
ज्वालामुख्यां [5] तथा जिह्वा देव उन्मत्तभैरवः ।
अम्बिका सिद्धिदा देवी
स्तनं जालन्धरे [6] मम ॥ ८ ॥
भीषणो भैरवस्तत्र देवी त्रिपरनाशिनी ।
हार्दपीठं वैद्यनाथे [7] वैद्यनाथस्तु भैरवः ॥ ९ ॥
देवता जयदुर्गाख्या
नेपाले [8] जानु मे शिव ।
कपाली भैरवः श्रीमान् महामाया च देवता ॥ १० ॥
मानसे [9] दक्षहस्तो मे देवी दाक्षायणी हरः ।
विरजा चोत्कले [10] ख्याता नाभिर्मे जयभैरवः ॥ ११ ॥
गण्डक्यां [11] गण्डकश्चण्डी जगन्नाथस्तु भैरवः ।
बहुलायां [12] वामबाहुर्बहुलाख्या च देवता ॥ १२ ॥

भीरुको भैरवस्तत्र सर्वसिद्धिप्रदायकः ।
उज्जयिन्यां[१३] कूर्परश्च मङ्गला कपिलाम्बरः ॥ १३ ॥
चट्टले[१४] दक्षबाहुर्मे भैरवश्चन्द्रशेखरः ।
व्यक्तरूपा भगवती भवानी तत्र देवता ॥ १४ ॥
विशेषतः कलियुगे वसामि चन्द्रशेखरे ।
त्रिपुरायां[१५] दक्षपादो देवता त्रिपुरा नलः ॥ १५ ॥
त्रिस्रोतायां[१६] वामपादो भ्रामरी भैरवोम्बरः ।
योनिपीठं कामरूपे[१७-२६] कामाख्या तत्र देवता ॥ १६ ॥
यत्रास्ते त्रिगुणातीता व्यक्ता पाषाणरूपिणी ।
यत्रास्ते माधवः साक्षाच्चिदानन्दोऽथ भैरवः ॥ १७ ॥
तत्र श्रीभैरवी देवी तत्र च क्षेत्रदेवता ।
प्रचण्डचण्डिका तत्र मातङ्गी त्रिपुराम्बिका ॥ १८ ॥
वगला कमला तत्र भुवनेशी सधूमिनी ।
एतानि दशपीठानि शंसन्ति दशभैरवाः ॥ १९ ॥
क्षीरग्रामे[२७] महादेव भैरवः क्षीरकण्ठकः ।
युगाद्या सा महामाया दक्षाङ्गुष्ठं पदो मम ॥ २० ॥
नकुलीशः कालीपीठे[२८] दक्षपादाङ्गुलीषु मे ।
अङ्गुलीषु च हस्तस्य प्रयागे[२९] ललिता भवः ॥ २१ ॥
जयन्त्यां[३०] वामजङ्घा च जयन्ती क्रमदीश्वरः ।
भुवनेशी सिद्धिरूपः किरीटाख्ये[३१] किरीटकः ॥ २२ ॥
कन्याश्रमे[३२] च पृष्ठं मे निमिषो भैरवस्तथा ।
सर्वाणी देवता तत्र
कुरुक्षेत्रे[३३] च गुल्फतः ॥ २३ ॥
स्थाणुर्नाम्ना च सावित्री देवता
मणिवेदके[३४] ।
मणिबन्धे च गायत्री सर्वानन्दस्तु भैरवः ॥ २४ ॥
श्रीहट्टे[३५] च मम ग्रीवा महालक्ष्मीस्तु देवता ।
भैरवः सम्बरानन्दो देशे देशे व्यवस्थितः ॥ २५ ॥
काञ्चीदेशे[३६] च कङ्कालो भैरवो रुरुनामकः ।
देवता देवगर्भाख्या
नितम्बः कालमाधवे[३७] ॥ २६ ॥
भैरवोऽत्रासिताङ्गश्च देवी काली सुसिद्धिदा ।
दृष्ट्वा दृष्ट्वा नमस्कृत्य मन्त्रसिद्धिमवाप्नुयात् ॥ २७ ॥

शोणाख्या भद्रसेनस्तु नर्मदाख्ये [३८] नितम्बकः ।
रामगिरौ [३९] स्तनान्यश्च शिवानी चण्डभैरवः ॥ २८ ॥
उमावने [४०] केशजालं भूतेशः परभैरवः ।
संहाराख्य ऊर्द्धदन्तेऽनले [४१] नारायणी शुचौ ॥ २९ ॥
अधोदन्ते महारुद्रो वाराही पञ्चसागरे [४२] ।
करतोयातटे [४३] कर्णे वामे वामनभैरवः ॥ ३० ॥
अपर्णा देवता तत्र ब्रह्मरूपाकरोद्भवा ।
श्रीपर्वते [४४] दक्षकर्णस्तत्र श्रीसुन्दरी परा ॥ ३१ ॥
सर्वसिद्धीश्वरी देवी सुन्दरानन्दभैरवः ।
कपाली च भीमरूपा वामगुल्फो विभाषके [४५] ॥ ३२ ॥
अधरश्च प्रभासे [४६] मे चन्द्रभागा यशस्विनी ।
वक्रतुण्डो भैरवश्च
ओष्ठो भैरवपर्वते [४७] ॥ ३३ ॥
अवन्ती च महादेवी लम्बकर्णस्तु भैरवः ।
चिवुके भ्रामरी देवी विकृताख्यो जनस्थाने [४८] ॥ ३४ ॥
गण्डो गोदावरीतीरे [४९] विश्वेशो विश्वमातृका ।
रत्नवत्यां [५०] दक्षस्कन्धः कुमारी भैरवी शिवा ॥ ३५ ॥
मिथिलायां [५१] महादेवी वामस्कन्धो महोदरः ।
एतास्ते कथिताः पुत्र पीठनाथाधिदेवताः ॥ ३६ ॥
क्षेत्राधीशं विना देव पूजयेत्पीठदेवताम् ।
भैरवैर्ह्रियते सर्वं जपपूजादिसाधनम् ॥ ३७ ॥
अज्ञात्वा भैरवं पीठे पीठशक्तिश्च शङ्कर ।
प्राणनाथ न सिध्येत्तु कल्पकोटिजपादिभिः ॥ ३८ ॥
न देयं परशिष्याय निन्दकाय दुरात्मने ।
शठाय क्रूरकार्याय दत्वा मृत्युमवाप्नुयात् ॥ ३९ ॥
दद्याच्छान्ताय शिष्याय मन्त्री मन्त्रार्थसिद्धये ॥ ४० ॥

B

Modified Text of the Pīṭhanirṇaya as found in Manuscript H (with slight emendation of the faulty language of the original)

श्रीशिव उवाच ।
षट्कर्मसाधनं देवि कस्मिन् स्थाने प्रशस्तकम् ।
मातः परावरे नित्ये सर्वज्ञानमहेश्वरि ॥
कथ्यतां मे सर्वपीठं तथा षट्कर्मसाधनम् ।
शक्तिभैरवदेव्यश्च साधूनां हितकाम्यया ॥

श्रीदेव्युवाच ।

शृणु वत्स प्रवक्ष्यामि दयालु भक्तवत्सल ।
यानि विना न सिध्यन्ति जपसाधनसत्क्रियाः ॥
पञ्चाशदेकपीठानि चैवं भैरवदेवताः ।
प्रधानं पीठकं देव यथा भैरवदेवताः ॥
यत्र साधनं प्रशस्तं तथा षट्कर्म भैरव ॥
गङ्गाद्याः सततं सर्वाः समुद्राश्च तथा नदाः ।
सर्वतीर्थानि सर्वत्र ममाङ्गे शृणु भैरव ॥
अङ्गप्रत्यङ्गपातेन विष्णुचक्रक्षतेन च ।
ममास्य वपुषो देव हिताय च त्वयां शृणु ॥
ब्रह्मरन्ध्रं हिङ्गुलायां भैरवो भीमलोचनः ।
कुट्टवी सा महाकाली त्रिगुणा या दिगम्बरी ॥
शर्कर्य्यां दक्षनेत्रं मे देवी महिषमर्दिनी ।
क्रोधीशो भैरवस्तत्र सुगन्धनामकाननः ॥
ताराद्यायां वामनेत्रं ताराख्या तारिणी परा ।
उन्मत्तो भैरवस्तत्र सर्वलक्षणसंयुतः ॥
मानसे दक्षहस्तो मे तत्र दाक्षायणी हरः ॥
विजये उत्कले ख्याते नाभिर्मे अम्बभैरवः ।
सोऽयञ्च सिद्धिदः साक्षाद् देवी मङ्गलचण्डिका ॥
सदने दक्षकूर्पं(?) मे भैरवश्चण्डसंज्ञकः ।
व्यक्तरूपा भगवती भवानी यत्र देवता ॥
सुगन्ध (?) नासिका यत्र देवस्त्र्यम्बकभैरवः ।
आनन्दा देवता तत्र सर्वसिद्धिप्रदायिनी ॥
काश्मीरे कण्ठदेशश्च त्रिसन्ध्येश्वरभैरवः ।
महामाया भगवती गुणातीता वरप्रदा ॥
ज्वालामुख्यां तथा जिह्वा भैरवो वटकेश्वरः ।
अम्बिका सिद्धिदा नाम्नी स्तने जालन्धरे मम ॥
भीषणो भैरवस्तत्र देवी त्रिपुरमालिनी ॥
वामस्तनं वक्त्रकेश्वरे भैरवश्चन्द्रशेखरः ।
देवता भैरवी तत्र सर्वपीठेषु नायिका ॥
नासा मे नवखण्डे च वैद्यनाथश्च भैरवः ।
देवता दुर्गाख्या च सा सर्वसिद्धिप्रदायिनी ॥
नेपाले जयदुर्गाख्या तत्र वै तालुकं शिव ।
कपाली भैरवस्तत्र महामारी च देवता ॥

विशेषतः कलियुगे वसामि चन्द्रशेखरे ॥
त्रिपुरायां दक्षपादो देवी त्रिपुरसुन्दरी ।
भैरवस्त्रिपुरो देवः सर्वसम्पत्प्रदायकः ॥
त्रिस्रोतायां वामपादो देवता भ्रामरी स्वयम् ।
योनिपीठं कामगिरौ कामाख्या देवता स्वयम् ॥
यत्रास्ते त्रिगुणात्मिका व्यक्ताव्यक्तस्वरूपिणी ।
यत्र श्रीभैरवी देवी यत्र नक्षत्रदेवता ॥
प्रचण्डचण्डिका चैव मातङ्गी त्रिपुरात्मिका ।
वगला कमला तत्र भवानी हरनायिका ॥
महाकाली स्वयं तत्र भद्रकाली तथापरा ।
सर्वशक्तिः स्वयं तत्र सर्वभैरवदेवताः ॥
महाकालः स्वयं तत्र सर्वदेवसमन्वितः ।
सर्वत्र विरला चाहं कामरूपे गृहे गृहे ॥
एतानि वरपीठानि शंसन्ति च भैरवाः ।
एषां ते देवताः सर्वास्तथा क्षेत्राधिदेवताः ॥
अङ्गुलीषु च सर्वेषु प्रयागे ललिता स्वयम् ॥
कुरुक्षेत्रे तथा देवा भैरवाः पुण्यभाजनाः ।
क्षेत्रेशी देवता तत्र सर्वपापविनाशिनी ॥
विन्ध्यशेखरमासाद्य पतिता चाङ्गुली मम ।
सर्वेशो भैरवो नामा तत्र तिष्ठति नित्यशः ॥
जयन्त्यां वामजङ्घा मे जयन्ती कुमुदेश्वरी ।
कोंके कोंकेश्वरी देवी भैरवो रुरुनामकः ॥
मेखले[1] मेखली देवी वामाङ्गुली प्रभेदतः ।
[तत्र च भैरवश्चण्डनामकः स महाबलः] ॥
गौरीशिखरमारुह्य पुनर्जन्म न विद्यते ।
तत्राहं भवता सार्द्धं वसामि नियतं शिव ॥
भूतधात्री महादेवी भैरवः क्षीरखण्डभाक् ।
युगाद्या सा महाविद्या विख्याता भुवनत्रये ॥
नकुलीशः कालीघाटे कालिका तत्र देवता ।
तत्र मे पतिता वत्स केशा मस्तकसंयुताः ॥

[1] It is tempting to suggest the emendation मेकले referring to the old Mekala country about the Amarkantak hills. But the author may have actually had in his mind Mekhliganj in the Cooch Bihar State in North Bengal. Cf. Mekhalā of the Rudrayāmala list quoted above (p. 18).

करतोयां समारभ्य यावद्दिक्करवासिनीम् ।
शतयोजनविस्तीर्णं योनिचक्रं महेश्वर ।
देवा मरणमिच्छन्ति किं पुनर्मानुषादयः ॥
भुवनेशी सिद्धिरूपा किरीटाख्यायां किरीटिका ।
देवेशो भैरवस्तत्र सर्वमङ्गलदायकः ॥
फुल्लरायामाभरणं देवता विमला च वै ।
संवर्त्तो भैरवो देव सर्वदेवनमस्कृतः ॥
वाराणस्यां विशालाक्षी देवता कालभैरवः ।
तत्र मे पतितं लिङ्गं (?) स्वयमेव सदाशिव ॥
मणिकर्णिकेति विख्याता कुण्डले च मम श्रुतेः ॥
अयोध्यायाश्च मे हारो भैरवो हरिहरात्मकः ।
तत्र सा देवता पूर्णा महालक्ष्मीः सुखप्रदा ॥
कन्यास्तु मे (कन्याश्रमे ?) कात्यायनी वामदेवश्च भैरवः ।
तत्र मे पतितं चर्म नमीषो नाम एव च ॥
कुमारी देवता तत्र सर्वाणः सर्व भैरवः ।
तत्र मे पतितं रोम तस्माद् भैरवदेवता ॥
स्थाननामा च सावित्री देवता मणिवेदका (°वेदके ?) ।
मणिबन्धे च गायत्री सर्वानन्दश्च भैरवः ॥
श्रीशैले च मम ग्रीवा महालक्ष्मीश्च देवता ।
भैरवः संभृतानन्दो देशे देशे व्यवस्थितः ॥
काञ्चीदेशे च कङ्काली भैरवो मदनः स्वयम् ।
तत्र मे पतिते देव नितम्बे देववल्लभ ॥
देवता वेदगर्भाख्या माधवो भैरवः स्वयम् ।
तत्र मे पतिता विद्या तथा च कालमाधवे ॥
भैरवः शुङ्गनामा च देवी काली सुसिद्धिदा ।
मणिद्वीपे महाबाहो पतितं मे सुवस्त्रकम् ।
दृष्ट्वा स्मृत्वा महादेव मन्त्रसिद्धिमवाप्नुयात् ॥
कुजवारे भूततिथौ निशार्द्धे यस्तु साधकः ।
नत्वा प्रदक्षिणीकृत्य मन्त्रसिद्धिमवाप्नुयात् ॥
सोमाख्ये भद्रसेनश्च तत्र भद्रा च देवता ।
वामपार्श्वे शुभाख्या च नर्त्तकी दण्डभैरवः ॥
उमानाम्नी केशपाशे भूतेशः पूर्णभैरवः ।
संहाराख्ये चोर्द्धदन्तो देवी नारायणी शुचौ ॥

अधोदन्तो महारुद्र वाराही सप्तसागरः (°सागरे ?)[1] ॥
करतोयातटे शय्या तत्र वामनभैरवः ।
अपर्णा देवता तत्र सर्वेशो भैरवः स्वयम् ॥
श्रीपर्वते नूपुरञ्च सुन्दरी तत्र देवता ।
सुन्दरो भैरवो देव योगिनीवल्लभप्रभुः ॥
सिद्धेश्वरी महाविद्या समुद्रो भैरवः स्वयम् ।
दन्तावलीषु मे देव जाता भैरवदेवताः ॥
प्रभासे धर्म्मकं देव तत्र कपालिनी परा ।
भैरवः सर्वदेवस्य सर्वभैरवनायकः ॥
गोदावरीमहातीर्थे हरिद्वारे च विभ्यसे ।
वक्रेशो भैरवस्तत्र भैरवी देवता स्वयम् ॥
ओष्ठं वैवस्वते तीर्थे हरिता त्रिपुटा तथा ।
भैरवः सोमहन्ता च सर्वदेवी तथापरा ॥
चिबुके डामरी (भ्रामरी) देवी विकटाख्या जले स्थले
गण्ड गर्गा सुपर्वा च विश्वेशो विश्वमातृका ।
दण्डपाणिभैरवस्य वामगण्डे च राकिणी ॥
शैलखण्डस्थखण्डे मे सर्वभौतिकदेवताः ।
रत्नावल्यां स्कन्धदेशः कुमारो भैरवः स्वयम् ॥
देवता च शिवा देवी भैरवस्य स्वयं शिवः ॥
मिथिलायां वामदेशे उग्रदेवी महोदरी ।
सेतुबन्धे महाभीमो भैरवो देवता जया ।
लोमखण्डे च देवेशस्तैलाङ्गे (तैलङ्गे ?) चण्डनायिका ॥
चण्डेशो भैरवस्तत्र नित्यं तत्र वसाम्यहम् ॥
भैरवो दीर्घदर्शी च चक्रपाणिश्च भैरवः ।
क्षेत्रवती महादेवी सर्वसम्पत्प्रदायिनी ॥
पृथिव्यां यानि तीर्थानि याश्च भैरवदेवताः ।
पर्वतेषु श्मशानेषु गङ्गासागरसङ्गमे ॥
वैष्णवी सा महादेवी माधवो भैरवः स्वयम् ।
महाकायो महायोगो भैरवः सर्वविघ्नकृत् (°हृत्) ॥
कलौ नीलाचलक्षेत्रं तथा च भुवनेश्वरः ।
विमला विरजा राज्ञा जगन्नाथस्य भैरवः ॥
तत्र मे पतितं देव उच्छिष्टं शुद्धिता तथा ।
भुवनेशो भैरवस्तत्र वसामि च द्वया सदा (त्वया सह ?) ॥

---

1 Note the attempt to correct पञ्च into सप्त. See *supra*, p. 53, note 9.

उच्छिष्टचण्डालिनी देवी सर्वपीठेश्वरी परा ॥
चक्रद्वीपे शूलपाणिर्देवता चक्रधारिणी ।
तत्र मे पतितश्चास्त्रं तेन जातो महोरगः ॥
एतत्ते कथितं देव पीठनाथादिदैवतम् ॥
क्षेत्राधीशं विना देव पूजयेत् पीठदेवताम् ।
भैरवीरहितं सर्वं जपसाधनकं क्रियाः (?) ॥
अज्ञात्वा भैरवं पीठं शक्तिश्च कुलभैरवम् ।
प्राणनाथ न सिध्यन्ति कल्पकोटिजपादिभिः ॥
न देयं परशिष्याय निन्दिताय दुरात्मने ।
शठाय वञ्चकायाशु दत्वा मृत्युमवाप्नुयात् ॥
देयं शिष्याय शान्ताय नैष्ठिकाय ममाज्ञया ।
एषु स्थानेषु देवेश षट्कर्मसाधनं चरेत् ॥
साधकाय कुलीनाय मन्त्री मन्त्रार्थसिद्धये ।
दद्याच्चैव महादेव अन्यथा पतनं भवेत् ॥

APPENDIX II

Puranic Text containing 108 Names of the Mother-goddess.

नामाष्टोत्तरशतम्

Mts = Matsya Purāṇa: *a* Veṅkaṭeśvara Press ed.; *b* Ānandāśrama ed.; *c* Vaṅgavāsī ed. (ch. 13, verses 26–53).
DBh = Devībhāgavata, Vaṅgavāsī ed. (Bk. VII, ch. 30, verses 55–83).
Pdm = Padma Purāṇa-Sṛṣṭikhaṇḍa, Vaṅgavāsī ed. (ch. 17, verses 184–211).
Skd = Skanda Purāṇa-Āvantyakhaṇḍa, Vangavāsī ed. (Revākhaṇḍa, ch. 98, verses 64–92).

[1] वाराणस्यां विशालाक्षी नैमिषे लिङ्गधारिणी [2] ।

---

[1] Pdm begins the section with the additional line: सावित्री पुष्करे नाम तीर्थानां प्रवरे शुभे and reads कर्णिके for पुष्करे in verse 4.

It is interesting to note that a number of the holy places mentioned here are also known from the *Viṣṇusaṃhitā* (ch. 85) as *tīrthas* suitable for performing funerary rites. The list of 54 in the *Viṣṇusaṃhitā* includes: Puṣkara, Gayāśīrṣa, Akṣayavaṭa, Amarakaṇṭaka, Varāhaparvata, Narmadātīra, Yamunātīra, Gaṅgā, Kuśāvarta, Binduka, Nīlaparvata, Kanakhala, Kubjāmra, Bhṛgutuṅga, Kedāra, Mahālaya, Naḍantikā, Sugandhā, Śākambharī, Phalgutīrtha, Mahāgaṅgā, Trihalikāgrāma, Kumāradhārā, Prabhāsa, Sarasvatī, Gaṅgādvāra, Prayāga, Gaṅgāsāgarasaṅgama, Naimiṣāraṇya, Vārāṇasī, Agastyāśrama, Kaṇvāśrama, Kauśikī, Sarayūtīra, Śonajyotiṣāsaṅgama, Śrīparvata, Kālodaka, Uttaramānasa, Vaḍavā, Mataṅgavāpī, Saptārṣa, Viṣṇupada, Svargamārgapada, Godāvarī, Gomatī, Vetravatī, Vipāśā, Vitastā, Śatadrutīra, Candrabhāgā, Irāvatī, Sindhutīra, Dakṣiṇa-Pañcanada and Ausaja. Cf. the *Prāṇatoṣaṇī* lists quoted above, pp. 25, note 3; 28, note 2. Note also the long list of *Pitṛtīrthas* or *Śrāddhatīrthas* in the *Padma Purāṇa*, Sṛṣṭikhaṇḍa, ch. 11. For an important but later list of Śākta *tīrthas*, see *DBh*, VII, 38, 5–30.

[2] DBh—गौरीमुखनिवासिनी ।
क्षेत्रे वै नैमिषारण्ये प्रोक्ता सा लिङ्गधारिणी ॥

The elaboration (cf. p. 58, note 9) points to later modification of the original text.

प्रयागे ललिता देवी[1] कामाक्षी[2] गन्धमादने ॥ १ ॥
मानसे कुमुदा नाम विश्वकाया तथाम्बरे[3] ।
गोमन्ते गोमती नाम मन्दरे कामचारिणी ॥ २ ॥
मदोत्कटा चैत्ररथे जयन्ती हस्तिनापुरे[4] ।
कान्यकुब्जे तथा गौरी रम्भा मलयपर्वते[5] ॥ ३ ॥
एकाम्रके[6] कीर्त्तिमती विश्वां[7] विश्वेश्वरे[8] विदुः ।
पुष्करे पुरुहूतेति केदारे मार्गदायिनी[9] ॥ ४ ॥
नन्दा[10] हिमवतः पृष्ठे गोकर्णे भद्रकर्णिका[11] ।
स्थाण्वीश्वरे[12] भवानी तु विल्वके[13] विल्वपत्रिका ॥ ५ ॥
श्रीशैले माधवी नाम[14] भद्रा भद्रेश्वरे[15] तथा ।
जया वराहशैले तु[16] कमला कमलालये ॥ ६ ॥
रुद्रकोट्यां च[17] रुद्राणी काली कालञ्जरे गिरौ[18] ।
[19] महालिङ्गे तु कपिला मर्कोटे[20] मुकुटेश्वरी ॥ ७ ॥

---

1 DBh—प्रोक्ता ।

2 DBh—कामुकी ; Pdm, Skd—कामुका ।

3 Skd—°परे ; DBh—प्रोक्ता दक्षिणे चोत्तरे तथा ।
विश्वकामा भगवती विश्वकामप्रपूरिणी ॥ (Cf. p. 66, note 2.)

4 Skd—जयन्ती हास्तिने पुरे ।

5 DBh—गौरी प्रोक्ता कान्यकुब्जे रम्भा तु मलयाचले ।

6 Mts *ab*—एकाभ्रके ; DBh—एकाम्रपीठे सम्प्रोक्ता देवी सा कीर्त्तिमत्यपि ।
विश्वे विश्वेश्वरीं प्राहुः पुरुहूताञ्च पुष्करे ।
केदारपीठे सम्प्रोक्ता देवी सन्मार्गदायिनी ॥ (Cf. note 3 above; also p. 66, note 2.)

7 Pdm—विल्वा ।

8 Pdm (v.l.)—विश्वेश्वरी ।

9 Pdm—कर्णिके पूरुहूतेति केदारे मार्गदायिका । Skd—पुरुहूता च ।

10 DBh—मन्दा ; Skd—हिमवतः प्रस्थे ।

11 Pdm—भद्रकालिका ।

12 Mts, DBh, Skd—स्थानेश्वरे ।

13 Mts *ab*—विल्वले. Cf. विन्दुक in the *Viṣṇusaṃhitā*.

14 Pdm—देवी ; DBh—प्रोक्ता ।

15 Mts *c*—महेश्वरे ; Skd—भद्रे भद्रेश्वरीति च ।

16 DBh—वराहशैले तु जया ।

17 Pdm—रुद्रकोट्यान्तु ; DBh—रुद्राणी रुद्रकोट्यान्त ; Skd—रुद्रकोट्यान्तु कल्याणी ।

18 Skd, Pdm, Dbh—तथा ।

19 DBh reads this line after the following line,

20 Skd, DBh—माकोट ; Pdm—कर्कोटे मङ्गलेश्वरी ।

शालग्रामे[1] महादेवी शिवलिङ्गे जलप्रिया ।
मायापुर्यां कुमारी तु सन्ताने ललिता तथा ॥ ८ ॥
[2]उत्पलाक्षी[3] सहस्राक्षे कमलाक्षे[4] महोत्पला ।
गङ्गायां[5] मङ्गला नाम[6] विमला पुरुषोत्तमे ॥ ९ ॥
विपाशायाममोघाक्षी पाटला पुण्ड्रवर्द्धने[7] ।
नारायणी सुपार्श्वे तु त्रिकूटे[8] भद्रसुन्दरी[9] ॥ १० ॥
विपुले विपुला नाम[10] कल्याणी मानसाचले[11] ।
कोटवी कोटितीर्थे तु[12] सुगन्धा माधवे वने[13] ॥ ११ ॥
गोदाश्रमे[14] त्रिसन्ध्या तु गङ्गाद्वारे रतिप्रिया[15] ।
शिवकुण्डे[16] शिवानन्दा[17] नन्दिनी देविकातटे ॥ १२ ॥
रुक्मिणी द्वारवत्यान्तु राधा वृन्दावने वने[18] ।
देवकी मथुरायान्तु पाताले परमेश्वरी ॥ १३ ॥
चित्रकूटे तथा सीता विन्ध्ये विन्ध्यनिवासिनी[19] ।
[20]सह्याद्रावेकवीरा तु हरिश्चन्द्रे[21] तु चन्द्रिका ॥ १४ ॥

---

1 Skd—शालिग्रामे ।

2 DBh reads this line after the following line.

3 Pdm—उत्पलाख्या ।

4 Skd, Pdm, DBh—हिरण्याक्षे ।

Cf. गोवर्धनं हरिश्चन्द्रं पुरश्चन्द्रं पृथूदकम् ।
सहस्राक्षं हिरण्याक्षं तथा च कदली नदी ॥ पद्मपुराण । सृष्टिखण्ड । ११ । ४२

5 Pdm, DBh—गयायां ; Skd—गयायां विमला नाम मङ्गला पुरुषोत्तमे ।

6 DBh—प्रोक्ता ।

7 Pdm—पुण्ड्वर्द्धने । The accounts of Hiuen Tsang appear to support this form of the name.

8 Mts—विकूटे ।

9 DBh—चन्द्र° ।

10 DBh—देवी ।

11 Skd, Mts, DBh—मलयाचले । After this line DBh reads the last line of verse 14 and the first of verse 15

12 Skd—°तीर्थेषु ।

13 Pdm—माधवी° ; Skd—गन्धमादने (cf. verse 1). Cf. सुगन्धा in the *V.S.*

14 Pdm—गोदावर्यां ; Mts *a* (v.l.)—कुब्जाचके. Cf. कुब्जाम्र in the *V.S.*

15 Pdm—हरिप्रिया ।

16 DBh—शिवकुक्षे ; Skd—शिवचण्डे ।

17 Mts *a* (v.l.)—सुनन्दा तु ; *b* (v.l.), DBh—शुभानन्दा ; Skd—सभानन्दा ।

18 Pdm—तथा ।

19 Mts—विन्ध्याधिवासिनी ।

20 DBh reads this line after the following one.

21 Mts *a* (v.l.)—हर्मचन्द्रे ; Skd—चण्डिका । For the name हरिश्चन्द्र, see *Padma Purāṇa*, Sṛṣṭikhaṇḍa, ch. 11, v. 42 quoted in note 4 above.

रमणा रामतीर्थे तु यमुनायां मृगावती ।
करवीरे महालक्ष्मीरुमादेवी [1] विनायके ॥ १५ ॥
अरोगा [2] वैद्यनाथे तु महाकाले महेश्वरी ।
अभयेत्युष्णतीर्थे तु [3] चामृता विन्ध्यकन्दरे ॥ १६ ॥
माण्डव्ये [4] माण्डवी नाम स्वाहा माहेश्वरे [5] पुरे ।
छागलाण्डे [6] प्रचण्डा तु चण्डिकामरकण्टके [7] ॥ १७ ॥
सोमेश्वरे वरारोहा प्रभासे पुष्करावती ।
देवमाता [8] सरस्वत्यां पारावारतटे माता [9] ॥ १८ ॥
महालये महाभागा [10] पयोष्ण्यां पिङ्गलेश्वरी ।
सिंहिका कृतशौचे तु कार्त्तिकेये यशस्करी [11] ॥ १९ ॥
उत्पलावर्त्तके लोला सुभद्रा शोणसङ्गमे [12] ।
माता सिद्धपुरे [13] लक्ष्मीरङ्गना [14] भरताश्रमे ॥ २० ॥
जालन्धरे विश्वमुखी तारा किष्किन्ध्यपर्वते [15] ।
देवदारुवने पुष्टिर्मेधा काश्मीरमण्डले ॥ २१ ॥
भीमादेवी हिमाद्रौ तु [16] तुष्टिर्वस्त्रेश्वरे [17] तथा ।
कपालमोचने शुद्धिर्माता [18] कायावरोहणे ॥ २२ ॥

---

1 Skd—रूपादेवी ।

2 Mts *b* (v.l.), DBh, Skd—आरोग्या ।

3 Skd—°तीर्थे तु मृगी वा ; Pdm—पुष्पतीर्थेतु चामृता ; DBh—नितम्बा विन्ध्य° ।

4 DBh—माण्डवे ; Skd—माण्डुकीनाम ।

5 Skd—महेश्वरे ; DBh—माहेश्वरी° ।

6 DBh—छगलण्डे ; Skd—छागलिङ्गे ; Pdm—वेगले तु प्रचण्डाथ ।

7 Mts—मकरन्दके ; *b* (v.l.)—मरकण्टे ।

8 Skd—वेदमाता ।

9 Pdm—पारापारे तटे स्थिता ; DBh—पारावारातटे स्मृता ; Skd—पारा पारातटे शुभे ।

10 Pdm—महापद्मा ।

11 Pdm—तु शङ्करी ; DBh—°त्वतिशाङ्करी ; Skd—कार्त्तिके चैव शाङ्करी ।

12 Pdm—सिन्धुसङ्गमे ।

13 DBh—सिद्धवने ; Skd—सिद्धवटे ; Pdm—उमा सिद्धवने ।

14 Pdm, DBh—लक्ष्मीरनङ्गा ; Skd—लक्ष्मीस्तरङ्गा ।

15 Skd—किष्किन्ध° ।

16 Pdm—च ।

17 DBh—तुष्टिर्विश्वेश्वरी ; Mts—पुष्टिर्विश्वेश्वरे ; Skd—पुष्टिर्वस्त्रेश्वरे ।

18 Pdm—शुद्धा माता ।

शङ्खोद्धारे ध्वनिर्नाम [1] धृतिः पिण्डारके तथा ।
काला [2] तु चन्द्रभागायामच्छोदे शिवकारिणी [3] ॥ २३ ॥
वेणायाममृता नाम [4] बदर्यामुर्वशी तथा ।
औषधी [5] चोत्तरकुरौ कुशद्वीपे कुशोदका ॥ २४ ॥
मन्मथा हेमकूटे तु मुकुटे [6] सत्यवादिनी ।
अश्वत्थे वन्दनीया [7] तु निधिर्वैश्रवणालये ॥ २५ ॥
गायत्री वेदवदने पार्वती शिवसन्निधौ ।
देवलोके [8] तथेन्द्राणी ब्रह्मास्येषु [9] सरस्वती ॥ २६ ॥
सूर्यविम्बे प्रभा नाम मातॄणां वैष्णवी मता ।
अरुन्धती सतीनान्तु रामासु च तिलोत्तमा ॥
चित्ते [10] ब्रह्मकला नाम शक्तिः सर्वशरीरिणाम् ॥ २७ ॥ [11]
एतदुद्देशतः [12] प्रोक्तं नामाष्टशतमुत्तमम् ।
अष्टोत्तरञ्च तीर्थानां शतमेतदुदाहृतम् ॥ २८ ॥

APPENDIX III

Evolution of the Dakṣayajña Story.

दक्षयज्ञकथामूलम्

(*a*) प्रथिष्ट यस्य वीरकर्ममिष्णदनुष्ठितं नु नर्यो अपौहत् ।
पुनस्तदा वृहति यत् कनाया दुहितुरा अनुभृतमनर्वा ॥

---

1 Mts *a*—धरा नाम ।

2 DBh—कला ।

3 DBh—शिवधारिणी; Pdm—सिद्धिदायिनी; Skd—शक्तिधारिणी ।

4 Pdm—देवी ।

5 Mts *b*—औषधी; DBh—औषधिश्चोत्तर°। Cf. औसज in the *V.S.*

6 DBh, Pdm, Skd—कुमुदे ।

7 Skd—वन्दिनीका ।

8 DBh—वेदलोके ।

9 Pdm, Skd—ब्रह्मास्ये तु ।

10 Pdm—चित्रे ।

11 Skd adds after this line: शूलेश्वरी भृगुक्षेत्रे भगो सौभाग्यसुन्दरी ।

12 Pdm—एतज्ज्ञात्वा मया;

DBh—इमान्यष्टशतानि स्युः पीठानि जनमेजय ।
तत्संख्यकास्तदीशान्यो देव्यश्च परिकीर्तिताः ॥
सतीदेव्यङ्गभूतानि पीठानि सन्ति तानि च ।
अन्यान्यपि प्रसिद्धानि यानि मुख्यानि भूतले ॥

मध्या यत्कार्त्वमभवदभीके कामं कृण्वाने पितरि युवत्याम् ।
मनानग्रेतो जहतुर्वियन्ता सानौ निषिक्तं सुकृतस्य योनौ ॥
पिता यत् स्वां दुहितरमधिष्कन् क्ष्मया रेतः संजग्मानो निषिञ्चत् ।
स्वाध्योऽजनयन् ब्रह्म देवा वास्तोष्पतिं व्रतपां निरतक्षन् ॥

(ऋग्वेद, १०।६१।५-७)

(*b*) प्रजापतिर्ह वै स्वां दुहितरमभिदध्यौ दिवं वोषसं वा मिथुन्येनया स्यामिति। तां सम्बभूव। तद्वै देवानामाग आस य इत्थं स्वां दुहितरमस्माकं स्वसारं करोतीति। ते ह देवा उचुः। योऽयं देवः पशूनामीष्टेऽतिसंधं वा अयं चरति य इत्थं स्वां दुहितरमस्माकं स्वसारं करोति विध्येममिति। तं रुद्रोऽभ्यायत्य विव्याध। तस्य सामि रेतः प्रचस्कन्द। तथेन्नूनं तदास। तस्मादेतदृषिणाभ्यनूक्तम्। पिता यत्स्वां दुहितरमधिष्कन् क्ष्मया रेतः संजग्मानो निषिञ्चदिति। तदाग्निमारुतमित्युक्थं तस्मिंस्तदाख्यायते यथा तद्देवा रेतः प्राजनयन्। तेषां तदा देवानां क्रोधो व्यैदथ प्रजापतिमभिषज्यंस्तस्य तं शल्यं निरकृन्तन्। स वै यज्ञ एव प्रजापतिः। ते होचुः। उपजानीत यथेदं नामुयासत्कनीयो ह्या हुतेर्यथेदं स्यादिति। ते होचुः। भगायैनद्दक्षिणत आसीनाय परिहरत तद्भगः प्राशिष्यति तद्यथाहुतमेवं भविष्यतीति। तद्भगाय दक्षिणत आसीनाय पर्याजह्रुः। तद्भगोऽवेक्षां चक्रे। तस्याक्षिणी निर्ददाह। तथेन्नूनं तदास। तस्मादाहुरन्धो भग इति। ते होचुः। नो न्वेवात्राशमत्पूष्णऽएनत् परिहरतेति। तत्पूष्णे पर्याजह्रुः। तत्पूषा प्राश। तस्य दतो निर्जघान। तथेन्नूनं तदास। तस्मादाहुरदन्तकः पूषेति। *** (शतपथब्राह्मण-माध्यन्दिनशाखा। १।७।४। १–७।

(*c*) प्रजापतिर्वै स्वां दुहितरमभ्यध्यायद्दिवमित्यन्य आहुरुषसमित्यन्ये। तामृश्यो भूत्वा रोहितं भूतामभ्यैत्। तं देवा अपश्यन् न कृतं वै प्रजापतिः करोतीति। ते तमैच्छन्य एनमारिष्यत्येतमन्योन्यस्मिन्नाविन्दन्। तेषां या एव घोरतमास्तन्व आसंस्ता एकधा समभरंस्ताः संभृता एष देवोऽभवत्तदस्यै तद्भूतवन्नाम भवति वै स योऽस्यै तदेवं नाम वेद। तं देवा अब्रुवन्नयं वै प्रजापतिरकृतमकरिमं विध्येति। स तथेत्यब्रवीत् स वै वो वरं वृणा इति वृणीष्वेति। स एतमेव वरमवृणीत पशूनामाधिपत्यम्। तदस्यैतत्पशुमन्नाम पशुमान् भवति योऽस्यै तदेवं नाम वेद। तमाभ्यायत्याविध्यत्। स विद्ध ऊर्ध्व उदप्रपततमेतं मृग इत्याचक्षते। य उ एव मृगव्याधः स उ एव स या रोहित्सा रोहिणी य एवेषुस्त्रिकाण्डा स एवेषुस्त्रिकाण्डा। तद्वा इदं प्रजापते रेतः सिक्तमधावत्तत्सरोऽभवत्। ते देवा अब्रुवन् मेदं प्रजापते रेतो दुषदिति। यदब्रुवन् मेदं प्रजापते रेतो दुषदिति तन्मादुषमभवत्। *** (ऐतरेयब्राह्मण। ३।३३)

(*d*) प्रजापतिर्वै रुद्रं यज्ञान्निरभजत्। सोऽकामयत मेऽयमस्मा आकूतिः समृद्धिर्यो मा यज्ञान्निरभाक्षीदिति। स यज्ञमभ्यायम्याविध्य तदाविद्धं निरकृन्तत। तत् प्राशित्रमभवत्तदुदयच्छत्तद्भगाय पर्यहरंस्तत्प्रतीक्षेत। तस्य चक्षुः परापतत्तस्मादाहुरन्धो वै भग इत्यपि हृतं नेच्छेद्यमिच्छति तत् सवित्रे पर्यहरंस्तत्प्रत्यगृह्णात् तस्य पाणी प्रतिच्छेद तस्मै हिरण्मयौ प्रत्यदधुस्तस्माद्धिरण्यपाणिरिति स्तुतस्तत् पूष्णे पर्यहरंस्तत् प्राश्नात्तस्य दन्ताः परोप्यन्त तस्मादाहुरदन्तकः पूषा पेष्टभाजन इति। *** (गोपथब्राह्मण। २।१)।

(*e*) कस्यचित्त्वथ कालस्य दक्षनामा प्रजापतिः।
पूर्वोक्तेन विधानेन यक्ष्यमाणोऽन्वपद्यत॥
ततस्तस्य मखं देवाः सर्वे शक्रपुरोगमाः।
गमनाय समागम्य बुद्धिमापेदिरे तदा॥
ते विमानैर्महात्मानो ज्वलनार्कसमप्रभैः।
देवस्यानुमते गच्छन् गङ्गाद्वारमिति श्रुतिः॥
प्रस्थिता देवता दृष्ट्वा शैलराजसुता तदा।
उवाच वचनं साध्वी देवं पशुपतिं पतिम्॥
भगवन् क्व नु यान्त्येते देवाः शक्रपुरोगमाः।
ब्रूहि तत्त्वेन तत्त्वज्ञ संशयो मे महानयम्॥

महेश्वर उवाच॥

दक्षो नाम महाभागे प्रजानां पतिरुत्तमः।
हयमेधेन यजते तत्र यान्ति दिवौकसः॥

उमोवाच॥

यज्ञमेतं महादेव किमर्थं नाधिगच्छसि।
केन वा प्रतिषेधेन गमनं ते न विद्यते॥

महेश्वर उवाच॥

सुरैरेव महाभागे पूर्वमेतदनुष्ठितम्।
यज्ञेषु सर्वेषु मम न भाग उपकल्पितः॥
पूर्वोपायोपपन्नेन मार्गेण वरवर्णिनि।
न मे सुराः प्रयच्छन्ति भागं यज्ञस्य धर्मतः॥

उमोवाच॥

भगवन् सर्वभूतेषु प्रभावाभ्यधिको गुणैः।
अजय्यश्चाप्यधृष्यश्च तेजसा यशसा श्रिया
अनेन ते महाभाग प्रतिषेधेन भागतः।
अतीव दुःखमुत्पन्नं वेपथुश्च ममानघ॥

भीष्म उवाच ॥

एवमुक्ता तु सा देवी तदा पशुपतिं पतिम् ।
तुष्णीम्भूताभवद्राजन् दह्यमानेन चेतसा ॥
अथ देव्या मतं ज्ञात्वा हृद्गतं यच्चिकीर्षितम् ।
स समाज्ञापयामास तिष्ठ त्वमिति नन्दिनम् ॥
ततो योगबलं कृत्वा सर्वयोगेश्वरेश्वरः ।
तं यज्ञं स महातेजा भीमैरनुचरैस्तदा ॥
सहसा घातयामास देवदेवः पिनाकधृक् ॥ * * *

(महाभारत ।१२।२८३।१९–२३) ।

(*f*) * * * केचिद्बभञ्जुः प्राग्वंशं पत्नीशालां तथापरे ।
सद आग्नीध्रशालाश्च तद्विहारं महानसम् ॥
रुरुजुर्यज्ञपात्राणि तथैकेऽग्नीननाशयन् ।
कुण्डेष्वमूत्रयन् केचिद्बिभिदुर्वेदिमेखलाः ॥
अबाधन्त मुनीनन्ये एके पत्नीरतर्जयन् ।
अपरे जगृहुर्देवान् प्रत्यासन्नान् पलायितान् ॥
भृगुं बबन्ध मणिमान् वीरभद्रः प्रजापतिम् ।
चण्डेशः पूषणं देवं भगं नन्दीश्वरोऽग्रहीत् ॥
सर्वं एवर्त्विजो दृष्ट्वा सदस्याः सदिवौकसः ।
तैरर्द्यमानाः सुभृशं ग्रावभिर्नैकधाद्रवन् ॥
जुह्वतः स्रुवहस्तस्य श्मश्रूणि भगवान् भवः ।
भृगोर्लुलुञ्चे सदसि योऽहसत् श्मश्रु दर्शयन् ॥
भगस्य नेत्रे भगवान् पातितस्य रुषा भुवि ।
उज्जहार सदःस्थोऽक्ष्णा यः शपन्तमसूसुचत् ॥
पूष्णो ह्यपातयद्दन्तान् कालिङ्गस्य यथा बलः ।
शप्यमाने गरिमणि योऽहसद्दर्शयन् दतः ॥ * * *

(भागवतपुराण ।४।५।१४–२१)

(*g*) * * * वीरभद्रोऽपि दीप्तात्मा शक्रस्यैवोद्यतं करम् ।
व्यष्टम्भयददीनात्मा तथान्येषां दिवौकसाम् ॥
भगस्य नेत्रे चोत्पाट्य करजाग्रेण लीलया ।
निहत्य मुष्टिना दन्तान् पूष्णश्चैवमपातयत् ॥
तथा चन्द्रमसं देवं पादाङ्गुष्ठेन लीलया ।
घर्षयामास बलवान् स्मयमानो गणेश्वरः ॥
वह्नेर्हस्तद्वयं छित्त्वा जिह्वामुत्पाट्य लीलया ।
जघान मूर्ध्नि पादेन मुनीनपि मुनीश्वराः ॥
तथा विष्णुं सगरुडं समायान्तं महाबलः ।
विव्याध निशितैर्बाणैः स्तम्भयित्वा सुदर्शनम् ॥ * * *

(कूर्मपुराण ।१।१५।६०–६४) ।

APPENDIX IV

Date of the Tantrasāra.

The celebrated Tantric encyclopedia entitled *Tantrasāra*, composed or rather compiled by the great Bengali leader of Tantric thought named Kṛṣṇānanda, is well known to all students of the Tantra literature. In the colophons added to some of the chapters of the *Tantrasāra* the author calls himself 'Mahāmahopādhyāya-Kṛṣṇānanda-Vāgīśa-Bhaṭṭācārya'; but later writers usually refer to him as Kṛṣṇānanda Āgamavāgīśa. *Vāgīśa* seems to have been an abbreviated form of *Āgamavāgīśa*.

The late Mr. N. N. Vasu gave the following description of the family, to which Kṛṣṇānanda Āgamavāgīśa, author of the *Tantrasāra*, belonged, in the *Vārendra-Brāhmaṇa-Vivaraṇa* Volume of his *Vaṅger Jātīya Itihāsa* (in Bengali): 'This family is known in the community of the Vārendra Brāhmaṇas as the Kāśyapa-gotrīya Maitras of Maṇḍalajānī. It originally flourished at Āgameśvarī-talā at Śrīdhāma-Navadvīpa; but later, owing to an expansion of the family, its members scattered themselves over different parts of Bengal. A branch of the family still lives at Śrīdhāma and is devoted to the worship of the goddess Āgameśvarī' (p. 157). A number of traditions about Kṛṣṇānanda's religious life have also been quoted in the work. In connection with the date of Kṛṣṇānanda Āgamavāgīśa, Mr. Vasu says (*loc. cit.*), 'Kṛṣṇānanda, Śrīcaitanya and Raghunātha Śiromaṇi were co-students at the Catuṣpāṭhī of the same Guru at Navadvīpa. At first Kṛṣṇānanda and Caitanya were great friends; but dissension separated them when Caitanya preferred to worship Kṛṣṇa according to the principle known as the Sakhī-bhāva. Kṛṣṇānanda requested his friend not to take up the new course, but was insulted; and from that time they began to preach the Śākta and Vaiṣṇava doctrines separately. Kṛṣṇānanda attained perfection with the Śakti-mantra and conceived and popularized the form of the image of the goddess Kālī.[1] Before this, Kālī was usually worshipped at a Ghaṭa. The Ghaṭa established for the purpose of worshipping the goddess by Kṛṣṇānanda at the temple of Āgameśvarī at Navadvīpa still exists and a large number of Śāktas flock to it for worshipping Mahāmāyā.'

The story narrated by Mr. Vasu invites comments. In the first place, we know that Kṛṣṇānanda began his work with an adoration to Lord Kṛṣṇa, identified with Viṣṇu (*Tantrasāra*, Vaṅgavāsī edition, p. 1):

नत्वा कृष्णपदद्वन्द्वं ब्रह्मादिसुरपूजितम् ।
गुरुञ्च ज्ञानदातारं कृष्णानन्देन धीमता ॥

---

[1] According to a tradition recorded by Vasu, Kṛṣṇānanda was ordered by the goddess Kālī in a dream to popularize the form of her image. On being questioned as to how the form could be realized, the goddess replied that it would be revealed to the devotee the next morning. Early next day when Kṛṣṇānanda came out of his house, he found a young cowherdess engaged in preparing cowdung cakes. She was standing in the *ālīḍha* pose (with the right knee thrown to front and the left leg firm behind in a slanting position) and had a large ball of cowdung in her left hand and a small one in the right, upraised to be set on a wall in the form of a cake. On the sudden consciousness of her being noticed by Kṛṣṇānanda the woman felt very much ashamed and pressed her tongue, that lolled, with her teeth (cf. Bengali लज्जाय जिव काटा which gives an expression to the feeling of shame). The appearance of the cowherdess as seen by Kṛṣṇānanda that morning was popularized by him as the form of the image of Dakṣiṇa-Kālī. Kṛṣṇānanda began to worship small images of this type made of mud by himself every day to be immersed early next morning in the waters of the Ganges. Later the king of Navadvīpa introduced the worship of large images of the same type on the newmoon of the month of Kārttika.

This seems to show that Kṛṣṇānanda Āgamavāgīśa was not initiated into the Śakti-mantra, but was a Tantric devotee who received his initiation into the Vaiṣṇava formula.[1] In the Śyāmā or Kālī section of the *Tantrasāra*, the author quotes the opinions of various Tantra works, but does not express any special view of his own (cf. *op. cit.*, p. 472ff; also Pūrṇānanda's *Śyāmārahasya*, ed. R. N. Chatterji, pp. 11-12).

In the second place, it is extremely difficult to regard Kṛṣṇānanda Āgamavāgīśa as a co-student of the celebrated Vaiṣṇava saint Caitanya of Navadvīpa and the great Bengali logician Raghunātha Śiromaṇi. Caitanya was born on the full-moon day of Phālguna in Śaka 1407, corresponding to the 18th February, 1486 A.D., and died at the age of 48 on the seventh *tithi* of the bright half of Āṣāḍha in Śaka 1455 (1533 A.D.). *Vide* D. C. Sen, *Vaṅgabhāṣā O Sāhitya*, 5th edition, pp. 256, 266; R. G. Bhandarkar's Collected Works, Vol. IV, pp. 118-19. According to the *History of Indian Logic* (pp. 463–65) by S. C. Vidyabhushan, Raghunātha Śiromaṇi flourished between 1477 and 1547 A.D., although recent writers on the subject suggest that the Śiromaṇi was born about 1460–65 A.D., composed his famous *Tattvacintāmaṇididhiti* about 1490–1500 A.D. and was therefore about a generation earlier than Caitanya (cf. *V.S.P.P.*, Vol. L, p. 13; LIII, pp. 1, 3). If, therefore, the story narrated by Mr. Vasu has to be believed, we have to assume that Kṛṣṇānanda was born about 1480 A.D. and died sometime about the middle of the sixteenth century. There is, however, evidence to show that the *Tantrasāra* was composed several years after 1577 A.D.

The great Tantric teacher Pūrṇānanda Paramahaṃsa, who was an inhabitant of the Mymensing District of Bengal (cf. Introduction to the Calcutta Sanskrit Series edition of the *Śrītattvacintāmaṇi*), wrote his famous work entitled *Śrītattvacintāmaṇi* in the Śaka year 1499 corresponding to 1577 A.D. This is clear from the following passage of the work: **श्रीमत्परमहंस-परिव्राजक-श्रीगुरु-ब्रह्मानन्द-मुखारविन्द-निस्यन्दमान-परमरहस्याति-रहस्य-निगममकरन्द-सन्दोहतुन्दिलानन्दः श्रीपूर्णानन्दपरमहंसः श्रीतत्त्वचिन्तामणिं चतुर्दशशताधिकनवनवतिशकाब्दे वितनोति ।** The *Śrītattvacintāmaṇi* by Pūrṇānanda has been quoted by Kṛṣṇānanda Agamavāgīśa in his *Tantrasāra* (p. 155). Now even if Pūrṇānanda and Kṛṣṇānanda were contemporaries, it is difficult to believe that in that age, when there was little facility of communication, Kṛṣṇānanda of Navadvīpa in the Nadia District could have information about the work of Pūrṇānanda of Mymensing and secure a copy of it immediately after its composition. The *Tantrasāra* thus does not appear to have been composed much earlier than *circa* 1600 A.D. If, under the circumstances, it is conjectured that the *Tantrasāra* was written by Kṛṣṇānanda when he was more than hundred years old, the story of Kṛṣṇānanda, Caitanya and Raghunātha Śiromaṇi having been co-students under the same Guru may not be altogether impossible. But such a suggestion, if not wholly absurd, is certainly rather improbable. It can hardly be accepted without any corroborative evidence. The *Tantrasāra*

---

[1] That Kṛṣṇānanda was not anti-Vaiṣṇava is even admitted by a tradition recorded by Vasu, according to which Śākta Kṛṣṇānanda had a brother named Sahasrākṣa who was a Vaiṣṇava. One day a number of bananas, preserved by Kṛṣṇānanda with a view to offering them to the goddess Āgameśvarī (Kālī), was, during his absence, dedicated by Sahasrākṣa to his own tutelary deity, the god Kṛṣṇa-Viṣṇu. At this Kṛṣṇānanda became very much annoyed. But when at night the Āgamavāgīśa was worshipping the goddess, he and his Vaiṣṇava brother, who happened to be near him, noticed with surprise that the goddess had Gopāla (child Kṛṣṇa) on her lap and was feeding him with bananas like a mother. Thereafter the two brothers realized that there was really no difference between the Vaiṣṇava and Śākta forms of worship.

also quotes Rāghava Bhaṭṭa (*loc. cit.*, p. 16 *et passim*), who wrote the *Padārthādarśa* commentary on the *Śāradātilaka* and flourished in 1493-94 A.D., and the *Tantrakaumudī* (*loc. cit.*, p. 374) composed by the Maithila Devanātha at the court of king Malladeva Naranārāyaṇa of Kamta (1555–87 A.D.; cf. *Pravāsī*, 1354 B.S., pp. 507-08).

In the preface to the *Kālikhaṇḍa* or Section I of the *Śaktisaṅgama Tantra*, published in the Gaekwad Oriental Series, Dr. B. Bhattacharya has made an attempt to determine the date of the composition of the *Śaktisaṅgama* and has incidentally discussed the date of the *Tantrasāra* by Kṛṣṇānanda Āgamavāgīśa. Dr. Bhattacharya says that Kṛṣṇānanda, author of the *Tantrasāra*, was a disciple of Pūrṇānanda Paramahaṃsa, author of the *Śrītattvacintāmaṇi*. As the preceptor, i.e. Pūrṇānanda, wrote his work in 1577 A.D., the disciple, i.e. Kṛṣṇānanda, in Dr. Bhattacharya's opinion, may have composed his *Tantrasāra* about thirty years later, that is to say, about 1607 A.D. Unfortunately however the suggestion that the author of the *Tantrasāra* was a disciple of that of the *Śrītattvacintāmaṇi* is absolutely unwarranted.

It is well known that Tantric devotees regard the Guru or preceptor as equal or even superior to all the gods as an object of veneration. Kṛṣṇānanda himself quotes the following verse in praise of the Guru from the *Jñānārṇava Tantra* in his *Tantrasāra* (p. 2):

गुरुः पिता गुरुर्माता गुरुर्देवो गुरुर्गतिः ।
शिवे रुष्टे गुरुस्त्राता गुरौ रुष्टे न कश्चन ॥

In this connection, the attention of scholars may be drawn to the views of various Tantra works quoted in the Guru-śiṣya-Prakaraṇa of the *Prāṇatoṣaṇī Tantra* (Vasumatī edition, pp. 91–103), especially to the following citations from the *Guru Tantra* and the *Guptasādhana Tantra* (cf. *ibid.*, pp. 94-95):

न गुरोरधिकं शास्त्रं न गुरोरधिकं तपः ।
न गुरोरधिकं मन्त्रो न गुरोरधिकं फलम् ॥
न गुरोरधिका देवी न गुरोरधिकः शिवः ।
न गुरोरधिका मूर्तिर्न गुरोरधिको जपः ॥

(गुरुतन्त्र)

गुरुर्ब्रह्मा गुरुर्विष्णुर्गुरुर्देवो महेश्वरः ।
गुरुस्तीर्थं गुरुर्यज्ञो गुरुर्दानं गुरुर्जपः ॥
गुरुरग्निर्गुरुः सूर्यः सर्वं गुरुमयं जगत् ॥

(गुप्तसाधनतन्त्र)

The section from Pūrṇānanda's *Śrītattvacintāmaṇi* quoted above, in which the author introduces himself as a disciple of another Tantrācārya named Brahmānanda Paramahaṃsa, demonstrates very clearly how much respectfully a Tantric devotee is expected to refer to his Guru. In his *Śyāmārahasya* Pūrṇānanda refers to himself as श्रीगुरुपादपद्मपरामोदामृतज्ञावितः पूर्णानन्दगिरिः । There is a distinct injunction as regards the mention of one's preceptor in the *Kulārṇava Tantra* from which the following verses have been quoted in the *Prāṇatoṣaṇī Tantra* (p. 103):

श्रीगुरुं कुलशास्त्राणि पूजास्थानानि यानि च ।
भक्त्या श्रीपूर्वकं देवि प्रणम्य च प्रकीर्तयेत् ॥
गुरुं नाम्ना न भाषेत जपकालादृते प्रिये ।
श्रीनाथदेवस्वामीति विवादे साधने वदेत् ॥

It is very interesting to note in this connection that the following lines of the *Tantrasāra* (p. 489) attributes a particular view to Pūrṇānanda Paramahaṃsa and refutes it categorically:

पूर्णानन्दमतेन लक्षजपे पुरश्चरणं; तत् सन्दिग्धमतं; नानातन्त्रे लक्षद्वयदर्शनात् लक्षद्वयेनैव पुरश्चरणं सिद्धमिति ।[1]

If Pūrṇānanda had been the preceptor of the author of the *Tantrasāra*, he would not certainly have been mentioned in the above passage merely as *Pūrṇānanda* but would have been called at least *Śrī-Pūrṇānanda* (if living).[2] This non-reverential reference to the author of the *Śrītattvacintāmaṇi* in the *Tantrasāra* shows beyond doubt that Kṛṣṇānanda Āgamavāgīśa was not a disciple of Pūrṇānanda Paramahaṃsa.

On the title page as well as in the introduction (p. 21) of the Vasumatī edition of the *Prāṇatoṣaṇī Tantra*, its author Rāmatoṣaṇa Vidyālaṅkāra is represented as the *vṛddhaprapautra* or great-great-grandson of Kṛṣṇānanda Āgamavāgīśa author of the *Tantrasāra*. Curiously enough the book itself proves clearly that the statement is wrong. Vasu's statement (*loc. cit.*) that the author of the book represents himself as the grandson of Sātu Ācārya seems also to be wrong. It is well known to the students of Tantra literature that Rāmatoṣaṇa's work was prepared and published under the patronage of Bābu Prāṇakṛṣṇa Viśvāsa of Khardaha near Calcutta, who was a great patron of Sastric learning. The author calls his work a *latā* (*vallī*, etc.) or creeper styled *Prāṇa-toṣaṇī* wherein parts of the names of both himself and his patron were cleverly accommodated. In a large number of passages in the work, Rāmatoṣaṇa refers to his indebtedness to Prāṇakṛṣṇa as well as to the latter's qualities, laudable activities and family relations. In many passages he also speaks of himself and his family. The following passage (p. 147):

श्रीप्राणकृष्णकृतिरस्य निदेशवर्त्ती
मैत्रेयवंशजकुलाश्रितचक्रवर्त्ती । etc.

says that Rāmatoṣaṇa Vidyālaṅkāra belonged to a Vaṃśaja (non-Kulin) family of the Maitreyas of the Vārendra Brāhmaṇa community. Elsewhere (p. 77) he refers to his father Kṛṣṇamaṅgala Vidyāvāgīśa and his mother Gaṅgādevī:

कृष्णमङ्गलविद्यावागीशसूनुः सतां मुदे
गङ्गादेवीसुतोऽकार्षीद्धर्मकाण्डं द्वितीयकम् ॥

---

1 Cf. *ibid.*, p. 488: अस्य पुरश्चरणं लक्षजपस्य पूर्णानन्दमतेन । The reference is to Ch. v of Pūrṇānanda's *S'yāmārahasya* which was composed later than his *S'rītattvacintāmaṇi* (1577 A.D.). The mention of Pūrṇānanda and the *S'rītattvacintāmaṇi* is noticed in the old and complete manuscripts of the *Tantrasāra* including one said to be copied in 1658 A.D. (probably during the author's lifetime).

2 Sometimes the Guru's name (if he was dead) was mentioned without honorific expressions when he was clearly said to have been one's preceptor: cf. *tripurānandena mad-guruṇā vyākhyātam* in Brahmānanda's *Tārārahasya*.

In another passage (p. 105) Rāmatoṣaṇa speaks of his elder brother Rāmalocana Vidyābhūṣaṇa who is said to have been the author of a commentary on the *Vāstuyāga* entitled *Vāstuyāgapradīpikā*; cf.

मदग्रजरामलोचनविद्याभूषणकृत-वास्तुयागप्रदीपिकाख्यतद्ग्रन्थशीर्षपञ्चरात्रे, etc.

There are several passages referring to Kṛṣṇānanda Āgamavāgīśa, author of the *Tantrasāra*, as a distinguished member of the family to which Rāmatoṣaṇa belonged; cf.

अस्मद्गोष्ठीगरिष्ठकृष्णानन्दागमवागीशेन स्वकृततन्त्रसारे सर्वं लिखितम् (p. 104);

अस्मद्गोष्ठीगरिष्ठकृष्णानन्दागमवागीशेन स्वकृततन्त्रसारग्रन्थे लिखिता (p. 143).

It is evident that the Āgamavāgīśa was an ancestor of the author of the *Prāṇatoṣaṇī Tantra*. Fortunately, however, there are some sections of the work which clearly define the relationship between Kṛṣṇānanda and Rāmatoṣaṇa and says that the former was the latter's *atyativṛddhaprapitāmaha*, i.e. great-grandfather's great-grandfather; cf.

अस्मदत्यतिवृद्धप्रपितामह-कृष्णानन्दागमवागीशेन तन्त्रसारे लिखिते (p. 116);

अस्मदत्यतिवृद्धप्रपितामह-सहृदयगोष्ठीगरिष्ठ-कृष्णानन्दागमवागीश-भट्टाचार्यैः स्वकृततन्त्रसारे लिखितम् (p. 75).

Rāmatoṣaṇa was therefore the *atyativṛddhaprapautra*, i.e. great-grandson's great-grandson, of Kṛṣṇānanda Āgamavāgīśa Bhaṭṭācarya and certainly not the latter's *vṛddhaprapautra* or great-grandson as asserted by the editor of the Vasumatī edition of the *Prāṇatoṣaṇī Tantra*. There is moreover a detailed genealogy in the work (p. 146) which makes the relation between the author of the *Prāṇatoṣaṇī* and that of the *Tantrasāra* absolutely clear.

Cf. धीमान् श्रीमान् भुवनविदिततन्त्रसारस्य कर्ता
कृष्णानन्दोऽजनि भुवि नवद्वीपदेशप्रदीपः ।
काशीनाथोऽभवदिह सुतस्तस्य सारावलीकृत्
विद्वान् मान्योऽजनि तदनुजो विश्वनाथाह्वयोऽतः ॥
गोपालो निर्णयकृतियशस्वी मधोः सूदनाम्ना (सूदनस्था)-
भूतां पुत्रौ मधुसुत इतः कालिदासः प्रसिद्धः ।
तत्पुत्रोऽभूद्रघुवरपरो नाथ एकान्तबुद्धि-
स्तत्सूनुस्त्वाभवदिह सुधीर्मङ्गलः कृष्णपूर्वः ॥
श्रीकृष्णमङ्गलसुतो नववल्लिकायाः
श्रीरामतोषण इदं कृतवान् द्वितीयम् । etc.

From the above details as well as those quoted before, the following genealogy of the Maitra or Maitreya family, to which Kṛṣṇānanda and Rāmatoṣaṇa belonged, may be prepared and offered in a tabular form:

- **Kṛṣṇānanda Āgamavāgīśa Bhaṭṭācārya, resident of Navadvīpa and author of the *Tantrasāra***
  - **Kāśīnātha, author of the *Sārāvalī***
  - **Viśvanātha**
    - **Gopāla, author of the *Nirṇaya***
    - **Madhusūdana**
      - **Kālidāsa**
        - **Nātharāma, or Nātha devoted to the god Rāma (said to be called Raghunātha in some *Kulapañjikās*)**
          - **Kṛṣṇamaṅgala Vidyāvāgīśa who married Gaṅgādevī**
            - **Rāmalocana-Vidyābhūṣaṇa, author of the *Vāstuyāga-pradīpikā***
            - **Rāmatoṣaṇa-Vidyālaṅkāra, author of the *Prāṇatoṣaṇī***

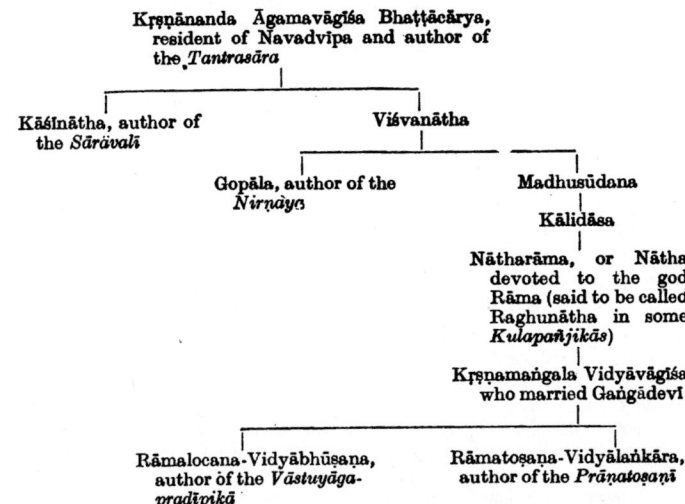

In the *Vārendra-Brāhmaṇa-Vivaraṇa* (p. 161) by the late Mr. N. N. Vasu there is a genealogical table of the Maitras of Maṇḍalajānī which slightly differs from the one quoted above. Although the details supplied by Rāmatoṣaṇa in his *Prāṇatoṣaṇī* appear to be authoritative, it has been suggested (*Pravāsī*, B.S. 1354, p. 506) that the *Sārāvalī* and the *Nirṇaya* have been wrongly ascribed to Kāśīnātha and Gopāla respectively. Another mistake of Rāmatoṣaṇa has been pointed out by quoting the following verse of Gopāla-Pañcānana's *Tantradīpikā* (MS.):

आगमवागीशपौत्रेण हरिनाथस्य सूनुना ।
श्रीगोपालेन विज्ञेन कृतेयं तन्त्रदीपिका ॥ (*loc. cit.*)

which is said to be supported by the *Kulapañjikās*. It will not be out of place to quote the corresponding portion of Mr. Vasu's table (said to be quoted from Yādava Cakravartin's *Kulaśāstradīpikā*) for easy reference and to point to the interesting fact that most of the names in the family exhibit Vaiṣṇava influence none of them being typically Śākta.

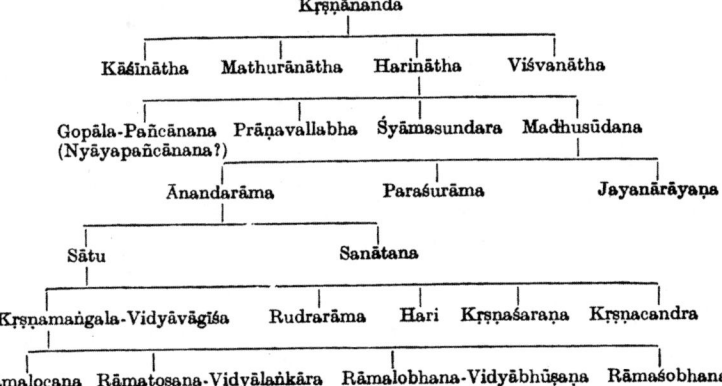

- **Kṛṣṇānanda**
  - **Kāśīnātha**
  - **Mathurānātha**
  - **Harinātha**
    - **Gopāla-Pañcānana (Nyāyapañcānana?)**
    - **Prāṇavallabha**
    - **Śyāmasundara**
    - **Madhusūdana**
      - **Ānandarāma**
        - **Sātu**
          - **Kṛṣṇamaṅgala-Vidyāvāgīśa**
            - **Rāmalocana**
            - **Rāmatoṣaṇa-Vidyālaṅkāra**
            - **Rāmalobhana-Vidyābhūṣaṇa**
            - **Rāmaśobhana**
          - **Rudrarāma**
          - **Hari**
          - **Kṛṣṇaśaraṇa**
          - **Kṛṣṇacandra**
        - **Sanātana**
      - **Paraśurāma**
      - **Jayanārāyaṇa**
  - **Viśvanātha**

It will be seen that Kṛṣṇānanda, author of the *Tantrasāra*, was the seventh in ascent from Rāmatosaṇa, author of the *Prāṇatoṣaṇī*, in the family. If, as is usual, a period of twenty-five years is counted for each generation, Kṛṣṇānanda has to be placed about 150 years before the time of Rāmatoṣaṇa. The date of the composition of the *Prāṇatoṣaṇī* is given in the work (p. 3) as: शाके नेत्रयुगाद्रिकाभ्रपरिमितेऽतीतेऽक्षयायान्तिथौ, that is to say, the *akṣayā tithi* (probably the *akṣaya-tṛtīyā* or the third *tithi* of the bright half of Vaiśākha) in the Śaka year 1742 (1820 A.D.). That the book was printed and published shortly before the 29th of Kārttika of the Bengali San 1231, corresponding to the 13th of November, 1824, is known from the *Samācāradarpaṇa* of that date cited by B. N. Banerji in his *Saṃvāda-patre Sekāler Kathā*, Vol. I, p. 60.[1] If then Rāmatoṣaṇa composed his *Prāṇatoṣaṇī* in 1820 A.D., it seems that his seventh ancestor Kṛṣṇānanda wrote his *Tantrasāra* about 1670 A.D.

In the preface to the Vaṅgavāsī edition of the *Tantrasāra*, the late Pandit Pañcānana Tarkaratna says that amongst various manuscripts of the work utilized in preparing the text of the above edition, one belonging to Pandit Haripada Smṛ-titīrtha, Professor of the Mulajor Sanskrit College, was found to have been copied in Śaka 1580 which would correspond to 1658 A.D. A recent note published in the *Pravāsī*, B.S. 1354, pp. 506–08, speaks of certain manuscripts of the *Tantrasāra* believed to be copied in Śaka 1601 (1679 A.D.), Śaka 1568 (1646 A.D.) and Śaka 1554 (1632 A.D.). These dates can be accepted only after careful examination. I had the opportunity of examining only the third of these manuscripts in the library of the Vaṅgīya Sāhitya Pariṣat and find that the third figure of the year supposed to be Śaka 1554 is extremely doubtful. In any case, however, there is no doubt that the *Tantrasāra* was composed by the great Kṛṣṇānanda Āgamavāgīśa Bhaṭṭācarya sometime in the seventeenth century. It may not be improbable that Kṛṣṇānanda flourished in *circa* 1595–1675 A.D. and composed the *Tantrasāra* in the earlier part of his life.

APPENDIX V

An Index of Pīṭhas.

'Ain = 'Ain-i-Akbarī; Ānanda = Ānandārṇava Tantra; Aṣṭādaśa = Aṣṭādaśapīṭha; Caṇḍī = Caṇḍīmaṅgala; Hevajra = Hevajra Tantra; Jñāna = Jñānārṇava Tantra; Kālikā = Kālikā Purāṇa; Kubjikā = Kubjikā Tantra; Nāma = Nāmāṣṭottaraśata (Appendix I); Nīla = Bṛhan-Nīlatantra; Pīṭha = Pīṭhanirṇaya or Mahāpīṭhanirūpaṇa (text edited above, pp. 42–58, with notes); Prāṇa = Prāṇatoṣaṇī Tantra; Rudra = Rudrayāmala; Sādhana = Sādhanamālā; Śiva = Śivacarita. The names of the Devī's limbs, the Devī and the Bhairava have been mentioned, in cases where they are indicated, in order to show the uncertainty of the traditions about them.

A

Abdhisaṅgama—Nīla, Prāṇa (Jyotirmayī). See Sāgarasaṅgama.

Acchoda—Nāma (Śivakāriṇī, Śivadhāriṇī, Siddhidāyinī, Śaktidhāriṇī); modern Achchhavat in Kashmir.

---

[1] Cf. *ibid.*, Vol. II, pp. 802-03 where the year of publication of the *Prāṇatoṣaṇī* is given as 1823 A.D. on the authority of the *Friend of India*, Vol. III, No. 11. The *Saṃvādpatre Sekāler Kathā*, Vol. I (2nd ed.), p. 486, gives the year of its composition as Śaka 1743; but the word *netra* indicates 'two' (not 'three') according to Sanskrit lexicons.

Ādipīṭha—Nīla.
Aditipura—Nīla.
Ādinātha—Nīla.
Āditya—Nīla.
Adrikūṭa—Nīla, Prāṇa (Rudrāṇī—Mahāyogin).
Ādyantapura—Nīla.
Agastyāśrama—Nīla, Prāṇa (Mahāvidyā, Mattamedhā); one of the many places especially in Southern India associated with Agastya's name; probably Agastipuri near Nasik.
Aila, Aileyakavana—Prāṇa, Nīla.
Airāvatī—See Irāvatī.
Akampa—Nīla.
Akṣayagrīva—Kubjikā (v.l. Hayagrīva); probably a mistake for Akṣayavaṭa.
Akṣayavaṭa—Nīla, Prāṇa (Akṣayā); the sacred banyan tree located at many *tīrthas*, notably at Prayāga or Allahabad in U.P. and at Gayā in Bihar.
Ālāpura—Aṣṭādaśa (Yugalā); possibly a mistake for Elāpura.
Amala—Nāma (v.l. Malaya); cf. Anala.
Amarakaṇṭaka—Nāma (v.l. Makarandaka, Marakaṅkaṭa—Caṇḍī); Nīla, Prāṇa (Amareśī); the source of the Sone and Narmada in the Eastern C.P.
Amaraparvata, Kanakāmaraparvata—Nīla; same as Meru.
Amareśa—Nīla, Prāṇa (Caṇḍī, Maheśvarī—Kuśatuṅgāra); on the south bank of the Narmada, opposite Onkarnath, and to the north-west of Khandwa.
Ambara—Nāma (Viśvakāyā, Viśvakāmā); modern Amber in the Jaipur State, Rajputana.
Ambikā—Kubjikā; Nīla; may be Ambikā-Kālnā in the Burdwan District.
Ambujapura—Nīla.
Āmrakeśvara—See Āmrātakeśvara.
Āmrātakapura—Nīla, Prāṇa (Sūkṣmā—Sūkṣma); Nīla (Surūpeśā). See Āmrātakeśvara, Āmrakeśvara.
Āmrātakeśvara—Jñāna. See Āmrātakapura.
Amṛtakauśika—Nīla, Prāṇa (Kauśikā). See Kauśikā.
Anala—Pīṭha (v.l. Śuci); Śiva (Mahāpīṭha; Ūrdhvadanta—Nārāyaṇī—Saṃkrūra); cf. the name of the Nala lake in the Ahmadabad region.
Ānanda—Nīla. See under *Nandataṭa*.
Anantapura—Nīla.
Aṅga—Rudra; east Bihar.
Animāpura—Nīla.
Aniruddhapura—Nīla.
Annapūrṇā—Nīla.
Antarvedī—Rudra; the Ganges-Jumna Doab between Prayāga and Haridvāra.
Araṇya—See Vareṇya.
Arbuda—Jñāna; Nīla (Kātyāyanī); Mount Abu in the Sirohi State, Rajputana.
Ardhanālaka—Kubjikā (v.l. Vardhamānaka).
Āryāvarta—Prāṇa (Mahāryā). For the Tantric Āryāvarta in the eastern U.P., see *I.C.*, VIII, p. 57.
Asurāntakapura—Nīla.
Āśusiddhipura—Nīla.
Aśvamedhapura—Nīla.

Aśvaprada—Nīla, Prāṇa; probably the Asvakranta hill near Gauhati in Assam.

Aśvatīrtha—Nīla, Prāṇa; at the confluence of the Gaṅgā and Kālīnadī near Kanauj.

Aśvattha—Nāma (Vandanīyā).

Aṭṭahāsa—Jñāna; Nīla (Bhīmākālī); Pīṭha (Oṣṭha—Phullarā—Viśveśa); Śiva (Upapīṭha; Oṣṭhāṃśa—Phullarā—Viśvanātha); Nīla, Prāṇa (Cāmuṇḍā); Prāṇa (Mahānandā—Mahānanda); near Labhpur in the Birbhum District, Bengal.

Aujasa, Aurasa—Nīla, Prāṇa (Vīryadā); fictitious; but cf. Ausaja in *Viṣṇu S.*

Avanti—Nīla, Prāṇa (Atipāvanī); the same as Ujjayinī or the country round it.

Avantyāśrama—Nīla, Prāṇa; probably mistake for Agastyāśrama.

Avimukta—Nīla, Prāṇa (Viśālākṣī—Mahādeva); same as Vārāṇasī, Kāśī.

Ayodhyā—Rudra; Kubjikā; Nīla, Prāṇa (Bhavānī); Śiva (Upapīṭha; Kaṇṭhahāra—Annapūrṇā—Harihara); modern Ajodhya in the Fyzabad District, U.P.

B

Badarī—Kubjikā; Nāma (Urvaśī); Nīla, Prāṇa (Śrīvidyā); same as Badarikāśrama (Badrinath in Gahrwal, U.P.) in the Himalayas.

Bāhudā—Nīla, Prāṇa (Anantā); identified with the Dhumela or Burha-Rapti, a tributary of the Rapti in Oudh.

Bahulā—Pīṭha (v.l. Bāhulā; Vāmabāhu—Bahulā, Bāhulā—Bhīruka): Śiva (Mahāpīṭha;—Vāmabāhu—Bahulā—Bhīruka); located at Ketugram near Katwa in the Burdwan District, Bengal.

Bāliḍāṅgā—Caṇḍī (Dakṣiṇahasta—Rājeśvarī); in the Hooghly District, Bengal.

Balipura—Nīla (Allā); may be the same as Mahābalipura or Mamallapuram (Chingleput District), 30 miles to the south of Madras.

Beṇā—Nāma (Amṛtā); the Beṇā (tributary of the Krishnā), the Peṅgaṅgā or the Waingaṅgā. See Veṇā.

Bhadra—Nāma (v.l. Bhadreśvara); Nīla, Prāṇa (v.l. Bhadrāśva;—Bhadrakarṇikā). See Bhadreśvara. Bhadrāśva is a mythical division of the Jambudvīpa.

Bhadrakāleśvara—Nīla, Prāṇa (Mahābhadrā, Bhadrakālī).

Bhadrakarṇa—Nīla, Prāṇa (Bhadrakarṇikā—Mahādeva); identified with Karṇapura or Karnali on the south bank of the Narmada.

Bhadreśvara—Nāma (v.l. Bhadra;—Bhadrā, Bhadreśvarī); Nīla, Prāṇa (Ramā); possibly Bhadreswar in the Hooghly District.

Bhairava—Nīla, Prāṇa (Bhairavī—Bhairava). See Bhairavaparvata.

Bhairavaparvata—Pīṭha (v.l. Bhīruparvata;—Oṣṭha, Ūrdhvoṣṭha—Avantī—Lambakarṇa, Namrakarṇa). See Bhairava; probably in West Malwa.

Bharatāśrama—Nāma (Aṅganā, Anaṅgā, Taraṅgā); Nīla, Prāṇa (Bhagavatī).

Bhīma—Nīla, Prāṇa (Bhīmeśvarī—Bhīmeśvara). See Bhīmā under *Himādri*. The *tīrtha* may also be connected with the Bhīmā, a tributary of the Krishna.

Bhīruparvata—See Bhairavaparvata.

Bhṛgu, Bhṛgupurī—Jñāna; Nīla (v.l. Guptapura;—Vrajeśvarī); identified with Balia in U.P. Bhṛgupura was also the name of Broach (Tawney, *Prab. Cint.*, trans., p. 136).

Bhṛgutuṅga—Nīla, Prāṇa; a mountain in Nepal.

Bījāpur—'Ain (Tuljā Bhavānī, Turjā Bhavānī); probably same as Pūrṇagiri. The shrine of Bhavānī actually stands at Tuljapur near Osmanabad in the Hyderabad State.

Bilva, Bilvaka—See Vilvala.
Brahmaśiras—Nīla, Prāṇa (Brahmāṇī).
Brahmāsya—Nāma; fictitious.
Brahmāvarta—Nīla, Prāna (Vrajeśvarī); in the eastern Punjab.

C

Caitraratha—Nāma (Madotkaṭā).
Cakradvīpa—Śiva (Upapīṭha;—Astra—Cakradhāriṇī—Śūlapāṇi); possibly one of the several Cakratīrthas.
Candanaparvata—Nīla (Mahānandā).
Caṇḍapura, Caṇḍīpura—Nīla (Pracaṇḍā).
Candrabhāgā—Nāma (Kālā, Kalā); Nīla, Prāṇa (Candrabhāgā); river Chenab in the Punjab.
Candrapura—Jñāna; Nīla (Sitā or Asitā); possibly Chanda in C.P.
Candrāsthira—Jñāna (v.l. Caraṣthira, Carasthita).
Carasthira—See Candrāsthira.
Carasthita—See Candrāsthira.
Caṭṭagrāma—Śiva (Mahāpīṭha; Dakṣiṇahastārddha—Bhavānī—Candraśekhara). See Caṭṭala.
Caṭṭala—Pīṭha (Dakṣiṇabāhu—Bhavānī—Candraśekhara). See Chaṭṭagrāma; in the Chittagong District of East Bengal.
Cauhāra—Jñāna; mentioned in the short list but not in the long one; possibly a wrong reading.
Chāgalaṇḍa—See Chāgaliṅga.
Chāgalāṇḍa—See Chāgaliṅga.
Chāgaliṅga—Nāma (v.l. Chāgalāṇḍa, Chagalaṇḍa;—Pracaṇḍā); Prāṇa (Balipriyā).
Chāyāchatrapura—Jñāna.
Chāyāpura—Nīla; a mistake for Chāyāchatrapura.
Citrakūṭa—Nāma (Sītā); in Bundelkhand, or less probably Chitor (Mewar).
Citta—Nāma; fictitious.

D

Dakṣa-Pañcanada—Nīla, Prāṇa (Dakṣiṇā). See Pañcanada. *Dakṣa* (from Sans. *dakṣiṇa*) means 'south'.
Dārukeśa—v.l. Āmrātaka. Cf. the Dvarakeswar river running through the Bankura District.
Dehalikā—Nīla, Prāṇa (Amba); possibly modern Delhi. But cf. Trihalikāgrāma of the *Viṣṇusaṃhitā*.
Devadāruvana—Nāma (Puṣṭi); in the region of Badrinath in the Himalayas, or modern Aundh in the Deccan.
Devakoṭa—Same as Devīkoṭṭa.
Devakoṭṭa—Same as Devīkoṭṭa.
Devakūṭa—Jñāna. Same as Devīkoṭṭa.
Devaloka—Nāma; fictitious.
Devidaikoṭha—Rudra. See Devīkoṭṭa.
Devikātaṭa—Nāma (Nandinī); river Devikā is the modern Deeg in the Punjab.
Devīkoṭa—See Devīkoṭṭa.
Devīkoṭṭa—Jñāna; Kālikā (Pada—Mahābhāgā); Nīla (Akhileṣvarī); modern Bangarh in the Dinajpur District, Bengal. Same as Devakoṭṭa, Devakoṭa, Devakūṭa, Devīkoṭa, Devīkūṭa, Devidaikoṭha.
Devīkūṭa—Kālikā; see Devīkoṭṭa.
Drāviḍa—Nīla, Prāṇa (Sarasvatī); the Tamil country in southern India.
Durgā—Nīla, Prāṇa; a tributary of the Sabarmati in Gujarat.

Dvāravatī—Nāma (Rukmiṇī); Nīla, Prāṇa; modern Dwarka in north-western Kathiawar.

E

Ekāgra—v.l. Ekāmra.
Ekāmra—Jñāna; Nāma (Kīrtimatī); Nīla (Ekā); modern Bhuvaneśvara in Orissa.
Elāpura—Jñāna; Nīla, Prāṇa (Vīrā); Nīla (Mahāsampat); modern Ellora in the Hyderabad State.

G

Gaṇakṣetra—Nīla, Prāṇa (Maṅgalā—Prapitāmaha); probably the same as Gaṇeśvara.
Gaṇḍaka—Same as Gaṇḍakī.
Gaṇḍakī—Pīṭha (Gaṇḍa—Gaṇḍakī—Cakrapāṇi); Śiva (Mahāpīṭha; details as in Pīṭha); river Gaṇḍakī is a tributary of the Ganges which it meets near Bakhtyarpur in the Patna District, Bihar.
Gandhamādana—Nāma (Kāmākṣī, Kāmukī, Kāmukā); a Himalayan peak at Badarikāśrama. In *Nāma*, verse 11, we have Gandhamādana as a v.l. for Mādhavavana, Mādhavīvana.
Gaṇeśvara—Prāṇa, Nīla.
Gaṅgā—Nāma (v.l. Gayā;—Maṅgalā); Nīla, Prāṇa (Śivāmṛtā); the sacred river Ganges.
Gaṅgādvāra—Nāma (Ratipriyā, Haripriyā); Nīla, Prāṇa (Nārāyaṇī, Vaiṣṇavī); the same as Haridvāra, the place where the Ganges enters the plain from the Himalayas.
Gaṅgārāmācala—v.l. Gaṅgāvāmācala.
Gaṅgāsāgara—Nīla, Prāṇa; near the Sāgar islands where the Bhāgīrathī enters the Bay of Bengal.
Gaṅgāvāmācala—Nīla, Prāṇa (Śivā); v.l. Gaṅgāvāṭācala; Gaṅgārāmācala.
Gaṅgāvāṭācala—v.l. Gaṅgāvāmācala.
Gaṅgāvilva—Prāṇa, Nīla.
Gaṅgodbheda—Prāṇa, Nīla.
Gargoccheda—Nīla, Prāṇa (v.l. Gaṅgodbheda).
Gauḍa—Rudra; in a narrow sense the Murshidabad District with the southern part of the present Maldah District; in a wider sense the western half or the whole of Bengal.
Gaurīśekhara—Śiva (Upapītha; Vasā—Yugādyā—Bhīma). Cf. Gaurīśikhara in Kāmarūpa (Pīṭha).
Gautameśvara—Nīla, Prāṇa; possibly one of the places called Gautamaśrama.
Gayā—Nāma (v.l. Gaṅgā;—Maṅgalā); Nīla, Prāṇa (Gayeśvarī); Aṣṭādaśa (Māṅgalyakoṭikā); the celebrated city in Bihar.
Ghaṇṭākarṇa—Kubjikā.
Ghāṭaśilā—Caṇḍī (Vāmapada—Rukmiṇī; actually *Raṅkiṇī*); a place between Kharagpur and Tatanagar or Jamshedpur on the Bengal-Nagpur Railway.
Giri—Tantrasāra; part of the name Merugiri wrongly regarded as a separate name.
Godāśrama—Nāma (v.l. Godāvarī, Kubjāmraka;—Trisandhyā). See Godāvarī.
Godāvarī, Godāvarītīra—Kubjikā; Pīṭha (Vāmagaṇḍa—Viśveśī, Rākiṇī—Viśveśa, Daṇḍapāṇi, Vatsanābha); Śiva (Mahāpīṭha;—Vāmagaṇḍa—Viśvamātṛkā—Viśveśa); Nīla, Prāṇa (Gaveśvarī); the celebrated river of the Deccan. See Godāśrama, Saptagodāvara.

Gokarṇa—Jñāna; Nāma (Bhadrakarṇikā, Kālikā); Nīla, Prāṇa (Bhadrā—Mahābala); Nīla (Sarvamaṅgalā); modern Gendia about 30 miles from Goa.

Gomanta—Nāma (Gomatī); located in the Goa region.

Gomatī—Nīla, Prāṇa (Vimukti); one of the many rivers of this name.

Gorakṣacāriṇī—See Gorakṣakāriṇī; cf. the *tīrtha* called Gorakṣa on the Gomanta. Another Gorakṣa is the town of Gorkha, 53 miles to the west of Katmandu in Nepal. Cf. also Gorakhpur in U.P.

Gorakṣakāriṇī—Kubjikā (v.l. Gorakṣacāriṇī).

Govardhana—Kubjikā; Nīla, Prāṇa (Ambikā); near Nasik in the Bombay Presidency.

H

Haṃsatīrtha—Nīla, Prāṇa; possibly connected with Haṃsamārga (probably Haṃsadvāra or the Niti Pass in Kumaon; identified with modern Hunza and Nagar; cf. *JUPHS*, XVII, pp. 48-49) in the Himalayas.

Haratīrtha—Nīla, Prāṇa (Gavīśvarī); probably the same as Harakṣetra or Bhuvanesvar.

Haridrā—Nīla; may be the same as Haridvāra.

Haridvāra—Śiva (Mahāpīṭha:—Jaṭhara—Bhairavī—Vakra); Prāṇa, Nīla. See Gaṅgādvāra.

Hariścandra—Nāma (v.l. Harmacandra;—Candrikā); Nīla, Prāṇa (Subheśvarī).

Hārīta—Nīla, Prāṇa (Hariṇākṣī); probably the same as Hārītāśrama near Udaipur in Rajputana.

Harmacandra—Nāma (v.l. Hariścandra)

Harocchedа, Harodbheda—Prāṇa, Nīla.

Hastināpura—Jñāna; Nāma (Jayantī); Nīla (Rājeśvarī Mahālakṣmī); in the Meerut District, U.P.

Hayagrīva—Kubjikā (v.l. Akṣayagrīva).

Hayakṣetra—Aṣṭādaśa; probably the same as Hayagrīva.

Hemakūṭa—Nāma (Manmathā); the Varṣaparvata lying to the north of the Kimpuruṣavarṣa that is situated to the north of the Himavat and the Bhāratavarṣa; apparently a part of the northern Himalayas.

Himādri—Nāma (Bhīmā); cf. Bhīmāsthāna near Shahbazgarhi (Peshawar District) of the Mahābhārata. See Himālaya, Himavat.

Himālaya—Nīla (Pārvatī). See Himavat, Himādri.

Himavat—Nāma (Nandā, Mandā). The Nandāsthāna is different from the Bhīmāsthāna and is no doubt the same as the celebrated Nandādevī peak in the Garhwal District, U.P. See Himādri, Himālaya.

Hiṅglāja—Caṇḍī (Nābhi; the Devīnāma is doubtful); same as Hiṅgulā; on the Aghor or Hingool river in Baluchistan.

Hiṅgulā, Hiṅgulāṭa—Kubjikā; Rudra; Pīṭha (Brahmarandhra—Koṭṭarī, Koṭṭavī, Koṭṭarīśā—Bhīmalocana); Śiva (Mahāpīṭha;—Brahmarandhra—Koṭṭarī—Bhīmalocana); Prāṇa; same as Hiṅglāja (Hinglaj) in Baluchistan where the goddess is locally called Bībī Nānī.

Hiraṇyākṣa—Nāma (v.l. Kamalākṣa;—Mahotpalā).

Hiraṇyapura—Jñāna; Nīla (Suvarṇā); modern Herdoun or Hindaun in the Jaipur State, about 70 miles from Agra.

Hṛṣīkeśa—Kubjikā; on the Ganges, about 24 miles to the north of Hardwar on the way to Badrinath.

I

Ilānta—Nīla.

Ilodayagiri—Nīla.

Indirāpura—Nīla.
Indrānandapura—Nīla.
Indrāṇī—Nīla.
Indranīla—Nīla, Prāṇa (Mahākānti); cf. the Himalayan peak Indrakīla mentioned in the *Kāvyamīmāṃsā*.
Indrīśvara, Indrīśvarīpura—Nīla.
Indumatī—Nīla, Prāṇa (Pūrṇimā).
Indupura—Nīla.
Induvatīpura—Nīla. Same as Indumatī.
Induvijayapura—Nīla.
Irāvatī—Nīla, Prāṇa (Ī); river Rāvī in the Punjab.
Īśāna—Nīla.
Īśānyaiśapura—Nīla.
Iṣṭhanābha—Nīla, Prāṇa (Svāyambhuvā—Svayambhū).
Iṣṭapura—Nīla.
Īśvara—Nīla.
Īśvarayoga—Nīla.

J

Jāhnavīsaṅgama—Nīla, Prāṇa (Tṛpti, Svadhā); Jāhnavī is another name of the Ganges, while *Saṅgama* indicates a confluence. But the confluence referred to here cannot be determined.
Jāhnavītaṭa—Nīla (Vijayā). Jāhnavī is another name of the Gaṅgā.
Jājpur—See Yājapura (Jahājapura in the *Aṣṭādaśa*), Yāgapura, Virajā, Utkala; in the Cuttack District, Orissa. See also Nabhigayā.
Jālandhara—Hevajra; Kālikā (in the north;—Caṇḍī—Mahādeva); Kālikā (Stanadvaya;—Caṇḍī); Rudra; Jñāna; Kubjikā; Nāma (Viśvamukhī); Nīla (Nāgarī, Jvālāmukhī), Pīṭha (Stana—Tripuramālinī, Tripuranāśinī—Bhīṣana); Śiva (Mahāpīṭha;—Vāmastana—Tripuramālinī—Bhīṣaṇa); in the Punjab. '*Ain* speaks of the goddess at Nagarkot-Kangra as Jālandharī which is the same as Jvālāmukhī. The *Ānandārṇava* gives the name of the Pīṭha as Jālandhra. The Jālandhara Pīṭha is now located near Jvālāmukhī.
Jālandharagiri—Same as Jālandhara.
Jālandhra—See Jālandhara.
Jālaśaila—Same as Jālandhara.
Jaleśvara—Jñāna; in the Balasore District, Orissa.
Janasthāna—Śiva (Mahāpīṭha) and Pīṭha (Civuka—Bhrāmarī—Vikṛta, Vikṛtākṣa); on the Godāvarī in the Nasik region of the Bombay Presidency. V.l. Jalasthala.
Japyeśvara—Nīla, Prāṇa (Triśūlinī—Triśūlin); probably the same as Jalpeśvara in the Jalpaiguri District, Bengal.
Jayanta—Nīla, Prāṇa (Jayantī); probably the same as Jayantī.
Jayantā—Same as Jayantī.
Jayantī—Śiva (Mahāpīṭha) and Pīṭha (Vāmajaṅghā—Jayantī—Kramadīśvara); in the Sylhet District, Assam (now East Pakistan) See Jayanta, Jayantā, Jayantikā.
Jayantikā—Jñāna. See Jayantī.
Jayapura—Nīla (Jayā); may be Jaipur in eastern Rajputana.
Jvālā—Aṣṭādaśa (Vaiṣṇavī); possibly Jvālāmukhī is intended.
Jvālāmukhī—Kubjikā; 'Ain; Nīla, Prāṇa; Pīṭha (Jihvā—Siddhidā, Ambikā—Unmatta); Śiva (Mahāpīṭha;—Jihvā—Ambikā—Vaṭakeśvara, Unmatta); in the Kangrah District, Punjab.
Jvalantī—Rudra; probably the same as Jvālāmukhī.
Jyotiḥsara—Prāṇa, Nīla.

K

Kailāsa—Jñāna; Nīla (Bhuvaneśvarī); in the Himalayas.

Kālamādhava—Pīṭha (Nitamba—Kālī—Asitāṅga); Śiva (Mahāpīṭha;—Vāmanitamba—Kālī—Asitāṅga). See Mādhava.

Kalamba-kubja—Nīla, Prāṇa; represented as a combination of two names.

Kālañjara—Nāma (Kālī); Nīla, Prāṇa (Kālī—Nīlakaṇṭha); in the Banda District, U.P.

Kāleśvara—Jñāna (v.l. Kāmeśvara); cf. *Ṣaṭpañcāśaddeśavibhāga*, verses 10 and 40 (*I.* ., VIII, p. 33ff.).

Kālīghāṭa—Pīṭha (Muṇḍa—Jayadurgā—Krodhīśa, Krodheśa); Śiva (Mahāpīṭha;—Dakṣiṇapādāṅguli—Kālī—Nakuleśa). *Pīṭha* refers to the *devasthāna* at Juranpur near Katwa (Burdwan District), while *Śiva* speaks of the more important Kalighat in the southern suburb of Calcutta. For the same confusion see Kālīpīṭha. In the original part of *Pīṭha*, Kalighat is referred to as Kālīpīṭha. See also Kālīghaṭṭa.

Kālīghaṭṭa—Nīla, Prāṇa (Guhyakālī); Nīla (Kālī); same as Kālīghāṭa

Kaliṅga—Rudra; the Purī-Ganjam region in a narrow sense, but often it indicated the whole coast land down to the Godavari in the south.

Kālīpīṭha—Pīṭha (Dakṣiṇapādāṅguli—Kālī—Nakuleśa, Nakulīśa); Śiva (Upapīṭha;—Śiroṃśa—Caṇḍeśvarī—Caṇḍeśvara). See Kālīghāṭa, Kālī ghaṭṭa.

Kālīpura—See Kanyāpura.

Kālodaka—Nīla, Prāṇa (Kālī).

Kāmagiri—Pīṭha (in Kāmarūpa;—Mahāmudrā or Yoni—Kālī—Umānanda, Śivānanda, Rāvānanda, Rāmānanda); near Gauhāti in Assam. See Kāmarūpa, which is also called Kubjikā Pīṭha in the *Kālikā P.*

Kāmakoṭa, Kāmakoṭi, Kāmakoṭṭa—Jñāna; Nīla (Kāmeśvarī).

Kamalā—Kubjikā. See Kamalālaya.

Kamalākṣa—Nāma (v.l. Hiraṇyākṣa).

Kamalālaya—Nīla, Prāṇa (Kamalākṣī—Kamalākṣa).

Kāmarūpa—Hevajra; Nīla, Kālikā (in the east;—Kāmeśvarī—Kāmeśvara; Kālikā (Yoni—Kāmākhyā); Sādhana; 'Ain; Rudra; Jñāna; Kubjikā; Ānandārṇava; Caṇḍī (Madhyadeśa—Kāmarūpa-Kāmākhyā); Pīṭha (see Kāmagiri); Śiva (Mahāpīṭha;—Yoni—Kāmākhyā, Nīlapārvatī—Rāvānanda, Umānanda). *Pīṭha* associates the Gaurīśikhara with this place, while *Kālikā* places the *sthānas* of Dikkaravāsinī and Lalitakāntā in the Kāmarūpa country which corresponds to the Gauhati District of Assam and the adjoining region. The temple of Kāmākhyā stands on the Nīlakūṭa or Nīlaparvata, called the Kāmarupa-parvata by Rājaśekhara in the *Kāvyamīmāṃsā*. This blue hill is the same as Kāmagiri.

Kāmeśvara—Jñāna (v.l. Kāleśvara); cf. Kāmeśvaranātha at Karon in the Balia District, U.P. Kāmeśvara and Mahāgaurī (Kāmākhyā) were tutelary deities of the ancient kings of Assam (*Kāmarūpaśāsanāvalī*, Intro., p. 32, n. 2).

Kāmodaka—Nīla, Prāṇa (v.l. Kālodaka).

Kāmrāj—'Ain (Śāradā); in Kashmir. The reference is to modern Sardi.

Kanakāmaraparvata—Same as Meru, Amaraparvata.

Kanakhala—Nīla, Prāṇa (Śraddhā); Prāṇa (Śivogrā—Ugra); near Haridvāra (Hardwar).

Kāñcī—Rudra; Nīla, Prana (Kanakakāñcī); Pīṭha (Kaṅkāla—Devagarbhā—Ruru); Śiva (Mahāpīṭha;—Kaṅkāla—Vedagarbhā—Ruru). The earlier references are to modern Conjeeveram in the Chingleput District, Madras; but some late works (composed in Bengal) possibly speak of a locality on the Kopāi in the Birbhum District, Bengal.

Kāñcikāpurī—Aṣṭādaśa. The name is the same as Kāñcī.

Kaṇvāśrama—Nīla, Prāṇa (v.l. Kanyāśrama); possibly one of the several places associated with the name of Kaṇva.

Kānyakubja—Jñāna; Nāma (Gaurī); Nīla (Brahmāṇī); in the Farrukhabad District, U.P.

Kanyāpura—Nīla (v.l. Kālīpura;—Kanyā); see Kaṇvāśrama, Kanyāśrama.

Kanyāśrama—Pīṭha (Pṛshṭha—Sarvāṇī—Nimiṣa); located in eastern India at Kumārīkuṇḍa near the Kumira railway station in the Chittagong District.

Kapālamocana—Nāma (Śuddhi). One of the several places known by this name in different parts of India.

Karatoyātaṭa—Pīṭha (Vāmakarṇa, Talpa—Aparṇā—Vāmana, Vāmeśa); Śiva (Mahāpīṭha;—Vāmakarṇa—Aparṇā—Vāmeśa). The Pīṭha is located at Bhavānīpura near the bank of the Karatoyā in the Bogra District, North Bengal.

Karavīra, Karavīrapura—Nāma (Mahālakṣmī); Pīṭha (v.l. Śarkarāra;—Trinetra—Mahiṣamardinī—Krodhīśa, Krodheśa); Prāṇa (Satī); the capital of Brahmāvarta and on the Dṛṣadvatī in the Eastern Punjab according to the *Kālikā Purāṇa;* but usually identified with Kolhapur (called Karvir) in the South Maratha country.

Karkoṭa—Nāma (v.l. Mākoṭa); modern Karra, about 40 miles north-west of Allahabad; according to local tradition, Satī's hand fell at this place.

Karṇasūtra—Kubjikā. See Karṇatīrtha.

Karṇatīrtha—Nīla, Prāṇa. See Karnasūtra.

Kārttikeya—Nāma (Yaśaskarī, Saṅkarī, Atiśaṅkarī); possibly modern Baijnath near Almora in the Kumaon District, U.P.

Kāśī—Kubjikā; Nīla, Prāṇa (Annapūrṇā); in U.P. Same as Vārāṇasī, Avimukta. Vaṃśīdāsa connects it with Satī's *keśa.*

Kāśmīra (Kāshmīr)—Jñāna; Nāma (Medhā); Aṣṭādaśa (Sarasvatī); 'Ain (see Kāmrāj); Śiva (Mahāpīṭha) and Pīṭha (Kaṇṭha—Mahāmāyā—Trisandya, Trisandhyeśvara).

Kaṭaka—Śiva (Upapīṭha;—Carmāṃśa—Kaṭakeśvarī—Vāmadeva); modern Cuttack in Orissa.

Kaulagiri—Jñāna; same as Kolvagiri.

Kauśikī—Nīla, Prāṇa; river Kosi running through Nepal and Bihar.

Kavarī—Nīla, Prāṇa; same as Kāverī.

Kāverī—Nīla, Prāṇa (Kapileśvarī); river in the Tamil country in Southern India. See Kavarī.

Kāyāvarohaṇa—Nāma (Mātā); also called Kāyāvatāra, associated with the tradition of Nakulīśa, an incarnation of Śiva; same as Kārvān in the Dabhoi Taluk of the Baroda State.

Kedāra—Jñāna; Nāma (Mārgadāyinī); Nīla (Vāradā); Prāṇa; in the Himalayas. See Kedāreśvara.

Kedāreśvara—Nīla, Prāṇa (Sanmārgadāyinī). See Kedāra.

Keśajāla—Pīṭha (v.l. Vṛndāvana); Śiva (Upapīṭha;—Keśa—Umā—Bhūteśa). See Vṛndāvana. The name is apparently due to a textual confusion.

Kirīṭa, Kirīṭakoṇā—Pīṭha (Kirīṭa—Bhuvaneśī, Vimalā—Siddhirūpa, Samvarta); Śiva (Upapīṭha;—Kirīṭa—Bhuvaneśī—Kirīṭin); Prāṇa (Kirīṭeśvarī). The *tīrtha* is located at Vaṭanagara near Lālbāg in the Murshidabad District, Bengal.

Kiṣkindhyaparvata—Nāma (Tārā); in the modern Hyderabad State, or modern Kekind in the Jodhpur State.

Kokāmukha—Śiva (Mahāpīṭha;—Kŏk or Kukṣi—Kokeśvarī—Kokeśvara); modern Barāhchhatra (Varāhakṣetra) on the Kauśikī in Nepal.

Kolvagiri—Jñāna; possibly modern Coorg or Koḍagu which means 'steep mountains' (Pargiter, *Mark. Pur.*, trans., p. 364 n.); but more probably it has to be identified with Kolāpura or Kolhapur (*I.C.*, VIII, p. 49). See Kaulagiri, Karavīra, Mahālakṣmī.

Koṭa—Nāma (v.l. Mākoṭa), possibly Koṭatīrtha at Kalanjar.

Koṭimudrā—Rudra; possibly same as Koṭitīrtha.

Koṭitīrtha—Nāma (Koṭavī); one of the several places of this name.

Kṛṣṇabeṇyā (Kṛṣṇabeṇvā)—Nīla, Prāṇa (Bhedinī); river Krishna running through the Deccan.

Kṛtaśauca—Nāma (Siṃhikā).

Kṣīragrāma—Kubjikā; Caṇḍī (Pṛṣṭha—Yogādyā); Pīṭha (Dakṣiṇapādāṅguṣṭha—Yugādyā—Kṣīrakhaṇḍa, Kṣīrakaṇṭha); Śiva (Mahāpīṭha; —Dakṣiṇapādāṅguṣṭha—Yogādyā—Kṣīrakhaṇḍa). See Kṣirikā; modern Khirgram near Katwa in the Burdwan District, Bengal.

Kṣīrapura—Nīla (Yugādyā, Kṣīrā); same as Kṣīragrāma.

Kṣirikā—Jñāna. See Kṣīragrāma.

Kubjāmraka—Nāma (v.l. Godāvarī, Godāśrama); near Hṛṣīkeśa in the Himalayas; the same as Kanakhala according to some authorities.

Kulānta—See Kūpānta.

Kumāra, Kumāradhāma—Nīla, Prāṇa (Kaumarī); possibly the same as Cape Comorin.

Kumuda—Nāma (v.l. Mukuṭa;—Satyavādinī).

Kuñcapaṭṭana—Aṣṭādaśa (Cāmuṇḍā); a mistake for Krauñca° (Banavasi).

Kūpānta—Jñāna (v.l. Kulānta).

Kurukṣetra—Kubjikā; Nīla, Prāṇa (Śivā—Sthāṇu); Prāṇa (Aruṇekṣaṇā, Raṇekṣaṇā); Pīṭha (Dakṣiṇagulpha—Sāvitrī—Sthāṇu); Śiva (Mahāpīṭha;—Dakṣiṇagulpha—Saṃvarī, Vimalā—Saṃvarta); near Thanesar in the eastern Punjab.

Kuśadvīpa—Nāma (Kuśodakā); one of the seven mythical Dvīpas of the world; cf. Kusha, the old Persian name of Ethiopia. See Kuśāvarta.

Kuśāvarta—Nīla, Prāṇa; a tank at Tryambak near Nasik or a Ghat at Hardwar.

L

Lagnikāśrama—Nīla, Prāṇa; possibly a mistake for Nagnikāśrama.

Lakṣmaṇocchedа, Lakṣmaṇodbheda—Prāṇa, Nīla.

Lalitā, Lalitāpura—Nīla, Prāṇa (Lalitā); possibly Lalitpur in the Jhansi District, U.P.

Laṅkā—Aṣṭādaśa (Śaṅkarī); Śiva (Upapīṭha) and Pīṭha (Nūpura—Indrākṣī—Rākṣaseśvara); modern Ceylon, but the *Aṣṭādaśa* makes separate mention of Laṅkā and Siṃhaladvīpa. The word *laṅkā*, means 'an island' and may indicate any island in the sea or a river.

Liṅga—Nīla, Prāṇa (Liṅgavāhinī); Nīla (Bhairavī).

M

Madanta—Nīla, Prāṇa (Madantī).

Madantikā—Nīla, Prāṇa.

Mādhava—Kubjikā. See Mādhavavana, Mādhavīvana, Kālamādhava.

Mādhavavana—Nāma (v.l. Mādhavīvana, Gandhamādana;—Sugandhā); probably the same as Madhuvana or Mathurā. See Mādhava.

Mādhavīvana—See Mādhavavana.

Madhupurī—Rudra; Kubjikā; same as Mathurā (Muttra) in U.P.

Madhurā—Nīla, Prāṇa (Devakī, Mādhavī); same as Mathurā.

Madreśvara—See Bhadreśvara; cf. Madra in the Sialkot region of the Punjab.

Magadha, Māgadha—Rudra; Pīṭha (Dakṣiṇajaṅghā—Sarvānandamayī—Vyomakeśa); modern Patna-Gaya region in South Bihar.

Mahābala—Prāṇa (Prabalā); possibly owing to confusion with Mahāvana.

Mahābodhi—Nīla, Prāṇa (Mahābuddhi); modern Bodhgayā (possibly *Bodhigayā*) in the Gaya District, Bihar.

Mahāgaṅgā—Nīla, Prāṇa; the river Alakanandā in the Himalayas.

Mahākāla—Nāma (Maheśvarī); Prāṇa (Mahākālī—Mahākāla); cf. god Mahākāla at Ujjain.

Mahākarṇa—Kubjikā.

Mahālakṣmī, Mahālakṣmīpura—Jñāna; Nīla (Ambikā); possibly the same as Kolhapur where stands the great shrine of the goddess Mahālakṣmī. But the *Jñānārṇava* makes a distinction between Kolvagiri and Mahālakṣmī. See Karavīra, Kolvagiri.

Mahālaya—Nīla, Prāṇa (Mahābhāgā—Rudra); Nāma (Mahābhāgā, Mahāpadmā); same as Oṅkāranātha or Amareśvara.

Mahāliṅga—Nāma (Kapilā).

Mahānāda—Nīla, Prāṇa (Māheśvarī).

Mahānadī—Nīla, Prāṇa (Mahodayā); the celebrated river running through Orissa.

Mahānala—Prāṇa, Nīla.

Mahāpathapura—Nīla (Māheśvarī); possibly a mistake for Maheśvarapura.

Mahātīrtha—Nīla, Prāṇa (Mahodarī); Nīla, Prāṇa (Haṃseśvarī).

Mahāvana—Nīla, Prāṇa (Bhadrā, Bhadrakālī, Bhadreśvarī); the same as Purāṇa-Gokula, six miles from Mathurā.

Mahāviṣṇupada—Nīla, Prāṇa; possibly the same as Viṣṇupada.

Mahendra, Mahendrapura—Jñāna; Nīla, Prāṇa (Mahāntakā—Mahāntaka); Nīla (Jagadīśvarī); the celebrated peak in the Ganjam District of Orissa. The records of the Gaṅga kings speak of Śiva Gokarṇeśvara on the Mahendra.

Maheśvarapura—Nāma (Svāhā); same as Māhiṣmatī, Māheśvarapura, Māheśvarīpura; modern Maheśvara in the Indore State, C.P.

Māheśvarapura—See Maheśvarapura.

Maheśvarīpura—See Maheśvarapura.

Māhiṣmatī—Kubjikā; modern Maheśvara in the Indore State or less probably Mandhātā in the Nimar District, C.P.

Māhvara—Aṣṭādaśa (Ekavīrakā). See Sahyādri.

Maināka—Nīla, Prāṇa (Akhilavardhinī); one of the several peaks or mountains of this name.

Makarandaka—See Amarakaṇṭaka.

Mākoṭa—Nāma (v.l. Koṭa, Karkoṭa;—Mukuṭeśvarī, Maṅgaleśvarī); Nīla, Prāṇa (Muṇḍakeśvarī—Mahākoṭa).

Mālava—Jñāna (v.l. Mānava); Nīla, Prāṇa (v.l. Malinī;—Raṅginī); Nīla (v.l. Mānava;—Mahāvidyā); Śiva (Mahāpīṭha;—Vāmajānu—Śubhacaṇḍī—Tāmra); modern Malwa, the eastern part of which was known as Ākara or Daśārṇa with its capital at Vidiśā, and the western part as Avanti or Apara-Mālava with its capital at Ujjayinī. Cf. Mānava, Mānasa, Malaya.

Malaya—Nāma (Rambhā); Nāma (v.l. Mānasa;—Kalyāṇī); cf. Mānasācala. Malaya has been identified with the southern part of the Western Ghats to the south of the Nilgiri.

Mānava—Jñāna (v.l. Mālava).

Mānasācala—Nāma (v.l. Malayāchala;—Kalyāṇī).

Mānasasarovara—Nāma (Kumudā); Nīla, Prāṇa (Gaurī); Pīṭha (Dakṣiṇahasta—Dākṣāyaṇī—Hara, Amara); Śiva (Mahāpīṭha;—Dakṣiṇahastārdha, Vāmahasta—Dākṣāyaṇī—Hara); the source of the Śatadru (Satlej) in the Himalayas.

Maṇḍaleśvara—Nīla, Prāṇa (Khāṇḍavī—Śaṅkara); Prāṇa (Karavīrā—Acaleśvara).

Mandara—Nāma (Kāmacāriṇī); Prāṇa (Bhuvaneśvarī); the Mandār hill in the Bhagalpur District, Bihar, or a mythical mountain in the Western Sea (Arabian Sea).

Māṇḍavya—Nāma (v.l. Māṇḍava;—Māṇḍavī, Maṇḍukī); same as Māṇḍavyapura (modern Mandor) in the Jodhpur State, Rajputana.

Maṅgalakoṭa, Maṅgalakoṭara (°koṭṭaka)—Nīla, Prāṇa (Maṅgalā); at the junction of the Ajay and Kunur in the Burdwan region.

Maṇibandha—Śiva (Mahāpīṭha;—Vāmamaṇibandha—Gāyatrī—Śaṅkara, Śarvāṇa); Pīṭha (see Maṇiveda); the name seems to have been created out of a confused text.

Maṇikarṇikā (at Vārāṇasī)—Pīṭha (Kuṇḍala—Viśālākṣī—Kāla). See Vārāṇasī (modern Benares) in U.P.

Māṇikī—Aṣṭādaśa; probably a wrong reading.

Maṇipura—Kubjikā; possibly a place in the Manipur State in eastern India is indicated.

Maṇiveda—Pīṭha (Maṇibandha—Gāyatrī—Sarvānanda); Śiva (Mahāpīṭha; —Dakṣiṇamaṇibandha—Sāvitrī—Sthāṇu); possibly the same as Maṇipura.

Marakaṅkaṭa—See Amarakaṇṭaka.

Māruteśa, Māruteśvara—Jñāna; Nīla.

Mātaṅga—Nīla, Prāṇa (Mātaṅgī); same as Mātaṅgavāpī, modern Mātaṅgāśrama at Bakraur on the Phalgu, opposite Bodhgaya in the Gaya District, Bihar.

Mātaṅgavāpī—Nīla, Prāṇa; same as Mātaṅga.

Mathurā—Nāma (Devakī). See Madhurā, Madhupurī; modern Muttra in U.P.

Mātṛdarśa—Nīla, Prāṇa (Jaganmātā).

Mātṛgaṇa—Nāma (fictitious); Nīla, Prāṇa.

Māyā—Nīla, Prāṇa. See Māyāpurī, Māyāvatī, Māyāpura.

Māyāpura—Jñāna; Nīla (Māyā). See Māyā, Māyāpurī, Māyāvatī; the Haridvāra (Hardwar) region.

Māyāpurī—Nāma (Māyāvatī). See Māyā, Māyāpura, Māyāvatī.

Māyāvatī—Rudra; Kubjikā; same as Māyā, Māyāpura, Māyāpurī, i.e. the Hardwar region.

Meghavana—Nīla, Prāṇa (Meghasvanā).

Mehāra—*Sarvānandataraṅgiṇī*; a small Pargana in the Tippera District, East Bengal.

Mekhalā—Rudra; Mekalā, capital of Mekaladeśa in the Amarkantak region. Cf. also Mekliganj in the Coch Bihar State, Bengal.

Meru—Tantrasāra; Nīla (v.l. Amaraparvata;—Svargalakṣmī); same as Merugiri.

Merugiri—Jñāna; a mythical mountain; same as the mythical Sumeru, often identified with the Hindukush.

Mithilā—Rudra; Pīṭha (Vāmaskandha—Umā—Mahodara); Śiva (Mahāpīṭha;—Vāmaskandha—Mahādevī—Mahodara); modern Janakpur in the Nepalese Tarai.

Mukuṭa—Nāma (v.l. Kumuda).

Muṇḍapṛṣṭha—Nīla, Prāṇa (Śivā); the Brahmayoni hill at Gayā, particularly its portion containing the Viṣṇupada temple.

Munīśvara—Nīla, Prāṇa (Śuddhabuddhi).

N

Nābhigayā—Same as Gayānābhi or Jājpur (Orissa). Vaṃśīdāsa connects it with Satī's navel.

Nādavaṭa—Prāṇa, Nīla.

Nāgapurī—See Yāgapurī.

Nagarakoṭa-Kangra—'Ain (Jālandharī, probably the same as Jvālāmukhī); Caṇḍī (Mastaka—Jvālāmukhī); same as Jvālāmukhī.

Nagarasambhava—Kubjikā. See Nāgarasambhava.

Nāgarasambhava—Same as Nagarasambhava.

Nāgatīrtha—Nīla, Prāṇa (Surasā).

Naimiṣa—Nāma (Liṅgadhāriṇī). See Naimiṣāraṇya.

Naimiṣāraṇya—Nīla, Prāṇa (Prajñā, Liṅgadhāriṇī—Maheśvara); Prāṇa (Sukathā); modern Nimkhar or Nimsar and Misrikh regions in the Sitapur District, U.P. See Naimiṣa.

Naipāla—Same as Nepāla.

Nalāhāṭī—Pīṭha (Nalā—Kālī—Yogeśa, Yogīśa); Śiva (Upapīṭha;—Śirāṇālī—Śephālikā—Yogīśa); identified with Nalahati in the Birbhum District, Bengal.

Nalasthāna—Śiva (Upapīṭha;—Dakṣiṇagaṇḍāṃśa—Bhrāmarī—Virūpākṣa); probably Nalahati mentioned separately.

Nandapura—Nīla, Prāṇa (Mahānanda); possibly the same as Nandipura.

Nandataṭa—Nīla, Prāṇa (v.l. Nandavaṭa; Mahānanda); possibly a mistake for Nandātaṭa. For an Ānandā Mahāpīṭha, see *Skand P.*, Brahmakhaṇḍa, Dharmāraṇyakhaṇḍa, ch. 37, v. 62.

Nandavaṭa—See Nandataṭa.

Nandipura—Pīṭha (Hāra—Nandinī—Nandikeśvara); Śiva (Upapīṭha;—Hārāṃśa—Nandinī—Nandikeśvara); near Sainthia in the Birbhum District, Bengal.

Nārikela—Kubjikā; cf. Nārikeladvīpa mentioned in literature and such localities as Nārikeldāṅgā (near Calcutta) in Lower Bengal.

Narmadā—Nīla, Prāṇa (Narmadā); Pīṭha (v.l. Śona;—Nitamba—Śonā—Bhadrasena); Śiva (Mahāpīṭha;—Dakṣiṇanitamba—Śoṇākṣī—Bhadrasena); the celebrated river rising from the Amarkantak and falling into the Gulf of Cambay.

Narmadoccheda, Narmadodbheda—Nīla, Prāṇa (Dāruṇā).

Nepāla, Naipāla—Kubjikā; Jñāna; Nīla (Puṇyadā); Pīṭha (Jānu—Mahāmāyā—Kapālī); Śiva (Mahāpīṭha;—Dakṣiṇajaṅghā—Mahāmāyā, Navadurgā—Kapālī); the reference may be to Katmandu, the capital of Nepal.

Nīlācala, Nīlaparvata—Nīla, Prāṇa (Vimalā); Śiva (Upapīṭha;—Ucchiṣṭa—Vimalā—Jagannātha). See Virajā, Utkala. The reference seems to be to the Purī temple (said to be on the Nīla mountain) in Orissa, although; but there was another Nīlaparvata in Kāmarūpa from which Kāmākhyā was called Nīlapārvatī.

Nīlavāhinī—Kubjikā.

O

Oḍḍiyāna—Same as Uḍḍiyāna.

Oḍiyāna—Same as Uḍḍiyāna.

Oḍra—modern Orissa, but sometimes confused with Oḍḍiyāna in the Swat valley.

Oghavatī—Nīla, Prāṇa (Mahāvidyā); the river Apagā (a branch of the Chitang) running by Thanesar and Pehoa in the Eastern Punjab.

Oṅkāra—Nīla (Gāyatrī); Jñāna (possibly v.l. Praṇava); modern Oṅkāreśvara or Oṅkāranātha, i.e. the island of Mandhata in the Narmadā (32 miles north-west of Khandwa) in the Nimar District, C.P.

P

Pampāsaras—Nīla, Prāṇa (v.l. Pañcāpsaras;—Ṣāraṅgā); near modern Hampe in the Bellary District, Madras.

Pañcakaṭī—wrong reading for Pañcavaṭī.

Pañcanada—See Dakṣapañcanada.

Pañcāpsaras—Nīla, Prāṇa; located differently by different writers.

Pañcasāgara—Śiva (Mahāpītha) and Pīṭha (Adhodanta—Vārāhī—Mahārudra); possibly the oceans are indicated, although their traditional number was four or seven. But cf. Pañcatīrtha.

Pañcatīrtha—Nīla, Prāṇa; near Hardwar.

Pañcavaṭī—Nīla, Prāṇa (Tapasvinī). See Janasthāna in which Pañcavaṭī was situated.

Pāṇḍu—Nīla, Prāṇa (Pāṇḍarānanā); possibly the same as the Pāṇḍya country in the southern corner of India.

Parameśvarapura—Nīla (v.l. Samaneśvarapura).

Pārasya—Nīla (Paramānanda); Persia.

Pārātaṭa—Nāma (v.l. Pārāvāratīra); Pārā is the same as the Pārvatī in Malwa.

Pārāvāratīra—Nāma (v.l. Pārātaṭa;—Mātā, Pārā, Pāvā).

Pāṭala—Nīla, Prāṇa (Pāṭaleśvarī); possibly Pāṭaliputra (near modern Patna) or Pāṭana (Patna<*Pattana*) is indicated.

Pātāla—Nāma Parameśvarī); possibly Pāṭala is indicated, but is reminiscent of the region of Patalene, the ancient city and district, located by classical writers about the mouths of the Indus.

Pauṇḍravardhana—Jñāna, Nīla (Suveśā); same as Puṇḍra, Puṇḍravardhana.

Payoṣṇī—Nāma (Piṅgaleśvarī); probably the river Paisuni, a tributary of the Jumna between the Ken and the Tons.

Piṇḍāraka—Nāma (Dhṛti); Prāṇa; 16 miles to the east of Dvārakā in Kathiawar. See Piṇḍārakavana.

Piṇḍārakavana—Nīla, Prāṇa (Dhanyā). See Piṇḍāraka.

Piṅgā—Prāṇa, Nīla.

Piyālamārga—Prāṇa, Nīla.

Prabhāsa—Nāma (Puṣkarāvatī); Nīla, Prāṇa (Īśvarī); Nīla, Prāṇa (Surapūjitā); Nīla, Prāṇa (Puṣkarekṣaṇā—Somanātha); Pīṭha (Udara, Adhara—Candrabhāgā—Vakratuṇḍa); Śiva (Mahāpīṭha;—Adhara—Candrabhāgā—Vakratuṇḍa); modern Somnath in the Junagarh State, Kathiawar.

Prabhāsakhaṇḍa—Śiva (Mahāpīṭha;—Marma—Siddhīśvarī—Siddhīśvara); probably in the Prabhāsa region, or one of the other two Prabhāsas near Kurukṣetra or Kauśāmbī.

Pradyumna—Aṣṭādaśa; probably Pandua in the Hooghly District.

Praṇava—possibly the same as Oṅkāra.

Prapā—Nīla, Prāṇa (Pāpanāśinī).

Prasaṅga—Prāṇa, Nīla.

Prayāga—Kubjikā; Jñāna; Rudra; Aṣṭādaśa (Mādhaveśvarī); Nīla (Triveṇī?); Nāma (Lalitā); Pīṭha (Hastāṅguli—Lalitā—Bhava) Śiva (Mahāpīṭha;—Dvi-hast-āṅguli—Kamalā—Veṇīmādhava); modern Allahabad in U.P. The temple of Veṇīmādhava lies at the confluence of the Ganges and the Jumna.

Pṛthūdaka—Nīla, Prāṇa (Mahāvegā); modern Pehoa in the Karnal District, Punjab.
Puṇḍra—Śiva (Upapīṭha;—Loma—Sarvākṣiṇī—Sarva). See Puṇḍravardhana.
Puṇḍravardhana—Nāma (v.l. Puṇyavardhana;—Pāṭalā); same as Puṇḍra, Paundravardhana; identified with modern Mahasthan in the Bogra District, Bengal.
Puṇyādri—Nīla (v.l. Puṣyādri;—Mahāpuṇyā); possibly the same as Pūrṇagiri.
Puṇyavardhana—Same as Puṇḍravardhana. For this form of the name, see Watters, *On Yuan Chwang's Travels in India*, II, p. 185.
Puraścandra—Nīla, Prāṇa (Pureśvarī).
Purasthira—Jñāna (v.l. Purasthita).
Purasthita—Jñāna (v.l. Purasthira).
Pūrṇa—Same as Pūrṇagiri.
Pūrṇagiri—Hevajra; Kālikā (in the south;—Pūrṇeśvarī—Mahānātha); Kālikā (Skandhagrīvā—Pūrṇeśvarī); Sādhana; Jñāna; Rudra; probably located by the 'Ain in the Bijapur region of the Bombay Presidency. Same as Pūrṇa, Pūrṇaśaila. The name may not be unconnected with that of the Pūrṇā (modern Paira), a branch of the Godavari. The *Ānandārṇava* gives the name of the Pīṭha as Pūrṇabhūdhara.
Pūrṇaśaila—Same as Pūrṇagiri.
Puruṣottama—Nāma and Prāṇa (Vimalā); same as Purī in Orissa.
Puṣkara—Nāma (Puruhūtā); Prāṇa (Kamalākṣī); Prāṇa (Purahūtā—Rājagandhi); near Ajmer in Rajputana.
Puṣpatīrtha—Nāma (v.l. Uṣṇatīrtha); possibly connected with the Puṣpagiri in the Malaya range.

R

Rāḍha, Rāḍhā—Rudra; Nīla, Prāṇa (Maṅgalacaṇḍī); in a narrow sense, the land watered by the Ajay in the Burdwan District, Bengal.
Rājabolahāṭa—Caṇḍī (Vāmahasta—Viśālalocanī); near Serampur in the Hooghly District, Bengal.
Rājagiri—Pīṭha (v.l. Rāmagiri); possibly a form of Rājagṛha. Cf. Rājaparvata.
Rājagṛha—Jñāna; modern Rajgir in the Gaya District, Bihar.
Rājaparvata—Nīla; probably the same as Rājagiri.
Rāmā—Nāma (fictitious).
Rāmagiri—Kubjikā; Nāma (Trisandhyā); Pīṭha (v.l. Rājagiri;—Stana, Nāsā, Nalā—Śivānī—Caṇḍa); Śiva (Mahāpīṭha;—Dakṣiṇastana—Śivānī—Caṇḍa); possibly modern Ramtek near Nagpur in C.P., or Chitrakūṭa in the Banda District, U.P.
Ramaṇa, Ramaṇaka—Nīla, Prāṇa (Durgā).
Rāmatīrtha—Nāma (Ramaṇā); Nīla, Prāṇa (Mahādhṛti); the ancient Rāmatīrtha in Sūrpāraka (modern Sopara) in the Thana District, Bombay, although in this case Rāmagiri may be indicated.
Rāmeśvara—Nīla, Prāṇa (Prabhā); Prāṇa (Mahāsiddhi); the celebrated Setubandha Rāmeśvara in the Ramnad District, Madras. See Setubandha. Another Rāmeśvara lies at the confluence of the Banas and the Chambal.
Rāmoccheda, Rāmodbheda—Prāṇa, Nīla.
Raṇakhaṇḍa—Śiva (Mahāpīṭha;—Dakṣiṇakaphoni—Bahulākṣī—Mahākāla); possibly the same as Bahulā separately mentioned.
Rāsavṛndāvana—Nīla, Prāṇa (Rādhā). See Vṛndāvana.

Ratnāvalī—Pīṭha (v.l. Ratnavatī;—Dakṣiṇaskanda—Kumārī—Śiva); Śiva (Mahāpīṭha;—Dakṣiṇaskandha—Śivā—Śiva); possibly the same as the city of Ratnavatī mentioned in the *Kāvyamīmāṃsā*, but may also be a locality in Bengal. Ratnāvalī is the name of a sacred tributary of the Vāgmatī in Nepal.

Ratnavatī—See Ratnāvalī.

Ṛṇamocana—Nīla, Prāṇa (Vimukti).

Rudrakoṭī—Nāma (Rudrāṇī, Kalyāṇī); either the *tīrtha* of this name in Kurukṣetra, or that near the source of the Narmadā.

S

Sāgarasaṅgama—Nīla, Prāṇa (Svāhā); possibly the same as Gaṅgāsāgarasaṅgama.

Sahasrākṣa—Nāma (Utpalā, Utpalākṣī)

Sahyādri—Nāma (Ekavīrā).

Śākambharīpura—Nīla, Prāṇa; modern Sambhar near Pushkar.

Śālagrāma—Nāma (Mahādevī); at the source of the river Gaṇḍakī or Gaṇḍak.

Śāligrāma—Same as Śālagrāma.

Śamaneśvarapura—Nīla (v.l. Parameśvarapura;—Mahāvrajeśvarī).

Sambheda—Nīla, Prāṇa (Śubhavāsinī); supposed to be about the mouth of the Indus.

Saṃhāra—Śiva (Upapīṭha;—Dantāṃśa—Śūreśī—Śūreśa); apparently due to a textual corruption (cf. *Pīṭha*, verse 39 and notes).

Śaṅkhasaṃharaṇa—Prāṇa; same as Śaṅkhoddhāra.

Śaṅkhoddhāra—Nāma (Dhvani, Dharā); the island of Baṭi (Beyt) at the south-western extremity of the Gulf of Cutch.

Santāna—Nāma (Lalitā).

Saptagodāvara—Nīla, Prāṇa (Śrī, Akhileśvarī); at Solangipur, 16 miles from Pithapuram in the Godavari District of the Madras Presidency.

Saptārci—Nīla, Prāṇa; possibly the same as Guptārci at Viṣṇupada, or Saptārṣa (Satara) in the south Maratha country.

Śāradā—Nīla, Prāṇa (Śāradā); modern Sardi in Kashmir.

Sarasvatī—Nāma (Devamātā); Nīla, Prāṇa; river in the eastern Punjab running by Pehoa.

Sarayū, Sarayūtīra—Nīla, Prāṇa (Śāradā); the celebrated river running through Oudh, now called Ghagra or Gogra.

Śarīrin—Nāma (fictitious).

Śarkara—Śiva (Mahāpīṭha;—Trinetra—Mahiṣamardinī—Krodhīśa); same as Śarkarāra.

Śarkarāra—Pīṭha (v.l. Karavīra); identified with Sukkur in Sindh.

Sarvaśaila—Śiva (Upapīṭha;—Kakṣāṃśa—Viśvamātā—Daṇḍapāṇi); a vague reference to 'all hills'.

Ṣaṣṭhīpura—Nīla (Ṣaṣṭhī).

Śatadru—Nīla, Prāṇa (Śatarūpā); river running through the Punjab; now called Satlej.

Satī—Nāma (fictitious).

Satīcala—Śiva (Upapīṭha;—Karāṃśa—Sunandā—Sunanda).

Setubandha—Nīla, Prāṇa (Rāmeśvarī). See Rāmeśvara, Śvetabandha.

Siddhapura—v.l. Siddhavaṭa; either Siddhaur near Barabanki in U.P. or Sidpur about 64 miles from Ahmedabad; but may also be one of the several Siddhāśramas.

Siddhavana—v.l. Siddhavaṭa.

Siddhavaṭa—Nāma (v.l. Siddhavana, Siddhapura;—Mātā Lakṣmī, Umā Lakṣmī).
Siddhitīra—Nīla, Prāṇa (Siddhidā).
Siṃhala, Siṃhaladvīpa—Kubjikā (v.l. Siṃhanāda); Rudra; Aṣṭādaśa; modern Ceylon.
Siṃhanāda—Kubjikā (v.l. Siṃhala).
Sindhusaṅgama—v.l. Śoṇasaṃgama. Sindhu is the Indus running through north-western India to the Arabian Sea.
Sirihaṭṭa—See Śrīhaṭṭa.
Śivacaṇḍa—v.l. Śivakuṇḍa.
Śivakuṇḍa—Nāma (v.l. Śivakuñja, Śivacaṇḍa;—Śivānandā, Śubhānandā, Sunandā, Sabhānandā).
Śivakuñja—v.l. Śivakuṇḍa.
Śivaliṅga—Nāma (Jalapriyā).
Śivapīṭha—Nīla, Prāṇa (Jvālāmukhī).
Śivasannidhi—Nāma (fictitious).
Someśvara—Nāma (Varārohā); possibly the same as Somanātha or Prabhāsa in Kathiawar.
Śoṇa—Pīṭha (v.l. Narmadā;—Nitambā—Narmadā—Bhadrasena); Śiva (Upapīṭha;—Nitambāṃśa—Bhadrā—Bhadreśvara); Prāṇa (Kaṇakeśvarī); celebrated tributary joining the Ganges near Patna in Bihar.
Śoṇasaṅgama—Nāma (v.l. Sindhusaṅgama;—Subhadrā); the reference may be to the Śona-Gaṅgā-Saṅgama near Patna.
Śrīgiri—Nīla, Prāṇa (Śrī); same as Śrīśaila.
Śrīhaṭṭa—Sādhana (v.l. Sirihaṭṭa); Pīṭha (v.l. Śrīśaila); Śiva (Mahāpīṭha;—Grīvā—Mahālakṣmī—Sarvānanda); modern Sylhet in Assam.
Śrīparvata—Pīṭha (Dakṣiṇakarṇa—Sundarī—Sundarānanda, Sunandānanda); Śiva (Mahāpīṭha;—Dakṣiṇakarṇa—Sundarī—Sundarānanda); Prāṇa (Śaṅkarī—Tripurāntaka). See Śrīśaila.
Śrīpīṭha—Jñāna; possibly the same as Śrīhaṭṭa.
Śrīpura—Nīla (Śrīramā); possibly Sirpur in the Raipur District, C.P.
Sthala—Nīla, Prāṇa (Sthalā—Sthala).
Sthāneśvara—Same as Sthāṇvīśvara.
Sthāṇu—meant for Sthāṇvīśvara according to a wrong reading in Prāṇa.
Sthāṇvīśvara—Nāma (Bhavānī); modern Thanesar in the Ambala District, Punjab.
Strīrājya—Rudra; associated with the land of the Nu-wangs in eastern Tibet, who are said to have been ruled by a woman styled Pinchiu. The Strīrājya is usually located in the Kumaon-Garhwal region of the Himalayas. Hiuen Tsang seems to locate a western Strīrājya about Makran (Walters, *op. cit.*, II, p. 257).
Subhadra—Nīla, Prāṇa (Bhavyā); cf. the name Subhadrā applied to the Irawadi.
Śuci—Pīṭha (v.l. Anala;—Ūrdhvadanta—Nārāyaṇī—Saṃkrūra, Saṃhāra); cf. Supārśva.
Sugandhā—Śiva (Mahāpīṭha) and Pīṭha (Nāsikā—Sunandā—Tryambaka); Prāṇa; modern Shikarpur on the Sondha (Sugandhā) near Barisal in South Bengal.
Śuklatīrtha, Śukratīrtha—Prāna (Śraddhā); near Broach in Gujarat.
Suparṇa—Nīla, Prāṇa (Utpalā—Sahasrākṣa); possibly the source of the Tons (Tamasā), tributary of the Jumna.
Supārśva—Nāma (Nārāyaṇī); cf. Suci.
Svargamārga—Nīla, Prāṇa (Svargadā).

Svargoccheda, Svargodbheda—Nīla, Prāṇa (Mahārātri).
Śvetabandha—Śiva (Upapīṭha;—Bhagnāṃśa—Jayā—Mahābhīma); apparently a mistake for Setubandha.

T

Tailaṅga—Śiva (Upapīṭha;—Lomakhaṇḍa—Caṇḍadāyikā—Caṇḍeśa); Telengana or the present Telugu speaking area in the Deccan. Dey, *G.D.*, s.v. Triliṅga, said to be first mentioned in Rājaśekhara's *Viddhaśālabhañjikā*.
Tamolipta—Nīla, Prāṇa (Tamoghnī); modern Tamluk in the Midnapur District, Bengal. Other old forms of the name were Tāmralipta, Tāmralipti, Dāmalipta, etc.
Tantra—Nīla, Prāṇa (Gautameśvarī).
Tārā—Śiva (Mahāpīṭha;—Netrāṃśatārā—Tāriṇī—Unmatta); identified with Tarapur near Nalahati in the Birbhum District, Bengal. See Ugratārā.
Tirotā—Pīṭha (v.l. Trisrotā); but it is a corruption of *Trihuta* in *Śiva*, though the latter form itself is a corruption of Sanskrit *Tīrabhukti*.
Tīrthasaṅgama—Nīla, Prāṇa (Saṅgamā).
Traipura—v.l. Tripura.
Trihuta—Śiva (Mahāpīṭha;—Vāmapada—Amarī—Amara); Tirhut (Sanskrit *Tīrabhukti*) indicating the northern part of Bihar. See Tirotā.
Trikūṭa—Nāma (Bhadrasundarī, Rudrasundarī); the mythical peak of Ceylon on which the city of Laṅkā was supposed to have been situated. There was another Trikūṭa in the northern Konkan.
Tripada—Nīla, Prāṇa (Caṇḍā); possibly Tirupati (Tripadī; but really Sans. *Śrīpati*) is indicated.
Tripura—Nīla (Sundarī); probably the same as Tripurā, and not Tewar near Jubbulpore.
Tripurā—Kubjikā; Pīṭha (Dakṣiṇapada—Tripurā, Tripurasundarī—Nala, Tripureśa, Tripurākṣa); Śiva (Dakṣiṇapada—Tripurā—Nala); the Tripurā (Hill Tipperah) State in Bengal. Udayapura or Rāṅgāmāṭi (modern Rādhākiśorapura), old capital of Tripurā, is indicated.
Trisrotā—Jñāna; Pīṭha (v.l. Tirotā;—Vāmapada—Bhrāmarī, Amarī—Īśvara, Amara); Śiva (Mahāpīṭha;—Dakṣiṇajānu—Caṇḍikā—Sadānanda); Śiva (Upapīṭha;—Padāṃśa—Pārvatī—Īśvara, Bhairaveśvara); the river Tista running through northern Bengal. *Śiva* mentions Trisrotā both as a Mahāpīṭha and as an Upapīṭha.
Triveṇī—Kubjikā; either the Yuktaveṇī near Allahabad or more probably the Muktaveṇī near Calcutta.

U

Uḍḍīnapura—Nīla; probably a mistake for Uḍḍīśa or Uḍḍīyāna.
Uḍḍīśa—Jñāna; same as Oḍra from Sanskrit *Oḍraviṣaya*, Prakrit *Oḍḍavisa*, *Oḍḍaïsa*; modern Orissa (*Oḍiṣā*).
Uḍḍiyāna, Uḍḍīyāna—Hevajra; Kālikā (in the west;—Kātyāyanī—Jagannātha); Kālikā (Urudvaya;—Kātyāyanī); Rudra; Jñāna; Kubjikā; land watered by the river Swat in north-western India, but sometimes confused with Oḍra (Orissa).
Udiyāna—Same as Uḍḍiyāna.
Ugratārā—Vaṃśīdāsa connects it with Satī's eyes. See Tārā.
Ujānī—Pīṭha (v.l. Ujjayinī, Urjanī, Ujjanī); Śiva (Mahāpīṭha;—Vāmakaphoni—Maṅgalacaṇḍī—Kapilāmbara); modern Kogram in the Burdwan District, Bengal.

Ujjanī—See Ujānī, Ujjayinī.
Ujjayinī—Jñāna; Aṣṭādaśa (Mahākālī); Nīla; Pīṭha (v.l. Ujānī, Ujjanī, Urjanī;—Kūrpara—Maṅgalacaṇḍī—Kapilāmbara); modern Ujjain in the Gwalior State; but see also Ujānī.
Urjanī—See Ujānī, Ujjayinī.
Uṣṇatīrtha—Nāma (v.l. Puṣpatīrtha;—Abhayā).
Utkala—Śiva (Mahāpīṭha;—Nābhi—Vijayā—Jaya); Aṣṭādaśa (Virajā); roughly speaking another name of Oḍra or Orissa. See Virajā.
Utpalāvartaka—Nāma (Lolā); cf. the name of Utpalāvatī, a river (modern Vyapar) in the Tinnevelly District, Madras, and that of Utpalāvata or Utpalāraṇya (modern Bithoor) near Cawnpore, U.P.
Uttarā—Śiva (Upapīṭha;—Vāmagaṇḍāṁśa—Uttariṇī—Utsādana); possibly the Uttaragā or Rāmgaṅgā in Oudh.
Uttarakuru—Nāma (Auṣadhi, Oṣadhi); a Himalayan tract, often supposed to have included the northern part of Garhwal.
Uttaramānasa—Nīla, Prāṇa (Nīlā); the Ganga lake at the foot of the Harmuk peak in Kashmir, or a sacred place at Gayā.

V

Vāgmatī—Kubjikā; river in Nepal, whose junctions with the Maradārikā, Maṇisrohiṇī, Rājamañjarī, Ratnāvalī, Cārumatī, Prabhāvatī and Triveṇī form respectively the Śānta, Śaṅkara, Rājamañjarī, Pramodā, Sulakṣaṇa, Jaya and Gokarṇa *tīrthas*; also old Tista (*Hist. Beng.*, II, p. 10).
Vaidyanātha—Kubjikā; Nāma (Arogā, Ārogyā); Pīṭha (Hṛdaya—Jayadurgā—Vaidyanātha); Śiva (Mahāpīṭha;—Hṛdaya—Jayadurgā, Navadurgā—Vaidyanātha); modern Deoghar-Baidyanāthdhām in the Santal Parganas District, Bihar.
Vaiśravaṇālaya—Nāma (fictitious).
Vaivasvata—Śiva (Mahāpīṭha;—Pṛshṭha—Tripuṭā—Śamanakarman, Nimiṣa).
Vakranātha—Śiva (Mahāpīṭha;—Manas—Pāpaharā—Vakranātha); possibly the same place is referred to in *Śiva* as both Vakreśvara and Vakranātha (cf. double mention of Trisrotā). See Vakreśvara. For *Pāpaharā* as the name or an epithet of the river at Vakreśvara, see *Pīṭha*, v. 50.
Vakreśvara—Pīṭha (Manas—Mahiṣamardinī—Vakranātha); Śiva (Mahāpīṭha;—Dakṣiṇabāhu—Vakreśvarī—Vakreśvara); near Dubrajpur in the Birbhum District, Bengal.
Vāmana—Jñāna; probably Vāmanasthalī (Banthali) near Junagarh, Kathiawar.
Vaṅga—Rudra; originally the land watered by the mouths of the Ganges, but later south-east Bengal.
Varāhaparvata, Varāhaśaila—Nāma (Jayā); Nīla; Prāṇa (Vārāhī); either Baramula in Kashmir, or Barahchhatra in Nepal.
Vārāhī—Kubjikā; cf. Varāhaparvata.
Vārāṇasī—Rudra; Aṣṭādaśa (Viśālākṣī); Nīla; Nāma (Viśālākṣī); Pīṭha (see Maṇikarṇikā); Śiva (Upapīṭha;—Kuṇḍala—Viśālākṣī, Annapūrṇā—Kālabhairava, Viśveśvara); modern Benares in U.P.
Vardhamāna—Kubjikā; possibly Burdwan in Bengal. But see Dey, *G.D.*, s.v.
Vareṇya—Prāṇa (v.l. Araṇya;—Sandhyā—Ūrdhvaretas).
Vaśiṣṭhatīrtha—Nīla, Prāṇa (Arundhatī); on Mount Abu in the Sirohi State, Rajputana, or on Mount Sandhyachal near Gauhati in Assam, or a place near Ayodhya.
Vastrapada—Nīla, Prāṇa (Bhuvaneśvarī—Bhava); possibly a mistake for Vastrāpatha (modern Girnar) in Kathiawar, although the Vastrapā

or Vastrāpada country seems to be located in the Mahābhārata (II, 48, 14; III, 80, 108) in the north-west.

Vastreśvara—Nāma (v.l. Viśvesvara;—Puṣṭi, Tuṣṭi); possibly the same as Vastrāpatha or Girnar in Kathiawar. See Vastrapada.

Vaṭaparvatikā—Nīla, Prāṇa (Pañcavargā); mentioned in a Pāla record and in Vijayarāma Sena's *Tīrthamaṅgala* (second half of the 18th century) and identified with the Vaṭeśvaraparvata situated near Pātharghāṭā in the Patna District, Bihar (*Bhāratavarṣa*, Jyaiṣṭha, B.S. 1350, p. 405).

Vaṭīparvatikā—Wrong reading of Vaṭaparvatikā.

Vedamastaka—Nīla, Prāṇa (Vedamātā); same as Vedaśiras.

Vedaśiras—Nīla, Prāṇa; same as Vedamastaka.

Vedavadana—Nāma (fictitious).

Vedeśa—Nīla, Prāṇa (Vedadā); possibly Vaidiśa or Vidiśā (modern Besnagar in the Gwalior State) is indicated.

Vegala—Nāma (v.l. Chāgaliṅga, Chagalaṇḍa, Chāgalāṇḍa).

Veṇā—See Beṇā.

Veṇumatī—Nīla, Prāṇa (Puṇyā).

Vibhāsa—Pīṭha (Vāmagulpha—Bhīmarūpā—Kapālī, Sarvānanda); Śiva (Mahāpīṭha;—Vāmagulpha—Bhīmarūpā—Kapālī); near Tamluk in the Midnapur District, Bengal.

Vidyāpura—Nīla, Prāṇa (Vidyā); probably the same as Vidyānagara or Vijayanagara (modern Hampe) in the Bellary District, Madras. Vidyānagara was possibly also a name of Rajahmundry or of a place near it in the Godavari District. Another Vidyānagara is supposed to be modern Bijaynagar at the confluence of the Sindh and the Para, 25 miles below Narwar.

Vijayā—Prāṇa, Nīla.

Vijayanta—Nīla, Prāṇa (Aparājitā).

Vilvaka—Nāma (v.l. Vilvala;—Vilvapatrikā); Nīla (Rupiṇī); Prāṇa. See Bilvaka.

Vilvala—See Vilvaka.

Vimalā—Kubjikā.

Vimaleśvara—Nīla, Prāṇa (Viśvā—Viśva); cf. the name of Vimalagiri (modern Palitana), a Jain *tīrtha* in Kathiawar.

Vināyaka—Nāma (Umā, Rūpā); one of the eight Vināyaka *tīrthas* in the Bombay Presidency, viz. Ranjangaon, Margaon, Theur, Lenadri, Ojhar, Pali, Madh and Siddhatek.

Vindhya—Kubjikā; Nāma (Vindhyavāsinī); Jñāna; Śiva (Mahāpīṭha;—Vāmapadāṅguli—Vindhyavāsinī—Puṇyabhājana). The temple of Vindhyavāsinī lies at Bindhyachal near Mirzapur in U.P. See Vindhyakandara, Vindhyagaṅgāsaṅgama.

Vindhyagaṅgāsaṅgama—Nīla, Prāṇa (Vindhyavāsinī). See Vindhya.

Vindhyakandara—Nāma (Amṛtā, Nitambā, Mṛgī); different from Bindhyachal near Mirzapur; cf. Vindhya.

Vipāśā—Nāma (Amoghākṣī); Nīla, Prāṇa (Mahābalā); modern Beas, a tributary of the Sindhu or Indus.

Vipula—Nāma (Vipulā).

Viraja, Virajapura, Virajā, Virajākṣetra in Utkala—Kubjikā; Jñāna; Nīla; Pīṭha (Nābhi—Vimalā, Vijayā—Jagannātha, Jaya); modern Jājpur on the Vaitaraṇī in the Cuttack District, Orissa. See Utkala, Yāgapurī, Jājpur, Yājapura, Nābhigayā.

Virāṭa—Pīṭha (Padāṅguli—Ambikā—Amṛta, Amṛtākṣa). The ancient Virāṭa country lay in the Jaipur-Alwar-Bharatpur region of Rajputana; but another country of that name was placed by late-medieval writers in northern Bengal (*I.C.*, VIII, p. 54).

Viśāla—Nīla, Prāṇa (Viśālā); possibly Viśālā-Badarī or Badarikāśrama in the Himalayas.
Viṣṇupada—Nīla, Prāṇa (Guptārci); Prāṇa (Viṣṇupriyā); probably the hill of that name at Gayā in Bihar. For another Viṣṇupada, see *Sel. Ins.*, I, p. 277.
Viśveśvara—Nāma (Viśvā, Vilvā).
Vṛndāvana—Pīṭha (v.l. Keśajāla;—Keśa—Umā—Bhūteśa); Nāma (Rādhā); modern Brindaban near Mathurā (Muttra) in U.P. See Rāsavṛndāvana.
Vyāghrapura—Nīla, Prāṇa (Hara); possibly the same as Buxar (really Vyāghrasaras) in the Shahabad District, Bihar.

Y

Yāgapurī—Nīla, Prāṇa (v.l. Nāgapurī;—Virajā); same as Virajā, Yājapura, Jājpur, Nābhigayā.
Yājapura—Caṇḍī (Dakṣiṇapada—Virajā). See Virajā, Yāgapurī, Utkala, Jājpur. The Assia range about a mile to the south of Jajpur in the Cuttack District, Orissa, is said to have borne the name Catuṣpīṭha-parvata.
Yamunā—Nāma (Mṛgāvatī); Nīla, Prāṇa (Kālindī); modern Jumna, the principal tributary of the Ganges.
Yaśora—Pīṭha (Pāṇi—Yaśoreśvarī—Caṇḍa); Śiva (Upapīṭha;—Pāṇi—Yaśoreśvarī—Pracaṇḍa); modern Jessore in Bengal, although the Pīṭha is located at Īśvarīpura (Khulna District) not far from Hasanabad in the 24-Parganas District.
Yugādyā—Pīṭha (v.l. Kṣīragrāma).

APPENDIX VI

Śiva and Śakti in the Orthodox Indian Pantheon.

The age covered by the composition of the Ṛgvedic hymns is considerably wide (between *circa* 1400 B.C. and 1000 B.C.). It is therefore no wonder, considering the popularity of the union of Aryan males with non-Aryan females, that the speech as well as the social and religious life of the Aryan peoples began to be modified as early as that age.[1] Attention

[1] Cf. 'The ideas of *Karma* and transmigration, the practice of *Yoga*, the religious and philosophical ideas centering round the conception of the divinity as Śiva and Devī and as Viṣṇu, the Hindu ritual of *Pūjā* as opposed to the Vedic ritual of *Homa*—all these and much more in Hindu religion and thought would appear to be non-Aryan in origin; a great deal of Puranic and epic myth, legend and semi-history is pre-Aryan; much of our material culture and social and other usages, e.g. the cultivation of some of our most important plants like rice and some vegetables and fruits like the tamarind and the cocoanut, etc., the use of the betel-leaf in Hindu life and ritual, most of our popular religions, most of our folk crafts, our nautical crafts, our distinctive Hindu dress (the *Dhotī* and the *Sāḍī*), our marriage in some parts of India with the use of vermilion and turmeric—and many other things—would appear to be legacy from our pre-Aryan ancestors' (S. K. Chatterji, *Indo-Aryan and Hindi*, p. 31). 'The Austric tribes of India appear to have belonged to more than one group of the Austro-Asiatic section—to the Kol, to the Khasi and to the Mon-Khmer groups. They were in the neolithic stage of culture and perhaps in India they learned the use of copper and iron. They brought with them a primitive system of agriculture in which a digging stick (*lag, lang, *ling—various forms of an old word *lak) was employed to till the hill-side. Terrace cultivation of rice on hills, and plains cultivation of the same grain were in all likelihood introduced by them. They brought, as the names from their language would suggest, the cultivation of the cocoanut (*nārikela*), the plantain (*kadala*), the betel vine (*tāmbula*), the betel-nut (*guvāka*), probably also turmeric (*haridrā*) and ginger (*śṛṅgavera*), and some vegetables like the brinjal (*vātiṅgana*) and the pumpkin (*alābu*). They appear not to have been cattle-breeders—they had no use for milk, but they were the first people to tame the elephant, and to domesticate the fowl. The habit of counting by twenties in some parts of North India (cf. Hindi *koḍī*,

may be drawn in this connection to the borrowing of the cerebral consonantal sounds from non-Aryan speech, to the speedy modification of the Ṛgvedic god Rudra and to the germ of theism, a non-Aryan institution later completely absorbed in Indian (i.e. mixed Aryo-aboriginal) religious life, to be traced possibly in the reference in the *Ṛgveda* (I, 22, 20) to the *Sūris* (meaning 'sectarian devotees of the god Viṣṇu' according to later works) as a class favoured by Viṣṇu. It is, however, interesting to note that, while the pre-Aryan Father-god was in the process of amalgamation with Aryan Rudra even in the early Vedic period, the absorption of the pre-Aryan Mother-goddess in the orthodox Indian religious life of later days took a considerably longer period of time.

The objects unearthed at the prehistoric (*circa* 2750 B.C.) sites of the Indus Valley prove the prevalence of the cult of the Father-god and Mother-goddess among the pre-Aryan peoples of India. The Mohenjodaro people worshipped a male god who may be regarded as the proto-type of Śiva. He is represented as seated in the *Yoga* posture, surrounded by animals, and has three visible faces with two horns on two sides of a tall head-dress. The ithyphallic (*ūrdhva-liṅga*) characteristic is also very marked. This apparently explains the later conception of Śiva as a *Yogin*, styled *Paśupati*, his *Liṅga* being specially important and his special attributes being the three eyes and the trident, probably associated respectively with the three faces and the two horns together with the head-dress. Some stone pieces looking exactly like the Śiva-liṅga have actually been discovered at Mohenjodaro. The *Liṅga* of the Father-god or Creator was worshipped apparently as a symbol not only of creation but also of virility. See Banerjea, *Dev. H. Icon.*, pp. 174ff.

The objects found at Mohenjodaro include many figurines of the Mother-goddess and point to the wide prevalence of her cult. Such figurines, discovered from prehistoric as well as later sites in different parts of India, are usually nude, but wear a peculiar head-dress, a wide girdle and a quantity of jewellery. A prehistoric terracotta seal from Harappa contains a representation of the same goddess who is shown upside down with her legs wide apart and a plant issuing from her womb and with a pair of tigers (cf. the association of the lion with the Indian Mother-goddess) towards the left, standing facing each other. The fundamental idea of the Mother-goddess cult was the belief in a female energy as the source of all creation. The Indus valley people appear to have also worshipped the *Yoni* as the symbol of this goddess just as they adored the *Liṅga* of the Father-god. Certain objects discovered at Mohenjodaro have their upper and lower surfaces undulating, while in some others the lower surface is flat but the upper one takes a quatre-foil form. Marshall regards these as representations of the *Yoni*, the female organ of generation symbolizing motherhood and fecundity. Yoni-rings of later date have been found from other sites. Certain disc-like objects, usually with well-carved decorative designs, have been found at old sites like Taxila and Rajghat and have been associated with the Yoni cult. See *op. cit.*, pp. 183ff.

Bengali *kuḍi*, 'score, twenty' from the Austric) appears to be the relic of an Austro-Asiatic habit. The later Hindu practice of computing time by days of the moon (*tithis*) seems also to be Austric in origin' (*op. cit.*, pp. 30-31). The 'notion of Brahman, the Supreme Spirit beyond the conception of the manifest gods, dwelling in the void by itself and creating the world out of itself, through its will or desire, can be looked upon as an Austric contribution in the evolution of Indian thought' (Chatterji in *Bhārata-kaumudī*, I, p. 206). India's script and architecture and the caste system are also pre-Aryan. For the contributions of the non-Aryans to Indian culture, see also *Pre-Aryan and Pre-Dravidian in India*, ed. P. C. Bagchi, Calcutta, 1929.

The *Ṛgveda* (VII, 21, 5; X, 99, 3) refers in a deprecatory manner to a class of people called *Śiśnadeva*. Whether they were Aryan (under the influence of an aboriginal cult) or non-Aryan in origin cannot be determined; but there is no doubt that at least the orthodox section of the Ṛgvedic Aryans disapproved of the phallic cult. The Ṛgvedic Rudra (literally, 'the howling one'), essentially the spirit of stormy clouds, was conceived as discharging brilliant shafts and killing men and cattle with his weapons as well as with diseases (I, 114; VII, 46). The giver of diseases was sometimes also regarded as the healer of them (I, 43, 4, etc.). Rudra's interesting epithet *Paśupa* (I, 114, 9) seems to point to his rapprochement with the pre-Aryan deity worshipped at Mohenjodaro even as early as the later Ṛgvedic age when some people also spoke of his 'universal sovereignty' (VII, 46, 20). In the Śatarudrīya section of the *Yajurveda* (*Taittirīya*, 4, 5, 1; *Vājasaneyi*, 16), Rudra's benign form is distinguished from his malignant appearance and he is called the heavenly physician, the god lying on the mountains (*Giriśa*), the wearer of matted hair (*Kapardin*), and the lord of paths, forests, cattle, forest-tribes and outcasts, thieves and robbers. He is also called Śarva (archer), Bhava (benign), Śaṃbhu (beneficent), Śiva (auspicious) and the wearer of tiger-skin. Thus the conception of a terrible destroyer as quite its opposite resulted from partially an attempt at appeasement by flattery and partially perhaps from his gradual amalgamation with the pre-Aryan Father-god. The Rudras, in the plural, are called *Gaṇa* (a tribe) and leaders of tribes (*Gaṇapati*) and of workmen, potters, cartmen, carpenters and Niṣādas who belonged to proto-Australoid forest-tribes. The *Atharvaveda* (cf. IV, 28; VI, 93, 2; VII, 87, 1; XI, 2, 1; XV, 5) refers to Bhava (called *Rājan*, the archer and the protector of the *Vrātyas* or outcasts), Paśupati, Ugra, Rudra, Mahādeva and Īśāna as distinct forms of the god. Śarva and Bhava, called *Bhūtapati* and *Paśupati*, are desired to remove their deadly poison to other places. In the Śūlagava sacrifice mentioned in the *Gṛihyasūtras* (*Āśvalāyana*, 4, 9), a bull was sacrificed to appease Rudra outside the limits of a village. This shows that the god was not exactly within the orthodox pantheon apparently owing to his association with non-Aryan tribes. He is called by the names Hara, Mṛḍa, Bhīma and Śaṅkara, and one is directed to adore Rudra at the time of traversing a path and a crossing of four roads, of passing by a heap of dung and a creeping serpent, of being overtaken by a tornado and of coming to a variegated scene, a sacrificial site and an old tree (*Hiraṇyakeśin*, 1, 5, 16; cf. *Pāraskara*, III, 15). The *Śvetāśvatara Upaniṣad* (cf. Chs. III–IV), which is earlier than the *Bhagavadgītā* (*circa* third century B.C.) and contains speculations approaching closely the Bhakti cult of later days, calls the god *Bhagavat*, the Great Soul and also Maheśvara in whose power stands Māyā and Prakṛti. It is also said that, knowing Śiva who is minuter than the minute, the creator and protector of the universe, the one having many forms and the one alone encompassing the world and concealed in all beings, men (*Brahmarṣis*) become free from all nooses and attain eternal peace. The god is further said to be the one unchangeable principle that existed before creation. The earliest exposition of the Pāśupata doctrine is found in the *Atharvaśiras Upaniṣad* (cf. R. G. Bhandarkar, *Vaiṣṇavism*, etc., p. 159) which is, however, not a very ancient work. The *Śiva-bhāgavatas* of Patañjali's *Mahābhāṣya* (originally composed in the second century B.C.), under *Pāṇini*, V, 2, 76, were apparently followers of the *Pāśupata-vrata* mentioned in this *Upaniṣad*. Thus the pre-Aryan Father-god, amalgamated with Vedic Rudra, gradually came to be, as Rudra-śiva, a great force in the composite religious life of India long before the birth of Christ, although even in later times often his non-Aryan origin and association were remembered and pointedly mentioned (cf. the legend about the destruction of Dakṣa's sacrifice, *supra*, p. 6). This shows that the influence of Śiva, worshipped by the pre-Aryans, was strong enough to overcome the reluctance of the orthodox Aryan element and to occupy a front seat in the Indo-Aryan pantheon in spite of opposition.

The pre-Aryans appear to have conceived the Mother-goddess as the wife of the Father-god; but, in the Vedic literature, the Mother-goddess is rarely referred to.[1] The *Yajurveda* (cf. *Taittirīya*, I, 8, 6) mentions Aṃbikā as Rudra's sister. In connection of the Śūlagava sacrifice in honour of Rudra, the *Gṛhyasūtras* speak of the 'wife of Bhava' (*Hiraṇyakaśin*, II, 3, 8) apparently as a subordinate deity. Sometimes Rudrāṇī, Śarvāṇī and Bhavānī are mentioned side by side (*Pāraskara*, III, 8). The *Kena Upaniṣad* gives a story in which Umā Haimavatī (daughter of the Himavat) disclosed the nature of Brahman (probably Śiva) to the gods (cf. R. G. Bhandarkar, *op. cit.*, p. 158). But she is not called Rudraśiva's wife. Aṃbikā's mention as Rudra's spouse in the interpolated tenth section of the *Taittirīya Āraṇyaka* (X, 18) is of course very late. Thus in the age covered by the Vedic literature, when the non-Aryan Father-god was considerably near the front rank in the orthodox Indian pantheon, the worship of the Mother-goddess does not appear to have been popular with the higher classes of the society. Even if she made any progress towards recognition, that was possibly as a subordinate to her husband Śiva. This may have been due mainly to the fact that the cult of the Mother-goddess as such was originally unknown to the Aryans who were moreover a patrilineal people unlike the matrilineal aboriginals. Even in the early centuries of the Christian era when the Liṅga cult was becoming widely popular among the people of different classes (although the phallic emblems were gradually being made symbolical by removing their earlier realistic character which was apparently disliked by the orthodox) and when the appearance of *Ommo* (*Umā* from the Dravidian *Amma* meaning the universal mother) on the coin of Huviṣka proves that the Mother-goddess cult became an important factor in Indian religious life, Śakti seems to have been subordinated to Śiva by the upper classes of people who moreover practically ignored the worship of *Yoni* as the symbol of the Mother-goddess. Certain *tīrthas* containing Yoni tanks are no doubt mentioned in the *Mahābhārata*; but the worship of *Yoni* is prescribed only in the late-medieval *Tantra*[2] works which were also not favoured universally by all classes of the society. This particular cult was specially disliked by the orthodox upper classes.

The representation of the bull, i.e. Śiva in his theriomorphic form, on an Indo-scythian coin of about the beginning of the Christian era, that of

---

[1] Her influence is slightly noticed in the conception of Vedic Aditi (spirit of the boundless sky), described as the mighty mother of the Ādityas and as associated with Dakṣa. See Macdonell, *Ved. Myth.*, sect. 41. But she is a minor deity of the Vedic pantheon and was gradually forgotten with the development of the Dākṣāyaṇī-Haimavatī conception of the Mother-goddess.

[2] Cf. also the late-medieval work *Bṛhaddharma* P., II, 1, 38.

योनिः साक्षात् भगवती लिङ्गं साक्षान्महेश्वरः ।
तयोस्तु पूजनेन स्यात् सर्वदैवतपूजनम् ॥

Also देवीं वर्त्तुं भगात्मिकाम् (II, 10, 53); देवीं कुर्याद्योनिरूपां सैव देवी प्रकीर्तिता (II, 27, 32).

See also सर्वासु खलु नारीषु ममाधिष्ठानमुत्तमम् ।
कुमारीषु च सर्वासु युवतीषु विशेषतः ।
आसां योनिं स्तनं दृष्ट्वा प्रथमेभ्यामनुस्मरन् ॥ (II, 11, 99-100).

Śiva in his anthropomorphic form such as on the pre-Christian Ujjain coins and on those of Gondophernes and the Kuṣāṇas belonging to the first and second centuries A.D. (the ithyphallic characteristic of Śiva or Harihara being apparent on a coin of Huviṣka), the discovery from all parts of India of innumerable symbolical phallic emblems of Śiva dating from about the beginning of the Gupta age (although certain realistically made Liṅgas such as that of Gudimallam and their representation on coins such as those from Ujjain have been assigned to dates prior to the beginning of the Christian era), the description of an exceptionally large number of Indian rulers of all parts of the country as exclusive devotees of Maheśvara or Śiva in records dating from the first century A.D. (cf. *Sel. Ins.*, I, pp. 125, 331, 387, 394, 419f., etc.), the mention of ten generations of Pāśupata *ācāryas* in a Mathurā inscription of 381 A.D. (*ibid.*, pp. 269ff.) and the evidence of the epics and the Purāṇas show beyond doubt that Śiva's status at least in the early centuries of the Christian era was practically the same as it is today in the religious life of India. See *Dev. H. Icon.*, Chs. IV-V. But the case of Śakti, in spite of her growing popularity with different classes of people as suggested by Huviṣka's coin, seems to have been different. The evidence of certain later sections of the *Mahābhārata* and the *Purāṇas* like the *Mārkaṇḍeya* no doubt shows that the Mother-goddess, conceived as the wife of Śiva, was nearing the front rank about the age of the imperial Guptas. But even in the period following this age we very often find her associated and apparently subordinated to Śiva. Attention may be drawn in this connection to the adoration of Kāmeśvara and Mahāgaurī in the early-medieval records of some kings of Kāmarūpa (*Kāmarūpaśāsanāvalī*, Intro., p. 32) where the most important deity was no doubt Kāmākhyā (Mahāgaurī). Interesting is also Hiuen Tsang's mention of Bhīmādevī of Gandhāra in association with Mahādeva worshipped by the *Tīrthikas* or *Pāśupatas*. It is well known that the Kāpālika sect of the Śaivas worshipped Śakti in association with Śiva (*supra*, p. 10, note 1). It is also to be noted that the Śūlkīs of Orissa, although their family-deity was Stambheśvarī, claimed to have been exclusively devoted to Maheśvara (D. R. Bhandarkar, *List*, Nos. 1697-98, 1700). The very name of the goddess shows that she was made out on a *Stambha* indicating a *Liṅga* (such Liṅgas with the representation of Śaktis being found in Eastern India; cf. *Hist. Beng.*, I, p. 452) and was thus subordinate to Śiva. A king of the Bhañja family of Orissa claims to have obtained boons from the goddess Stambheśvarī although he was a worshipper of Viṣṇu personally (*List*, No. 1493). There are similar other references to the worship (usually and especially by the aboriginals) of particular forms of the Mother-goddess; cf. Vindhyavāsinī mentioned in the *Harivaṃśa* (*circa* fourth century A.D.) and Vākpatirāja's *Gaüḍavaha* (eighth century). Jālandhara (Jvālāmukhī), Uḍḍiyāna (in the Swat valley), Kāmarūpa, Śrīhaṭṭa and Pūrṇagiri were regarded as the greatest seats of the Mother-goddess in works dating from the eighth century (*supra*, pp. 12ff.). Śiva was, however, usually worshipped along with the Mother-goddess in such seats (*Pīṭhas*) in a form styled Bhairava.[1] But the gradual increase in the importance of the Mother-goddess is also sometimes noticed as suggested by her independent installation for worship (cf. also *supra*, p. 10, note 1, l. 7). In the fifth century A.D., the Maukhari chief Anantavarman established the images of Bhūtapati and Devī in a cave in the Nagarjuni hills, while in another cave he installed an image of the Mother-goddess styled Devī, Bhavānī, Kātyāyanī and the one overpowering

---

[1] Cf. Mahiṣamardinī at the Śaiva establishments of Udaygiri (c. 400), Bhumara (c. 6th cent.), Mamallapuram (7th cent.), Bhubaneswar (Vaital Deul), etc.

the demon Mahiṣāsura. It should, however, be remembered that the chief was a worshipper of Śiva and Śakti and not of Śakti alone. The 'Divine Mothers', often associated with Mahāsena as in the records of the early Kadambas and Calukyas, are known to have usually been collectively adored (*Bṛhatsamhitā*, 60, 19). The construction of a temple for them, described as a 'terrible abode, full of *Ḍākinīs* (female ghouls), of the Mothers who utter loud and tremendous shouts of joy and who stir up the very oceans with the wind rising from the *Tantra* (magical rites)', by a Vaiṣṇava (the 'Mothers' being subordinate to Viṣṇu in this case) royal official for merit, is referred to in a Mandasor inscription of 423 A.D. (*Sel. Ins.*, pp. 284f.). For another early temple of the 'Divine Mothers', see the Deogarh rock inscription of about the sixth century A.D. (*E.I.*, XVIII, pp. 126f.). But whereas the kings of the Gupta age and their successors are usually described as devotees of Maheśvara, Śambhu, Aditya, Sugata, Buddha, Tathāgata, Bhagavat (Viṣṇu), Viṣṇu, Varāha, Cakrapāṇi, Narasiṁha, etc., we rarely find kings who were exclusively devoted to the worship of the Mother-goddess before the age of the Gurjara-Pratiharas (eighth to the eleventh century) of Kanauj, among whom Nāgabhaṭa II, Bhoja I and Mahendrapāla I claim to have been devotees of the goddess Bhagavatī (D. R. Bhandarkar, *op. cit.*, No. 25), while Mahīpāla had predilections for the worship of that goddess as well as of the sun-god (Tripathi, *Hist. Kanauj*, pp. 290-91).

Neither Śiva nor Śakti, however, has been free from aboriginal associations even to this day; but the latter bears the stigma in a far more marked degree than the former, although it has of course to be admitted that Śakti is now regarded as one of the *Pañcadevatā* (Sūrya, Ganeśa, Devī, Śiva and Viṣṇu) to be worshipped in all ceremonies (*Bṛhaddharma P.*, III, 9, 1). Certain late-medieval *Tantras* and other works dealing with the Śaiva and Śākta cults (e.g. *Annadāmaṅgala*, Vaṅgavāsī ed., p. 78) represent Śiva as an ardent lover of Koch girls. This trait, not found in earlier works, no doubt resulted from the identification of Śiva with a tribal deity of the Koch people after their Hinduization in the medieval period; but it shows that Śiva was particularly associated with non-Aryan barbarians even in comparatively modern times. We have already discussed (*supra*, p. 3, note 2) the contribu ion of the various non-Aryan elements in the Indian population to the conception of the Indian Mother-goddess as suggested by her names in Indian literature.[1] But the most glaring instance of her barbarian association in late-medieval and recent times is offered by the ceremony called Śabarotsava that was performed on the Daśamī *tithi* in connection with the autumnal worship of Durgā and is partially remembered in rural Bengal even to this day. The 'festivities on account of the excellent worship of the goddess Umā', celebrated by the people of Varendrī (North Bengal), is referred to by the twelfth century Bengali author Sandhyākaranandin in his *Rāmacarita* (III, 25).[2] People taking part in the Śabarotsava used to cover their bodies with leaves, etc., and to besmear them with mud and other things in the style of the Śabaras who are a proto-Australoid aboriginal people of south-eastern India. Two verses occurring both in the *Kālaviveka* (Bib. Ind. ed., p. 514) by the Bengali jurist Jīmūtavāhana (fifteenth century according to Jolly, but eleventh-twelfth century according to Kane, *Hist. Dharm.*, I, pp. 325-26) and in the *Kālikā Purāṇa*

---

[1] Names like *Kauśikī*, *Kātyāyanī* and *Dākṣāyaṇī* probably indicated deified ladies or deities worshipped by certain Aryan families or clans. See *supra*, p. 3, note 2.

[2] The oldest reference to the modern Bengali form of the worship of Durgā Mahiṣamardinī, accompanied by Kārttikeya, Gaṇeśa, Lakṣmī, and Sarasvatī, is found in the *Caṇḍīmaṅgala* (16th century).

(61, 21-22)[1] prove that the programme of this festivity included topics on and songs about the sex organs and possibly also about sexual intercourse with requisite movements of the body and that its violation incurred Bhagavatī's anger and curse. The *Bṛhaddharma Purāṇa* (III, 6, 81–83), a late-medieval Bengal work of about the seventeenth century,[2] introduces some modifications in the above programme when it says, 'People should not utter before others words which are expressive of such things as the male and female organs of generation; they should utter these during the days of the great worship of the goddess in the month of Āśvina. But even then they should never pronounce them before their mothers and daughters and before female disciples who have not yet been initiated to Śakti worship'. Still, however, the *Purāṇa* supports by arguments that a person worthy of worshipping the Mother-goddess should utter the indecent expressions with a view to pleasing her.[3]

---

1 Cf. सुवासिनीभिः कुमारीभिर्वेश्याभिर्नर्तकैस्तथा ।
शङ्खतूर्यनिनादैश्च मृदङ्गैः पटहैस्तथा ॥ १९
ध्वजैर्वस्त्रैर्बहुविधैर्लाजपुष्पप्रकीर्णकैः ।
धूलिकर्दमविक्षेपैः क्रीडाकौतुकमङ्गलैः ॥ २०
भगलिङ्गाभिधानैश्च भगलिङ्गप्रगीतकैः ।
भगलिङ्गादिशब्दैश्च (v.l. °लिङ्गक्रियाभिश्च) क्रीडयेयुरलं जनाः ॥ २१
परैर्नाक्षिप्यते यस्तु यः परान्नाक्षिपेद्यदि ।
क्रुद्धा भगवती तस्य शापं दद्यात् सुदारुणम् ॥ २२

2 The *Brahmavaivarta Purāṇa* (I, 10, 18 and 123), an East Indian adaptation of an old work and to be attributed to the fourteenth or fifteenth century (*supra*, p. 6, note 3), makes a distinction between the Ambaṣṭhas (probably the Ambaṣṭha-Kāyasthas of Bihar) and the Vaidyas (of Bengal), while the *Bṛhaddharma* (III, 14, 38–48) identifies the Vaidyas with the Ambaṣṭhas. Similarly, Kavikaṇṭhahāra's *Sadvaidyaulapañjikā* (1653 A.D.) is silent about the Ambaṣṭha origin of the Bengal Vaidyas (cf. Dacca ed., pp. 1-2), whereas Bharatamallika's *Candraprabhā* (1675 A.D.) definitely states that the Vaidyas were the same as the ancient Ambaṣṭhas (Calcutta ed., p. 4). The present-day Ambaṣṭhas of the Tamil land and Malabar (their early distribution in South India may have been wider) appear to be referred to as *Vaidyas* in inscriptions dating from the seventh century (*E.I.*, IX, p. 101; VIII, pp. 317–21; XVII, pp. 291ff.; *I.A.*, 1893, pp. 57f.). Their entry into Bengal during the rule of the Senas, hailing from Karṇāṭa or the Kanarese country in the Deccan, is very probable, as the Senas of Bengal must have patronized South Indians in the same way as the Muslim rulers of India entertained Musalmans of other countries at their courts. It is thus very probable that the crystallization of the professional community of the Vaidyas or physicians of Bengal into a caste was a result of their amalgamation with the tribal Ambaṣṭha-Vaidyas of Southern India. This seems to have been the background on which the theory identifying the Vaidyas with the Ambaṣṭhas of early Indian literature (Manu calling them physicians) was fabricated in the late-medieval period. The above facts would show that the date of the *Bṛhaddharma Purāṇa* is not much earlier than the seventeenth century. The reference to the stories of Kālaketu and Śrīmanta (III, 16, 45) seems to suggest for it more or less the same age as that of Mukundarāma's *Caṇḍīmaṅgala* (sixteenth century). It should also be noted that considerable influence of the late-medieval Tantric literature is discernible in this *Purāṇa* (cf. *supra*, p. 104, note 1). See Sircar, *The Ambahṣṭa Jāti* in *J.U.P.H.S.*, XVIII, pp. 148–61.

3 See *History of Bengal* (Dacca University), Vol. I, pp. 606-07. Cf.

शुक्रव्ययं वाग्व्ययं च नैव कुर्याद्वृथा क्वचित् ।
भगलिङ्गादिशब्दश्च नोच्चरेत् परगोचरम् ॥
उच्चरेदाश्विने मासि महापूजादिनेषु हि ।
मातॄणाञ्च सुतानाञ्च समीपे न तदापि च ॥
अशक्तिदीक्षितायाश्च शिष्यायाः सन्निधौ न च ।
देवी हि भगरूपेयं भगलिङ्गरसप्रिया ॥
तस्मात्तत्प्रियकाम्यायै तत्पूजायां तथा वदेत् ॥

POSTSCRIPT

The *Devībhāgavata*, VII, 38, 5–30, containing an important medieval list of Śākta *tīrthas* (cf. *supra*, p. 66, note 1), is quoted below so that the names may be compared with those in the other lists quoted earlier.

कोलापुरं महास्थानं यत्र लक्ष्मीः सदा स्थिता ।
मातुः पुरं द्वितीयञ्च रेणुकाधिष्ठितं परम् ॥
तुल्जापुरं तृतीयं स्यात् सप्तशृङ्गं तथैव च ।
हिङ्गुलाया महास्थानं ज्वालामुख्यास्तथैव च ॥
शाकम्भर्याः परं स्थानं भ्रामर्याः स्थानमुत्तमम् ।
श्रीरक्तदन्तिकास्थानं दुर्गास्थानं तथैव च ॥
विन्ध्याचलनिवासिन्याः स्थानं सर्वोत्तमोत्तमम् ।
अन्नपूर्णामहास्थानं काञ्चीपुरमनुत्तमम् ॥
भीमादेव्याः परं स्थानं विमलास्थानमेव च ।
श्रीचन्द्रलामहास्थानं कौशिकीस्थानमेव च ॥
नीलाम्बायाः परं स्थानं नीलपर्वतमस्तके ।
जाम्बुनदेश्वरीस्थानं तथा श्रीनगरं शुभम् ॥
गुह्यकाल्या महास्थानं नेपाले यत् प्रतिष्ठितम् ।
मीनाक्ष्याः परमं स्थानं यच्च प्रोक्तं चिदम्बरे ॥
वेदारण्यं महास्थानं सुन्दर्या समधिष्ठितम् ।
एकाम्बरं महास्थानं पराशक्त्या प्रतिष्ठितम् ॥
मदालसापरं स्थानं योगेश्वर्यास्तथैव च ।
तथा नीलसरस्वत्याः स्थानं चीनेषु विश्रुतम् ॥
वैद्यनाथे तु वगलास्थानं सर्वोत्तमं मतम् ।
श्रीमच्छ्रीभुवनेश्वर्या मणिद्वीपं मम स्मृतम् ॥
श्रीमत्त्रिपुरभैरव्याः कामाख्या योनिमण्डलम् ।
भूमण्डले क्षेत्ररत्नं महामायाधिवासितम् ॥

* * * *

गायत्र्याश्च परं स्थानं श्रीमत्पुष्करमीरितम् ।
अमरेशे चण्डिका स्यात् प्रभासे पुष्करेक्षिणी (°क्षणा) ॥
नैमिषे तु महास्थाने देवी सा लिङ्गधारिणी ।
पुरुहूता पुष्कराक्षे आषाढौ च रतिस्तथा ॥
चण्डमुण्डी महास्थाने दण्डिनी परमेश्वरी ।
भारभूतौ भवेद्भूतिर्नाकुले नकुलेश्वरी ॥
चन्द्रिका तु हरिश्चन्द्रे श्रीगिरौ शाङ्करी स्मृता ।
जप्येश्वरे त्रिशूला स्यात् सूक्ष्मा चाम्रातकेश्वरे ॥

शाङ्करी तु महाकाले शर्वाणी मध्यमाभिधे ।
केदाराख्ये महाक्षेत्रे देवी सा मार्गदायिनी ॥
भैरवाख्ये भैरवी सा गयायां मङ्गला स्मृता ।
स्थाणुप्रिया कुरुक्षेत्रे स्वायम्भुव्यपि नाकुले ॥
कनखले भवेदुग्रा विश्वेशा विमलेश्वरे ।
अट्टहासे महानन्दा महेन्द्रे तु महान्तका ॥
भीमे भीमेश्वरी प्रोक्ता स्थाने वस्त्रापथे पुनः ।
भवानी शाङ्करी प्रोक्ता रुद्राणी त्वर्द्धकोटिके ॥
अविमुक्ते विशालाक्षी महाभागा महालये ।
गोकर्णे भद्रकर्णी स्याद्भद्रा स्याद्भद्रकर्णके ॥
उत्पलाक्षी सुवर्णाक्षे स्थाण्वीशा स्थाणुसंज्ञिके ।
कमलालये तु कमला प्रचण्डा छगलण्डके ॥
कुरण्डले त्रिसन्ध्या स्यान्माकोटे मुकुटेश्वरी ।
मण्डलेशे साण्डकी स्यात् काली कालञ्जरे पुनः ॥
शङ्कुकर्णे ध्वनिः प्रोक्ता स्थूला स्यात् स्थूलकेश्वरे ।
ज्ञानिनां हृदयाम्भोजे हृल्लेखा परमेश्वरी ॥

INDEX

Abdhisaṅgama 80
Abhayā 27, 69
Abul Fazl, on the Pīṭhas 14
Ācārya-Sātu 77, 70
Acchoda, Achchhabal in Kashmir 28, 70, 80
Adhirājendra, Cola king 25n
Ādinātha 81
Ādipīṭha 22n, 81
Aditipura 81
Āditya 81, 105
Adrikula 32n, 81
Advayasiddhi 17
Ādyādināthapīṭha 22n
Ādyantapura 27n, 81
Ādyā Śakti 3n
Āgamavāgīśa Kṛṣṇānanda 74-80
Āgameśvarī 74, 75n
Āgameśvarī-talā at Śrīdhāma Navadvīpa 74
Agasty-āśrama, Agastipurī near Nāsik 26n, 28n, 66n, 81
Aghoraghaṇṭa 10n
Ahicchatra 16
Ahom 16
Ai, Kāmarūpa goddess 16n
Alḷa 27n, 81
Aileyaka-vana 81
Aindrī 28n.
'Ain-i-Akbarī 14, 16n, 34n, 80, 82, 86-87, 92
Airāvatī. Irāvatī 29n, 81
Aitareya Brāhmaṇa 5, 71
Akampāditya-pīṭha 22n
Akbar 14
Akhilavardhinī 30n
Akhileśvarī 30n, 38n
Akṣayā 28n
Akṣayādya-vaṭa 25n
Akṣayagrīva 19, 20n, 81
Akṣayavaṭa 25n, 28n, 66n, 81
Ālāpura, 18, 19n, 81
Albīrūnī 6n, 10n, 15, 25n
'Alī 25
Allahabad pillar inscription 15
Āma, king of Kanauj 25n
Amala, same as Malaya 27, 67
Āma-Nāgabhaṭa 25n
Amara 35-36, 41, 45n, 47n
Amarakaṇṭaka, source of Sone and Narmadā 25n, 27, 28n, 66n, 69, 81
Amaranātha, *tīrtha* in Kashmir 44n
Amaraparvata, same as Meru 81
Amareśa, on south bank of Narmadā 28n, 31n, 81, 107
Amareśapura 22n
Amareśī 81
Amarī 36, 41, 47n
Ambā 28n
Ambara, modern Amber in Rajasthan 27, 36, 47n, 60, 67, 81
Ambaṣṭha, their relation with Bengal Vaidyas 106
Ambikā, goddess at Ambikā-Kālnā in Burdwan Dist. 3 and n, 11n, 30n, 35, 37, 40, 44, and n, 48 and n, 57, 59-60, 62-63, 81, 103
Ambikāpīṭha 22n
Ambujākṣapura 22n
Ambujapura 81
amma, mother 3n
Amoghākṣī 27, 68
Āmrātakeśvara, 20, 21n, 22n, 23n, 31n, 81, 107
Amṛtā 27-28, 37, 57n, 69-70
Amṛtakauśika 81
Amṛtākṣa 37, 57
Anala 36, 40, 53 and n, 60
Ānandapīṭha 22n, 81
Ānandarāma 79
Ānandārṇava Tantra 17n, 80
Anaṅga 28, 69n, 82
Anaṅgavajra, son of king Gopāla 12
Anantapura 22n, 81
Anantavarman Coḍagaṅga 25n
Aṅga, East Bihar 18, 81
Aṅganā 28, 69, 82
aṅga-nyāsa 7n
aṅga-pratyaṅga of Devī 35-66
Animāpura 22n, 81
Aniruddhapura, 22n, 81
Annadāmaṅgala 3, 23, 35, 39, 42, 43n, 51n 59
Annapurṇā 28n, 41, 81, 107
Antarvedi, Ganges-Yamuna Doab between Prayāga and Haridvāra 18, 81
Anu-Bel-Ea, trinity of Babylonians 17n
Aparājitā 30n
Aparārka 12n
Aparṇā 3 and n, 36, 40, 54 and n, 61, 65, 98
Apte, V. S. 28n
Araṇya 81

Arbuda, Mt. Abu 20, 21n, 22, 23n, 81
Ardhanālaka 81
Ardhanārīśvara 24
Arogā 27, 69
Arogyā 27, 69n
Artemes 20n
Arundhatī 28, 70
Aruṇekṣaṇā 29n
Āryāvarta 30n, 81
Asitāṅga, Aśitāṅga 28n, 36, 40, 52 and n, 60
Aśoka-stūpa, at Puṣkalāvatī 10n
Assam tribes 16
Aṣṭādaśapīṭha 18 80-100
Asurāntakapura 22n, 81
Āśusiddhipura, 22n, 81
Aśvamedhapura 81
Aśvaprada, hill near Gauhati 81
Aśvatīrtha, near Kanauj 26n, 81
Aśvattha 28, 70, 82
Atharvaśiras Upaniṣad 10n
Atharvaveda 102-03
Atiśaṅkarī 27, 69n
Ātmapīṭha 11
Aṭṭahāsa in Birbhum Dist. 21 and n, 22n, 23n, 30n, 32n, 37, 38n, 39, 41, 43n, 57 and n, 82, 108
Aujasa 82
Aurasa 82
Auṣadhi 28, 70n
Ausaja 66n
Avantī, Ujjayinī and the country round it 82
Avantī, goddess 37, 40, 55 and n, 61
Avanty-āśrama 26n, 82
Avimukta, same as Vārāṇasī 32n, 82, 108
Ayodhyā in Faizabad Dist., U.P. 17, 19 and n, 27n, 30n, 41, 64, 82

Badal pillar inscription 9n
Badarī, Badrīnāth in Gahrwal 19 and n, 26n, 28, 30, 70, 82
Bagalā, Bagalāmukhī 48n, 60, 63
Bagchi, P. C. 12n, 101n
Bāhudā, a tributary of the Rāptī 82
Bahulā, Bāhulā, at Ketugrām in Burdwan Dist. 35, 40, 46 and n, 59, 82
Bahulākṣī 40
Baidyanātha 26n
Bāliḍāṅgā, near Dhaniākhāli in Hooghly Dist. 33 and n, 34, 82
Balipriyā 30n
Balipura, 22n, 82
Ballālasena, 12n
Banerjea, J. N. 11, 101
Banerji, B. N. 33n
Barbara 20n
Baṭakeśvara 62
Bāul of Bengal 24
Beṇā, tributary of the Kṛṣṇā 28, 70, 82
Betāi Caṇḍī of Betor near Sibpur in Howrah Dist. 24n
Bhadra 27, 67, 82
Bhadrā 27, 28n, 41, 64-65, 67
Bhadrakāleśvara 26n, 82
Bhadrakālī, Bhadrakālikā, 27 29n, 30n, 31n, 63, 67n, 82
Bhadrakarṇa, Karnali on the Narmadā 82
Bhadrakarṇī, Bhadrakarṇikā 27, 29n, 31n, 32n, 67, 108
Bhadrasena 36, 40, 53 and n, 61, 64
Bhadrāsundarī 27, 68
Bhadrāśva 31n
Bhadreśvara 26n, 27, 29n, 41, 67n, 82
Bhaga 5, 6 and n, 8, 10n, 71-73
Bhagavadgītā 102
Bhagavat 105
Bhāgavata Purāṇa, 6, 73
Bhagavatī, deity possessing *bhaga* 8, 82, 105
Bhairava, associated with Devī 3, 7, 11, 24-25, 32, 35-66, 80, 82, 104
Bhairava-parvata in W. Malwa 37, 40, 55 and n, 61, 82
Bhairavī 40, 48n, 108
Bhandarkar, D. R. 104
Bhandarkar, R. G. 10n, 75
Bhañja kings 104
Bharatabhāṣya 12n
Bhāratacandra, author of *Annadāmaṅgala*, 3, 4n, 23 , 37n, 39, 42, 50n, 58n
Bharatāśrama 28, 29n 69, 82
Bhāratī 29n
Bhāskaravarman 15
Bhattacharya, B. 12n, 76
Bhava 36, 50 and n, 60, 102
Bhavabhūti 10n, 16
Bhāvacūḍāmaṇi 4 and n
Bhavānī, goddess 15, 27, 30n, 32, 38n, 40, 47 and n, 60, 62-63, 67, 83, 87, 104, 108
Bhīmā, Bhīmādevī 9 and n, 28, 41, 69, 104, 107
Bhīmākālī 38n
Bhīmalocana 35, 39, 43, 59
Bhīmapīṭha, 32n
Bhīmarūpā 37, 41, 54 and n, 61
Bhīmaśaṅkara, at Ḍākinī near Poona, 46n
Bhīmā-tīrtha, Bhīmāstāna near Pañcanada (Punjab) 8, 9 and n, 11 and n
Bhīmeśvarī 32n, 108
Bhīruka 35, 40, 46, 60

Bhīru-parvata 37, 55n, 82
Bhīṣaṇa 28n, 35, 40, 45 and n, 59, 62
Bhogeśvarī 39n
Bhogī, voluntary victim for sacrifice 16n
Bhoja I, Gurjara-Pratihāra king 25n, 105
Bhramarāmbā, Bhramarāmbikā 18, 19n, 20n, 54n
Bhramaravāsinī 20 and n
Bhrāmarī 20n, 36-37, 40-41, 47, 55 and n, 60-61, 63, 65, 107
Bhṛgu 21 and n, 23n, 73
Bhṛgupura, Bhṛgupurī, Balia in U. P. 38n, 82
Bhṛgutuṅga 26n, 66n
Bhūtapati 104
Bhūteśa 36, 41, 53 and n, 60
Bhuvaneśī 13n, 36, 41, 48 and n, 50, 60, 64-65
Bhuvaneśvara 65
Bhuvaneśvarī 31n, 38n, 48n, 107
Bībī Nānī 85
Bijāpur 82
Bilva, Bilvaka (Vilvaka) 26-27, 66, 83, 90
Binduka 66n
Bramhakalā 28, 70
Brahman 6, 11n, 24, 28, 70
Brāhmaṇa 5-6
Brahmānanda 18n, 25n, 75-76, 77n
Brahmāṇḍa Purāṇa 5
Brahmāṇī 28n, 29n, 38n, 83, 88
Brahmaputra river 13n
Brahmaśiras 29 n, 83
Brahm-āsya 83
Brahmavaivarta Purāṇa 6n, 106 and n
Brahmāvarta 26n, 30n, 83
Brahmayāmala 17n
Brāhmī 28n
Bṛhaddharma Purāṇa 48n, 106n
Bṛhan-Nīlatantra 17n, 20n, 22n, 25n, 28n, 37n, 39n, 80-100
Bṛhatsaṁhitā 3n, 10n, 105
Bsam-yas monastery 16, 17n
Buddha 7, 10n, 48n, 105

Caitraratha, 27, 67, 83
Cakradhāriṇī 41, 66, 83
Cakradvīpa, 41, 63, 66
Cakrapāṇi 40, 65, 105
Cakravartin of Yādava line 79
Cālukya 105
Cāmuṇḍā 10n, 16, 28n, 30n
Cāmuṇḍā Tantra 48n
Caṇḍa 28n, 36-37, 40, 53 and n, 57, 61
Caṇḍā 30n
Caṇḍadāyikā 41
Caṇḍamahāroṣaṇa Tantra 11n
Caṇḍamuṇḍī 107
Candana-parvata 38n, 83
Caṇḍanāyikā 65
Caṇḍapura 39n, 83
Caṇḍeśa 37, 41, 57n, 65, 73
Caṇḍeśvara 41
Caṇḍeśvarī 41
Caṇḍī, section of *Mārkaṇḍeya Purāṇa* 20
Caṇḍī, Caṇḍikā 12 and n, 13 and n, 17 and n, 27, 28n, 31n, 32n, 35, 40, 46, 59, 69, 81, 86, 107
Caṇḍīmaṅgala of Mukundarāma 6 and n, 24 n, 33, 34n, 49n, 80-100
Caṇḍīpura 22n, 83
Candrabhāgā, Chenab 28, 29n, 37, 40, 55 and n, 61, 66n, 70, 83
Candracūḍāmaṇi 4 and n
Candragarbhasūtra 7
Candraprabhā 106n
Candrapura, Chanda in Madhya Pradesh 21 and n, 22n, 23n, 38n, 83
Candrāsthira 20, 21n, 83
Candrikā 27, 68, 107
Carasthira, Carasthita 20, 21n, 23n, 83
Carcikā 28n
Carcitānanda 41
Caṭṭagrāma 40
Caṭṭala, Chittagong in East Bengal 36, 47 and n, 60, 83
Caturānanda, Sahajayāna concept of 'four' 11n
Catuṣpīṭha conception 11 and n
Catuṣpīṭha-parvata, near Jājpur in Orissa 11n
Catuṣpīṭha Tantra 11
Cauhāra 18, 83
Chagala, Chāgala, Chagalaṇḍa, Chāgalāṇḍa, Chāgalaṇḍa, Chagalaṇḍaka 27, 32n, 69 and n, 83, 108
Chāgaliṅga, 26n, 27, 30n, 67n, 83
Chatreśvarī 39n
Chatterjee, R. N. 75
Chatterji, S. K. 10n
Chāyāchatrapura 21 and n, 23n, 83
Chāyāpura 22n, 83
Chinnamastā 48n
Christ 25
Chutiya of Assam 15
Cidambaram 107
Citrakūṭa in Bundelkhand 27, 68, 83
Citta 83

Ḍākinī 105
Dakṣa 5-6, 11n, 72
Dakṣa (Dakṣiṇa)-Pañcanada 83
Dakṣa-Prajāpati 5-6
Dakṣa-yajña-bhaṅga, section of Mukundarāma's *Caṇḍīmaṅgala* 33

Dakṣa-yajña-nāśa, legend of 5-6, 70-73
Dākṣāyaṇī 3n, 35, 40, 45, 59, 62
Dakṣiṇā 29n
Dakṣiṇa-Kālī image 74n
Dakṣiṇa- Pañcanada 66n
Ḍāmarī 65
Ḍāmunyā, in Burdwan Dist. 34
Daṇḍapāṇi 37, 41, 56, 65
Daṇḍinī 107
Dārukeśa 83
Daśāvatāra of Viṣṇu 39
Daśavidyā 3n
Dehalikā, Dehalikāśrama 28n, 83
Deogarh rock inscription 105
Deori, priest 15-16
Devadāruvana, Badrīnāth in Himalayas or Aundh in Deccan 28, 69, 83
Devagarbhā 36, 52 and n, 60
Devakī 27, 30n, 68
Devakoṭa, Devakoṭṭa, Devakūṭa 21 and n, 22n, 23n, 83
Devaloka 83
Devamātā 27, 69
Devanātha 75
Devī 3, 17, 24, 32-33, 35, 80, 100-106; presiding over Pīṭha 35-66
Devībhāgavata 6, 11n, 20n, 25, 66-70, 107
Devidaikoṭha 18, 83
Devikā river 27, 68
Devikā-taṭa 83
Devīkoṭa 38n, 83
Devīkoṭṭa, modern Bangarh in Dinajpur Dist. 17-18, 83
Devīkūṭa 13n, 17, 83
Devī-tīrtha 9n
Dharā 28, 70n
Dharmamāṇikya, king of Tripurā 47n
Dhṛti 28, 70
Dhūmāvatī 48n
Dhūminī 48n
Dhvani 28, 70
Dikkaravāsinī 13n, 17 and n, 64, 87
Dikṣu, Dikhu river 13n
Divine Mothers 28 and n, 70, 105
Drāviḍa 28n, 83
Durgā 3 and n, 25, 27n, 30n, 31n, 48n, 105-06; her worship 50n; tributary of Sābarmatī 83
Durmadā, v.l. Narmadā 28n
Dvāravatī, modern Dwarka 27 and n, 68, 84
Dyaus 5

Egypt 7
Eight Bhairavas 28n
Ekāgra 84
Ekāmra, Ekāmraka, Bhuvaneśvara in Orissa 20, 21n, 22n, 23n, 27, 38n, 67, 84
Ekavīrā 27, 68
Elāpura Ellora 21 and n, 22n, 23n 30n, 38n, 84
Elliot 14n

Fatimā 25
Female organ 3n, 7
Fīrūz, Sulṭān 15n

Gait, E. 16
Gajapura 22n
Gaṇakṣetra 31n, 84
Gaṇapati, 102
Gaṇḍaka 35, 46n, 59, 84
Gaṇḍakī, tributary of Ganges 35, 40, 46 and n, 59, 84
Gandhamādana, Himalayan peak 27, 67, 84
Gandhāra (Rawalpindi-Peshawar region) 9, 10n, 16
Gaṇeśvara 27n, 73, 84
Gaṅgā, Ganges 27, 28n, 66n, 68, 84
Gaṅgāvilva 84
Gaṅgādvāra, 26n, 27, 30n, 66n, 68, 72, 84
Gaṅgārāmācala 84
Gaṅgāsāgara-saṅgama 19 and n, 26n, 65, 66n, 84
Gaṅgāvāmācala 30n, 84
Gaṅgodbheda 84
garbhādhāna 8
Gargakṣetra 31n
Gargoccheda 84
Gauḍa 18, 84
Gauḍavaha 20
Gaurī 3, 27, 29n, 38n, 39n, 67; worshipped by Mongoloids of Himalayas 3n, 9
Gaurī-guru, father of Gaurī 9n
Gaurīśekhara 84
Gaurīśikhara 8, 9 and n, 11, 15, 41, 49, 63
Gautameśvara 26n, 84
Gaveśvarī, Gavīśvarī 28n, 30n
Gayā 9, 25n, 27, 28n, 68n, 84, 108
Gayaśīrṣa 66n
Gāyatrī 28 and n, 30n, 36, 38n, 40, 51 and n, 60, 64, 70, 107
Ghaṇṭākarṇa 19, 20n, 84
Ghaṇṭeśvara-Śiva 56n
Ghāṭaśilā, between Kharagpur and Tatanagar 33 and n, 84
Ghoṣa, modern Gusha 15

Ghṛṣṇeśa, at Śivālaya (Ellora) 47n
Giri-pīṭha 23, 84
Giriśa 3n
Godāśrama 27, 68, 84
Godāvarī 19 and n, 27, 29n, 40, 65, 66n, 68n, 84
Godāvarī-tīra 37, 55 and n, 61
Gode 12n
Gokarṇa, modern Gendia near Goa 21 and n, 22n, 23n, 27, 32n, 38n, 67, 85, 108
Gomatī 27, 29n, 66n, 67, 85
Gomanta, in Goa region 27, 67, 85
Gopāla, founder of Pāla dynasty 12, 75
Gopalan, R. 10n
Gopāla-Pañcānana 79
Gopatha Brāhmaṇa 5, 72
Gorakṣacāriṇī 19 and n, 85
Gorakṣakāriṇī 19 and n, 85
Govardhana 19, 20n, 26n, 30n, 85
Gṛhyasūtra 102-03
Guhyakālī 31n, 107
Guhyapīṭha 11
Guhyātiguhya Tantra 48n
Guptapura 22n
Guptasādhana Tantra 76
Gupta dynasty 5, 8
Gurjara-Pratihāra 105
Guru Tantra 76
Haft Iqlim 16n

Haṁsatīrtha, modern Humza and Nagar 26n, 85
Haṁseśvarī 30n
Hara 35, 40, 45 and n, 59
Haratīrtha, Harakṣetra or Bhuvaneśvara 30n, 85
Hari 35, 45n, 79
Haridrāpīṭha 22n, 38n, 85
Haridvāra 26n, 40, 65
Hari-Hara 24, 41
Hariṇākṣī 30n
Harinātha 79
Haripriyā 27, 68n
Hariścandra, Hariścandrapura 26n, 27, 30n, 68, 85, 107
Hārīta 26n, 30n, 85
Hārītī, Buddhist goddess 10n
Harivaṁśa 20n, 106
Harmacandra 27, 68n, 85
Harocchcda 85
Harodbheda 85
Hastināpura 21 and n, 23n, 27, 38n, 67, 85
Hayagrīva 19, 20n, 85
Hayakṣetra 85
Hazra, R. C. 10n, 12n

Hemakūṭa, part of N. Himalayas 28, 70, 85
Hevajra Tantra 12 and n, 80-100
Himācala 9
Himālaya 3n, 9 and n, 22n, 27-28, 67, 69, 85
Hima-parvata 39n
Himavat 85
Hiṅgalāja, Hiṅglāja, Hiṅgulā, Hiṅgulāta, modern Hinglaj in Baluchistan 18, 19 and n, 27n, 33n, 34n, 35, 39, 43 and n, 59, 62, 85, 107
Hiraṇyagarbha-mahādāna 8
Hiraṇyākṣa 27, 68n, 85
Hiraṇyapura, Herdoun(Hindaun) in Jaipur 21 and n, 22n, 23, 39n, 85
Hiuen Tsang 9, 10n, 11 and n, 15, 104
Hṛṣikeśa 19 and n, 85
Human sacrifice 10n, 16; at Raṅkiṇī temple 33n
Huviṣka 3n, 104

Ilānta 85
Ilāntendupura 22n
Ilodayagiri 22n, 85
Incest of Prajāpati 5-6
Indirāpura 22n, 86
Indrabhūti 16-17
Indrākṣī 37, 41, 57
Indrānandapura 22n, 86
Indrāṇī 28, 70, 86
Indranīla 26, 30n, 86
Indrapāla, records of 15n
Indreśvarī 39n
Indreśvara 86
Indreśvarīpura 86
Indumatī 29n, 86
Indupura 86
Induvatīpura 86
Induvijayapura 22n, 86
Irāvatī 29n, 66n, 81, 86
Īśāna 35, 45n, 86, 102
Īśānendīśvarīpura 22n
Īśānyaiśapura 22n, 86
Isis, sister and wife of Osiris 7
Isis-Osiris-Horus, triad of Egyptians 17n
Iṣṭanābha 86
Iṣṭanāmabhapura 22n
Iṣṭapura 86
Īśvara 36, 41, 47 and n, 86
Īśvarī 29n
Īśvarayoga 86

Jaganmātā, in Yoni form 3n, 30n
Jagannātha 12 and n, 35, 41, 45

and n, 46n, 59, 65; temple at Puri 25n
Jahājapura, modern Jājpur 19 and n
Jāhnavī 86
Jāhnavī-saṅgama 29n, 86
Jaintia 16
Jāhnavī-taṭa 39n, 86
Jājpur 86
Jālandhara, in Punjab 45n, 12 and n, 13 and n, 14 and n, 16, 17 and n, 18, 19 and n, 21 and n, 22n, 23n, 35, 38n, 40, 44, 59, 62, 69, 84, 104
Jālandharabandha 12n
Jālandhara-giri 13
Jālandharī 14
Jalapriyā 27, 68
Jālaśaila, seat of Caṇḍī and Mahādeva 12 and n, 13, 86
Jalasthala 37, 55
Jaleśvara, in Balasore in Orissa 12n, 21 and n, 23n, 86
Jaleśvarī 12n
Jāmadagnya 48n
Jambudvīpa 7
Janasthāna, Nasik region on Godāvarī 37, 40, 55, 61, 86
Japyeśvara 31n, 86, 107
Jarrett 14
jātakarman 8
Jaya 35, 40, 45n, 59
Jayā 27, 67
Jayadurgā 35, 37, 40, 45 and n, 56, 59, 62
Jayamaṅgalā 30n, 38n
Jayanārāyaṇa 79
Jayanta 26n, 86
Jayantā 86
Jayantī 27, 30n, 36, 40, 50 and n, 67, 86; Pīṭha at Sylhet in E. Bengal 50n, 60, 63
Jayantikā, Jayantī 21 and n, 23n, 86
Jayapura, Jaipur in Rajasthan 38n, 86
Jñānārṇava Tantra 18 and n, 20, 23, 76, 80-100
Jñānasiddhi 16
Job Charnock 34n
Jolā caste 6n
Julāhā, weaver 6n
Jvālā 86
Jvālāmukhī 14 and n, 17, 19 and n, 27n, 31n, 33 and n, 34n, 35, 38n, 40, 44 and n, 59, 62, 86, 107
Jvalantī 17, 86
Jyotiḥsara 86
Jyotirliṅga 46n

Kachāri 16
Kadamba 105
Kailāsa 21 and n, 22n, 23n, 38n, 87
Kakati, B. 15n
Kāla, time or death 3n, 36, 57
Kalā 28, 70n
Kālā 28, 70
Kālabhairava 47, 64
Kālamādhava 36, 40, 52 and n, 60, 87
Kalambakubja, Kalambakuñjaka 26n, 87
Kālāmukha 10n
Kālanidrā 3n
Kālañjara, in Banda Dist., U. P. 27 and n, 67, 87, 108
Kālapīṭha 36, 50n
Kalāvatī 31n, 38n
Kālaviveka 105
Kāleśvara 21 and n, 23n, 87
Kalhaṇa 15, 20
Kālī 3 and n, 15-16, 20n, 27, 29n, 36-37, 35n, 40, 48n, 52 and n, 56, 60, 74-75
Kālidāsa 5
Kālīghāṭa 24 and n, 24n, 37, 39, 41, 56, 87
Kālīghaṭṭa 27n, 31n, 39n, 87
Kālikā 24, 36, 41, 50 and n, 63, 87
Kālikā Purāṇa 6 and n, 12 and n, 13n, 16, 17 and n, 28n, 80-100
Kālindī 28n
Kāliṅga 18, 73, 87
Kālīpīṭha 36-37, 41, 43n, 50 and n, 56n, 60, 63, 87
Kālīpura 87
Kalkattā 34n
Kalki 48n
Kālodaka 26n, 29n, 66n, 87
Kālya 27n
Kalyāṇī 27, 67n, 68
Kāmagiri 13n, 36, 47, 48n, 63, 87
Kāmākhyā 13 and n, 14, 15 and n, 16n, 17, 33, 34n, 36, 46, 47 and n, 48n, 63, 87
Kāmakoṭa 38n, 87
Kāmakoṭi 87
Kāmakoṭṭa 21 and n, 22n, 23n, 87
Kāmākṣī 27, 67
Kāmakūṭa hill 13n
Kamalā 19, 20n, 27, 38n, 40, 48 and n, 60, 63, 67, 108
Kamalākṣī 28n, 32n
Kamalālaya 27, 32n, 67, 108
Kāmarūpa 9, 12 and n, 13, and n, 14 and n, 15, 16n, 17 and n, 19, 20n, 22n, 23n, 25n, 27, 30-31, 33, 34n, 37n, 39-40, 43n, 48n, 49 and n, 63, 67, 87, 104
Kāmeśa 37n
Kāmeśvara 13 and n, 21 and n, 23n, 48n, 87, 104

Kāmeśvarī 13 and n, 38n, 87
Kāmodaka 26n, 87
Kāmrāj 87
Kāmukā 27, 67n
Kāmukī 27, 67n
Kanakakāñcī 31n
Kanakāmaraparvata 38n, 31, 87
Kanakhala, near Hardwar 29n, 31n, 66n, 87, 108
Kāñcana, probably Kunchenjinga 13n
Kāñcī 17, 27n, 31n, 36, 40, 52 and n, 60, 64-87
Kāñcikāpurī 88
Kāñcīpura 107
Kangra 14
Kañja, same as Kunchenjinga 13n
Kaṇv-āśrama 26n, 66n, 88
Kanyā 38n
Kanyakāpura 38n
Kānyakubja 20, 21n, 22n, 23n, 27, 38n, 67, 88
Kanyāpura 88
Kanyāśrama 36, 37n, 51 and n, 60, 64, 88
kapāla 10n
Kapālakuṇḍalā 10n
Kapālamocana 28, 69, 88
Kapālin 28n, 35, 37, 40-41, 45 and n, 54n, 59, 61-62
Kāpālika 10n, 16, 104
Kāpālikavrata 10
Kapālinī 37, 54 and n
Kapilā 27, 67
Kapilāmbara 35, 40, 46 and n, 60
Kapilesvar 29n
Kapileśvara 35, 46n
Karālā 16
Karatoyā, river of North Bengal 13n, 49
Karatoyā-taṭa 36, 40, 54 and n, 61, 64-65, 88
Karavīra, Sukkur in Sind or Kolhapur in Maharashtra 27, 32n, 35, 44 and n, 69, 88
Karavīrapura 26n, 30n
Karkoṭa 27, 67n, 88
Karṇasūtra 19 and n, 88
Karṇāṭa 37n, 39, 43n
Karṇa-tīrtha 26n, 88
Kar, Sambhunath 19 and n
Kārttikeya 27, 69, 88
Kāśī 19 and n, 28n, 34n, 88
Kāśīnātha 79
Kāśmīra 16, 18, 19n, 20, 21n, 23n, 28, 35, 40, 44 and n, 59, 62, 69, 88
Kaṭaka 41, 88
Kaṭakeśvarī 41, 88
Kātyāyanī 3n, 12 and n, 13 and n, 17, 30n, 31n, 36, 38n, 53n, 64, 104
Kaulagiri 18, 88
Kaumārī 28n
Kauśikā 81
Kauśikī 3n, 26n, 29n, 66, 88, 107
Kauśītakipriya 29n
Kāverī 26n, 29n, 88
Kāvyamīmāṁsā 56n, 87
Kāyāvarohaṇa 28, 69, 88
Kedāra 21 and n, 22n, 23n, 26n, 27, 31n, 38n, 46n, 66n, 67, 88, 108
Kedāreśvara 88
Kesāi Khāti 15-16
Keśajāla 36, 41, 53n, 60, 88
Khotan 16
Kirātārjunīya 9n
Kirīṭa 27n, 31n, 36, 50 and n, 60, 64, 88
Kirīṭakoṇā 36, 41, 50n, 88
Kirīṭeśvarī 31n
Kirīṭin 41
Kīrtimatī 27, 67
Kishenganga river 15
Kiṣkindhya-parvata 28, 69, 88
Koch 16
Kokāmukha 40, 89
Kokeśvara 40
Kokeśvarī 40, 63
Kolāpura 107
Kolhāpura 18, 19n
Kol 20n
Kolva-giri (Kaula-giri) 18, 21 and n, 23n, 89
Koṭa 27, 67, 89
Koṭavī 27, 68
Koṭimudrā 18, 89
Koṭitīrtha 27, 68, 89
Koṭṭarī 35, 39, 43, 59
Koṭṭarīśā 35, 43n
Koṭṭavī 35, 43n
Kramadīśvara 36, 40, 50, 60
Krodha 28n
Krodheśa 37, 44n, 56n
Krodhīśa 35, 37, 39, 44, 56, 59, 62
Kṛṣṇa 25, 48n, 74, 75n
Kṛṣṇabeṇyā, Kṛṣṇbeṇvā 89
Kṛṣṇacandra 79
Kṛṣṇānanda Āgamavāgīśa 23, 74-80
Kṛṣṇanātha 36, 53n
Kṛṣṇaśaraṇa 79
Kṛṣṇaveṇā 26n, 29n
Kṛtaśauca 27, 69, 89
Kṣaṇā 31n
Kṣaṇamocana 30n
Kṣetrādhīśa, same as Bhairava 35
Kṣetravatī 65
Kṣīrikā, Kṣīragrāma 21 and n, 23n, 89
Kṣīragrāma, near Katwa in Burdwan Dist. 19, 20n, 21 and n, 23n, 33

and n, 36, 41, 49n, 60, 89
Kṣīrakaṇṭha 36, 49n, 60
Kṣīrakhaṇḍa 36, 41, 49
Kṣīra-pīṭha 38n
Kṣīrapura 22n, 89
Kubjāmra, Kubjāmraka 27, 66n, 68n, 89
Kubjikā Tantra 19 and n, 20n, 39, 80-100
Kulānta, Kulāntaka 18, 21 and n, 23n, 89
Kulapañjikā 79
Kulārṇava Tantra 18, 77
Kulaśāstradīpikā 79
Kumāra 37, 40-41, 56n, 65, 89
Kumāradhāma 28n
Kumāradhārā 66n
Kumārākhya 26n
Kumārasambhava of Kālidāsa 5
Kumārī 27, 37, 38n, 41, 56, 61, 65, 68
Kumuda 28, 70n, 89
Kumudā 27, 67
Kuñcapaṭṭana 89
Kuñja-giri, same as Kañja 13n
Kūpānta, Kulānta 21 and n, 23n, 89
Kuraṇḍala 108
Kūrma 48n
Kūrma Purāṇa 5, 10n, 73
Kurukṣetra 19 and n, 29n, 31n, 36, 41, 51 and n, 60, 63, 89, 108
Kurukullā 16
Kuśadvīpa 28, 70, 89
Kuśapriyā 30n
Kuśāvarta 26n, 27n, 30n, 66n, 89
Kuśodaka 28, 70
Kuṭuvī 62

Lagnikāśrama 26n, 89
Lakhyā, same as Lākṣā river 13n
Lākṣā 13n
Lakṣmaṇoccheda, °odbheda 89
Lakṣmī 107
Lakṣīṁkarā 16
Lalitā 26n, 271, 29n, 36, 50, 60, 63, 67-68, 89
Lalitakāntā 17 and n, 87
Lalitapura 29n, 89
Lambakarṇa 37, 55, and n, 61
Laṅkā 18, 19n, 37, 39, 41, 43n, 57, 89
Lévi, S. 12n
Liṅga, male organ 7-8, 89, 101
Liṅgadhāriṇī 27, 66 and n, 107
Liṅgākhya 31n, 39n
Liṅgavāhinī 31n
Lokeśvara 16
Lolā 27, 69
Lomakhaṇḍa 65

Ma, Cappadocian goddess 20n
Madālasā 107
Madanta 30n, 89
Madantī, Madantikā 30n, 89
Mādhava 19, 20n, 64-65, 89
Mādhava-vana, Mādhavī-vana 27, 68, 89
Mādhavī 27, 30n, 31n, 67
Madhupurī, same as Mathurā 17, 19 and n, 89
Madhurā, same as Mathurā 30n, 89
Madhusūdana 79
Madotkaṭā 27, 67, 83
Madreśvara 27, 67n, 90
Magadha, Māgadha, 18, 37n, 39, 57n, 90
Mahābala 90
Mahābhadrā 30n, 82
Mahābhāgā 17, 27, 69
Mahābhārata 5, 8, 9 and n, 13n, 25, 73, 103-04
Mahabhāṣya 102
Mahābhīmā 41, 65
Mahābodhi 90
Mahābuddhi 29n, 30n
Mahācala 32n
Mahādeva 10n, 12 and n, 14, 102
Mahādevī 27, 31n, 37, 40, 56n, 61, 68
Mahāgaṅgā 26n, 66n, 90
Mahāgaurī 13n, 15n, 48, 87, 104
Mahākāla temple at Ujjayinī 27, 40, 46n, 69, 90
Mahākālī 62-63
Mahākāntā 30n
Mahākarṇa 19 and n, 90
Mahāmāyā 3n, 14, 31n, 35-36, 40, 44 and n, 45 and n, 52n, 59, 62
Mahālakṣmī, Pīṭha-goddess 18, 19n, 27, 28n, 36, 39n, 40, 48n, 52, 60, 64, 69, 90
Mahālakṣmīpura 18, 21 and n, 22n, 25n, 90
Mahālaya 27, 32n, 69, 90, 108
Mahāliṅga 27, 67, 90
Mahāl Kalkattā 34n
Mahānāda 26n, 30n, 90
Mahānala 90
Mahānandā 29n, 30n, 32n, 38n, 83, 90, 108
Mahānātha 12 and n
Mahā-Nīlatantra 25n, 58n
Mahāpadmā 27, 69n
Mahāpathapura 90
Mahāpīṭha 39
Mah^-pīṭhanirūpaṇa, Pīṭhanirṇaya 3 and n, 4 and n, 23-24, 35, 38, 41-42, 59, 80-100
Mahārātri 79n
Mahārudra 36, 40, 53, 60
Mahāryā 30n

Mahāsena 105
Mahāsiddhi 30n
Mahāśmaśāna, at Padmāvatī in Gwalior (Gird) Dist., M.P. 10n
Mahātīrtha 90
Mahāvana 29n, 90
Mahāvegā 30n
Mahāvidyā 28n, 30n, 38n, 39, 48 and n, 49, 50n, 81
Mahāviṣṇupada 90
Mahāvratin 10n
Mahendra 21 and n, 22n, 23n, 32n, 90, 108
Mahendrapāla I 105
Mahendrapura 90
Mahendravarman I 10n
Māhendrī 28n
Maheśvara 9-10, 31n, 72, 104-05
Maheśvarapura, Māheśvarapura, on Narmadā 16, 27, 69, 90
Maheśvarī, Māheśvarī 27, 28n, 30n, 31n, 38n, 69, 81
Maheśvarīpura, Māheśvarīpura 27, 69n, 90
Mahīpāla 105
Mahiṣamardinī 35, 37, 39, 44, 57, 59, 62, 88
Mahiṣāsura 105
Māhiṣmatī 19, 20n, 90
Mahodara 37, 40, 56 and n, 61, 65
Mahodarī 29n
Māhvara 90
Maināka 30n, 90
Maithila Devanātha 76
Maitras of Maṇḍalajānī 74
Makarandaka 27, 69n, 81, 90
Mākoṭa 27, 32n, 67n
Makran 16
Malakūṭa 16
Mālatī 10n
Mālatīmādhava 10n, 16
Mālava 16, 21 and n, 23n, 30n, 35, 38n, 40, 45n, 90
Malaya 18, 21 and n, 23n, 27, 67, 90
Malay-ācala 27, 68n
Mālinī 30n
Mālinīvijaya 48n
Malladeva Naranārāyaṇa of Kāmtā 76
Mallikārjuna on Śrīśaila 46n, 54n
Mānasa 26n, 27, 29n, 35, 45, 59, 62, 67
Mānas-ācala 27, 68, 90
Manasāmaṅgala 24n, 34n
Mānasa-sarovara 40, 91
Mānava, Mālava 21 and n, 22n, 23n, 90
Mandā 27, 67n
Maṇḍaleśa 108
Maṇḍaleśvara 91
Mandara, Mandāra 27, 31n, 67, 91
Mandasor inscription 105
Māṇḍava 27, 69n
Māṇḍavī 27, 69
Māṇḍavya 27, 69, 91
Māndavyapura, Mandor near Jodhpur 25n
Māṇḍukī 27, 69n
Maṅgalā 27, 31n, 35, 46 and n, 47, 60, 68, 108
Maṅgalacaṇḍī, Maṅgalacaṇḍikā 35, 40, 46n, 62
Maṅgalakoṭa 27n, 31n, 91
Maṅgaleśvarapīṭha 32n,
Maṅgaleśvarī 26, 67n
Maṇibandha, 37n, 39, 40, 43n, 51n, 64, 91
Maṇidvīpa 64
Maṇikarṇikā at Vārāṇasī 36, 51n, 64, 91
Māṇikī 91
Maṇipura 19 and n, 91
Maṇiveda 35-36, 40, 51, 60, 64, 91
Manmatha 28, 70
Mantracūḍāmaṇi 4 and n, 39
Marakaṇṭaka, Marakaṅkaṭa 27, 69, 81, 91
Mārgadāyinī 27, 67, 108
Mārīcī 16
Mārkaṇḍeya Purāṇa 9, 20n, 28n, 104
Markoṭa 27, 67n
Marshall, J. 101
Māruteśa 91
Māruteśvara 21 and n, 22n, 23n
Mātā 27, 28, 69
Mātā Lakṣmī 28, 69
Mātaṅga 91
Mātaṅgavāpī 26n, 66n, 91
Mātaṅgī 29n, 48 and n, 60, 63
Mathurā 27, 68, 91
Mathurānātha 79
Mātṛdarśa 30n, 91
Mātṛgaṇa 26n, 91
mātṛkā 28n
Mātṛ-maṇḍala 10n
Mātṛ-tīrtha 9n
Matsya Purāṇa 5, 25 and n, 66-70
Mattamedhā 28n, 81
Mattavilāsa-prahasana 10n
Māyā 27n, 38n, 91
Māyāpura 21 and n, 22n, 23n, 38n, 91
Māyāpurī 27, 68, 91
Māyāvatī, Pīṭha near Hardwar 17, 19 and n, 91
Medhā 28, 69
Meghabalā 30n
Meghasvanā 30n
Meghavana 26n, 30n, 91
Mehāra, Pargana of Tippera Dist. 3n, 91
Mekalā 18
Mekhalā 18, 63 and n, 91

Mekhalī 63
Meru 91
Merugiri 21 and n, 23 and n, 91
Merupīṭha 23
Merusvanā 30n
Mīnākṣī 107
Mitākṣarā 10n
Mithilā 18, 37, 40, 56 and n, 61, 65, 91
Mohenjodaro 3n, 7, 101-02
Mother-goddess 3 and n, 5, 7-8, 9 and n, 10 and n, 14-17, 20 and n, 25, 43, 101-06; of Mohenjodaro 101-02
Mother of Demons 10n
Mṛgī 27, 69n
Muḥammad Shāh bin Tughlak Shāh, Sulṭān 15n
Mukundarāma, Bengali poet 6, 24n, 33-34
Mukuṭa 28, 70, 91
Mukuṭeśvarī 27, 67, 108
Muṇḍakeśvarī 32n
Muṇḍamālā Tantra 48n
Muṇḍapṛṣṭha 29n, 92
Munīśvara 29n, 92

Nābhigayā, Jājpur 34n, 92
Naḍantikā 66n
Nādavaṭa 92
Nāgabhaṭa II 105
Nāgapura 31n
Nāgapurī 92
Nagarakoṭa 14, 33 and n, 92
Nagarasambhava, Nāgarasambhava 19 and n, 92
Nāga-tīrtha 29n, 92
Nāgeśa, at Dārukavana 47n
Nagna-Śabara 3n
Nagnik-āśrama 26n
Naimiṣ-āraṇya 27, 29n, 66 and n, 92, 107
Naipāla 92
Nakuleśa, , Nakulīśa 36, 41, 50 and n, 60, 63
Nakuleśvarī 107
Nala 36, 41, 47 and n, 60
Nalāhāṭī, Nalhāṭī in Birbhum Dist. 37, 39, 41, 43n, 56 and n, 92
Nalasthāna 41, 92
Nalīśa 36, 50n
Nāmāṣṭottaraśata 80-100
Namrakarṇa 37, 40, 55n
Nana, on Kuṣāṇa coins 43n
Nanaia 20n
Nandā 27, 67
Nandapura 29n, 92
Nandavaṭa 92
Nandataṭa 30n, 92
Nandikeśvara 37, 57 and n
Nandinī 27, 37, 41, 57, 68
Nandipura 37, 39, 41, 43n, 57, 92
Nandīśvara 41
Nandīśvarī 73
Nānyadeva 12n
Narasiṁha 105
Nārasiṁhī 28n
Nārāyaṇī 27, 30n, 36, 40, 53 and n, 60, 64, 68
Nārikela 19 and n, 92
Narmadā 16, 26n, 28n, 29n, 36, 40, 53 and n, 61, 92
Narmadā-tīra 66n
Narmadoccheda 92
Narmadodbheda 92
Navadurgā 40
Navadvīpa 74
Nāyikā 28n
Nepāla 13n, 19 and n, 20, 21n, 22n, 23n, 35, 37n, 40, 45 and n, 59, 62, 92, 107
Nidhi 28, 70
Nīlā 29n
Nīl-ācala 34n, 41, 65, 92
Nīla-parvata 12n, 31n, 38n, 40, 66n, 87, 107
Nīla-Sarasvatī 107
Nīlavāhinī 19, 20n, 92
Nimiṣa 36, 40, 51, 60
Niṣāda 102
Nitambā 27, 69n
Non-Vedic element in Hinduism 100n, 101n
Nṛsiṁha 48n

Oḍiyāna, Uḍḍiyāna in Swat valley 12-13, 92
Oḍḍiyāna 12n, 13n, 17 and n, 92
Oḍra, seat of Kātāyanī and Jagannātha 12 and n, 13 and n, 92
Oghavatī, Āpagā river 26n, 30n, 93
Ommo, on coins of Huviṣka 3n, 103
Oṅkāra-pīṭha 21 and n, 22n, 23n, 38n, 46n, 92
Oṣadhi 28, 70
Osiris myth 7

Padārthādarśa 76
Padma Purāṇa 5, 25, 66-70
Padmasambhava 16, 17n
Padmavajra, author of *Hevajra Tantra* 12
Padmāvatī, Padam Pawaya in Gwalior (Gird) Dist., M.P. 10n, 16
Pākhaṇḍa, *Pākhaṇḍin* 10n
Palusha 9
Pampāsaras 30n, 93

Pañcakaṭī 93
Pañcanada (Punjab) 8, 9n, 29n, 93
Pañcāpsaras 93
Pañcasāgara 36, 40, 53, 60, 93
Pañcatantra 10n
Pañcatīrtha 93
Pañcavarga 30n
Pañcavaṭī 26n, 30n, 93
Pāṇḍarānanā, Pāṇḍavānanā 29n
Pāṇḍu, Pāṇḍya country 29n, 93
Pāṇini 10n, 102
Pāpaharā 40
Pāpamocana 38n
Pāpanāśinī 29n
Pārā 27, 69n
Paramānandā 38n
Parameśvarapura 93
Parameśvarī 27, 31n, 68
Parapīṭha 11
Paraśurāma 79
Pārasya, Persia 38n, 93
Pārā-taṭa 93
Pārāvāra-tīra 93
Parṇa-Śabarī, Buddhist deity borrowed from Parṇa-Śabaras 3n
Pārvatī 3 and n, 20n, 28, 32n, 39n, 41, 70
Pāśupata Yogin 10 and n, 16
Paśupati 72-73, 102
Paśupatinātha of Nepāl 45n
Pātāla 26n, 27, 29n, 68, 93
Pāṭalā 27, 68
Pāṭaleśvarī 19n
Patañjali 10n
Pauṇḍravardhana 20, 21n, 22n, 23n, 37n, 93
Pāvā 27, 69n
Pāvakya, Pārasya 22n
Payoṣṇī river 27, 69, 93
Phalgu-tīrtha 66n
Phallic worship 7, 101
Phullarā 37, 41, 57, 64
Piṇḍāraka, Piṇḍāraka-vana 26n, 28, 30n, 70, 93
Piṅga 93
Piṅgā 26
Piṅgaleśvarī 27, 69
Pīṭhas of Mother-goddess 3-8, 11-16, 17-18, 20 and n, 23-25, 32-66
Pīṭha-devatā, forms of Devī 35
Pīṭhamālā 4 and n
Pīṭhanirṇaya, *Mahāpīṭhanirūpaṇa* 3 and n, 4 and n, 9, 20n, 23-24, 34-35, 38-39, 41-42, 48n, 59, 80-100
Pīṭhanyāsa, Tantric ritual 4, 7 and n
Pīṭhasthala 3n
Pīṭhatattvanyāsa 14n
Pīṭhavinyāsa 7n
Piyālamārga 93
Plutarch 7
Prabalā 29n
Prabhā 28, 29n, 70
Prabhāsa, Prabhāsakhaṇḍa 26n, 27, 28n, 29n, 31n, 37, 40, 55 and n, 61, 65, 66n, 69, 93
Pracaṇḍā 27, 39n, 41, 69, 83, 108
Pracaṇḍacaṇḍikā 48 and n, 60, 63
Pradyumna 93
Prajāpati 5-6, 71-73
Prajñāpāramitā 11
Pramadā 30n
Prāṇatoṣaṇī Tantra 3, 14n, 23, 25n, 28n, 42, 66n, 76-100
Praṇava 93
Prāṇavallabha 79
Prapā 93
Prasaṅga 93
Pratāpgarh near Javlī 15
Prayāga 18, 19 and n, 21 and n, 22n, 23n, 27, 36, 40, 43n, 50 and n, 60, 63, 66n, 67, 93
Priyā 30n
Pṛthūdaka 26n, 36n, 94
Pulinda 20n
puṃsavana 8
Puṇḍra 41, 94
Puṇḍravardhana 27, 68, 94
Puṇyā 37n
Puṇyabhājana 41
Puṇyādri 94
Puṇyavardhana 27, 68n, 94
Puraścandra 30n, 94
Purasthira 94
Purasthita 20, 21n, 23n, 94
Pureśvarī 30n
Pūrṇa, Pūrṇaśaila, Pūrṇagiri 12 and n, 64, 94
Pūrṇā 37n
Pūrṇagiri 12 and n, 13 and n, 14n, 17 and n, 35, 94, 104
Pūrṇānanda 18n, 75, 76, 77 and n
Pūrṇanātha 12n
Pūrṇaśaila, seat of Pūrṇeśvarī and Mahānātha 12 and n, 20, 21n, 23n, 94
Pūrṇeśvarī 17 and n, 20, 21n, 23n
Pūrṇimā 29n
Pūruhūtā 27, 67
Puruṣottama 25n, 27, 31n, 68, 94
Pūṣan 5-6, 71-73
Puṣkalāvatī, Mirziyarat-Charsadda near Peshawar 10n
Puṣkara 25n, 27, 28n, 31n, 66n, 67, 94, 107
Puṣkarāvatī 27, 69
Puṣpatīrtha 27, 69n, 94
Puṣṭi 28, 69
Puṣyādri 22n

Rāḍhā, 18, 25n, 27, 31n, 68, 94
Rāghava Bhaṭṭa 76
Ragunātha Śiromani 74-75
Raghuvaṁśa 9n
Rahim 25
Rājabolahāṭa, near Serampur in Hooghly Dist. 33 and n, 34, 94
Rājagiri 36, 53n, 94
Rājagṛha 21 and n, 23n, 94
Rājalakṣmī 38n
Rājamālā, Bengali chronicle of Tripurā kings 4n, 20n
Rājaparvata 38n, 94
Rājataraṅgiṇī 10n, 15, 20
Rājeśvarī 33 and n
Rākiṇī 37, 56 and n, 65; same as Raṅkiṇī 33n
Rākṣaseśvara 37, 41, 57
Raktadantikā 107
Rāma 25, 48n
Ramā 29n, 38n
Rāmā 94
Rāmagiri, Ramtek in M. P. 19 and n, 36, 53, 61, 94
Rāmākiṇī 36, 53n
Ramaṇā 27, 69
Ramaṇa, Ramaṇaka 26n, 30n, 94
Rāmānanda 36, 47n
Rāmānuja 25n
Rāmaśobhana 79
Rāmatīrtha 26n, 27, 30n, 69, 94
Rāmatoṣaṇa Vidyālaṅkāra 23
Rambhā 27, 67
Rāmeśvara at Setubandha 26n, 29n, 30n, 47n, 94
Rāmeśvarī 31n
Rāmoccheda, Rāmodbheda 94
Raṇāditya 20
Raṇakhaṇḍa 40, 94
Raṇekṣaṇā 29n
Raṅkiṇī of Burdwan 33 and n
Rāsavṛndāvana 94
Ratipriyā 27, 68
Ratnāvalī 35,37,40, 56 and n, 65, 95
Ratnāvatī 37, 56 and n, 61, 95
Raudrī 38n
Rāvānanda 36, 40, 48n
Raychaudhuri 20n
retas of Prajāpati 5
Ṛgveda 5, 7, 71, 101-02
Ṛṇamocana 26n, 95
Rudra 3n, 5, 71, 102-03
Rudrakoṭi 27, 67, 95
Rudrāṇī 27, 38n, 81, 108
Rudrarāma 79
Rudra-Śiva 6, 102-03
Rudrasundarī 27, 68n
Rudrayāmala Tantra 12n, 17 and n, 18, 23, 80-100
Rukmiṇī 27, 33 and n, 68
Rūpā 27, 69n
Rūpiṇī 38n
Ruru 28n, 36, 46, 52 and n, 60, 63

Śabara 20n
Śabdakalpadruma 3, 7n, 42, 48n
Sabhānandā 27, 68n
Sachau, E. A. 15, 25n
Sadānanda 40
Sadāśiva 64
Sādhanamālā 12n, 13, 16, 39, 80-100
Sadiyā, Copper temple at 16
Sāgara-saṅgama 31n, 80, 95
Sahajayāna school of Buddhists 11 and n
Sahasrākṣa 27, 68, 75n, 95
Sahyādri 27, 68, 95
Śaila 36, 53n
Śaiva 3n, 10n, 22
Śākambharī 66n, 107
Śākambharīpura 26n, 95
Sakhī-bhāva 74
Śakra 72-73
Śākta 3n, 8, 22, 74, 75 and n
Śākta-tīrtha 66n
Śakti 3 and n, 8, 10n, 16, 24, 28, 30, 39-40, 100-06
Śaktidhāriṇī 28, 70n, 80
Śaktisaṅgama Tantra 15, 76
Śālagrāma 27, 68, 95
Śāligrāma 27, 68n, 95
Śamanakarman 40
Śamaneśvara-pīṭha 38n
Śamaneśvarapura 95
Samarānanda 36
Samayācāra Tantra 14n
Sambheda 95
Śambhu 10n, 102, 105
Śambhu-Śiva 10n
Saṁhāra 28n, 36, 41, 53, 60, 95
Saṁkrūra 36, 40, 53
Samudragupta 15
Saṁvarānanda 36, 52, 60
Saṁvarī 41
Saṁvarta 36, 41, 50
Samvṛtānanda 64
Sanātana 79
Śaṅkara 11n, 31n, 40
Śaṅkara Āgamācārya 18
Śaṅkarācārya 18
Śaṅkarī, Pīṭha-goddess 18, 19n, 27, 31n, 69n, 107-08
Śaṅkhoddhāra 28, 70, 95
Śaṅkhasaṁharaṇa 95
Śaṅkhasaṁhāriṇī 29n
Śani 6
Santāna 95
Śāntarakṣita, Śāntirakṣita 16

Saptagodāvara 95
Saptagodāvarī 27n, 30n
Saptārci 95
Saptārṣa 66n
Saptaśṛṅga 107
Sāradā, goddess 15, 29n, 30n, 44n, 95
Sāradā-pīṭha, modern Sardi in Kashmir 14
Sāradā-maṭha in Kashmir 15
Sāradātilaka Tantra 76
Sāradā-tīrtha 26n
Sarasvatī, same as goddess Sāradā, 18, 19n, 26n, 27, 28 and n, 30n, 66n, 69-70, 95
Sarayu 26n, 29n, 95
Sarayutīra 66n
Sāre Mākhe Ḍherī 10n
Śarīrin 95
Śarkarāra 44n, 59, 95
Sarkar, J. N. 15
Sarkar Satgaon 34n
Sarva 41, 102
Sarvākṣiṇī 41
Sarvamaṅgalā of Citpur, Calcutta 24n, 38n
Sarvāṇa 40
Sarvānanda 3n, 36, 37, 40, 51 and n, 52n, 60, 64
Sarvānandamayī 57n
Sarvānandataraṅgiṇī 3n
Sarvāṇī 31n, 36, 51, 60, 108
Sarvaśaila 41, 95
Sarveśa 37n
Sarveśvarī 41
Ṣaṣṭhī 38n
Ṣaṣṭhīpura 22n, 38n, 95
Sastri, H. P. 11 and n
Śatadravā (Śātadrava) 29n
Śatadru 29n, 95
Śatadru-tīra 66n
Śatapatha-Brāhmaṇa 5, 71
Śataprabhā 29n
Śatarūpā 29n
Satgaon 34n
Satī, daughter of Dakṣa 4n, 5, 6 and n, 7, 11n, 13n, 25, 30n, 32-35, 39n, 50n, 51n, 95
Satīcala 41, 95
Ṣaṭtriṁśanmata 10n
Sātu 77, 79
Satyavādinī 28, 70
Saurabheśvarī 38n
Sāvitrī 9n, 10n, 25, 30n, 36, 40, 51 and n, 60, 64, 66n, 72, 105
Sen, D. C. 75
Sephālikā 41
Set, brother of Osiris 7
Setubandha 31n, 65, 95
Shams-i-Shrirāj 'Afif 14n
Siddhapīṭha 3n, 6n, 19
Siddhapura 28, 69, 95
Siddhavana 28, 69n 95
Siddhavaṭa 28, 69n, 95
Siddeśvarī 40
Siddhi, perfection 3n
Siddhidā 29n, 35, 44 and n, 59, 62
Siddhidāyinī 28, 70n, 80
Siddhirūpā 36, 50 and n, 60
Siddhi-tīra 96
Sīmantonnayana 8
Siṁhala 18, 19 and n, 96
Siṁhanāda 19 and n, 96
Siṁhikā 27, 69
Sindhusaṅgama 28, 69n, 96
Sindhusthalī 38n
Śindhu-tīra 66n
Sircar, D. C. 24n
Sirihaṭṭa (Śrīhaṭṭa) 13, 14n, 96
Śiśnadeva, worshipper of Phallus 7
Sītā 27, 68
Sītākuṇḍa, on Chandranath hill 47n
Śiva 3 and n, 4n, 5-7, 10 and n, 11, 14, 16, 20n, 24 and n, 25,28, 31n, 37, 40, 56, 70, 100-06
Śivā 12n, 30n, 32n, 37, 39n, 40, 56n, 61
Śivabhadrā 37n
Śiva-bhāgavata 10n
Śivacaṇḍa 27, 68n, 96
Śivacarita 38, 39, 41n, 43n, 47n, 50n, 51n, 80-100
Śivadhāriṇī 28, 70n, 80
Śivadūtī 28n
Śivājī 15
Śiva-Kapāleśvara, in Cālukya inscription 10n
Śivakāriṇī 28, 70, 80
Śivakuṇḍa 27, 68, 96
Śivakuñja 27, 68n, 96
Śivaliṅga 27, 68, 96
Śiva-Mallikārjuna 16
Śivāmṛtā 28n
Śivānanda 36, 47n, 60
Śivānandā 27, 68
Śivānī 36, 40, 53 and n, 61
Śiva-Paśupati 3n
Śivapītha 31n, 96
Śiva Purāṇa 24n
Śivasannidhi 96
Śivātmikā 29n
Śivavallabhā 38n
Sixteen Mothers 28n
Skanda Purāṇa 24n, 25 and n, 66-70
Smith 29n
Ṣoḍaśī 48 n
Ṣoḍhānyāsa 7n
Somākhyā 64
Somanātha near Veraval in Junagarh Dist., Gujarat 96

Someśvara 26n, 27, 69, 96
Śoṇa 26n, 29, 36, 41, 53 and n, 96
Śoṇajyotiṣā-saṅgama 28, 66n, 69
Śoṇākṣī 40
Śoṇa-saṅgama 96
Śraddhā 29n
Śrī 29n, 48n
Śrīcaitanya 74-75
Śrīgiri 29n, 96, 107
Śrīhaṭṭa, same as Sirihaṭṭa 13, 36, 40, 52, 60, 96, 104
Śrīkṛṣṇa-Śatanāma 24n
Śrīnagara 107
Śrī-Nīlaparvata 26n
Śrīparvata 10n, 16, 31n, 36-37, 40, 51n, 54 and n, 65, 66n, 96
Śrīpīṭha, Śrīhaṭṭa 21 and n, 23n, 96
Śrīpura 22n, 38n, 96
Śrīśaila, in Karnool Dist., A.P. 16, 18, 19n, 20n, 21 and n, 22n, 23n, 27, 36, 38n, 41, 52, 64, 67
Śrītattvacintāmaṇi 75-76, 77 and n
Śrīvidyā 30n
Stambheśvarī 104
stana, hills regarded as breasts of Devī 8
Stanakuṇḍa 7-8, 9n, 15
Sthala 96
Sthāṇu 36 40, 51 and n, 60
Sthāneśvara 27, 67n
Sthāṇvīśvara, modern Thanesar 27, 32n, 51n, 67, 96
Strīrājya 18, 96
Stūpa 7
Subalā 29n
Śubhacaṇḍī 40
Subhadrā 28, 69, 96
Śubhānandā 27, 68n
Śubhavāsinī 29n
Śubheśvarī 30n
Śuci 36, 53, 60, 64, 96
Śuddhā 28, 69n
Śuddhabuddhi 29n
Śuddhi 28, 69, 88
Sugandhā, Shikarpur in Buckergunge Dist. 26n, 27, 35, 40, 44 and n, 59, 62, 66n, 68, 96
Sugatā 105
Sukathā 29n
Śukla-tīrtha 26n, 29n, 96
Śukra-tīrtha 29n
Śūlagava sacrifice 103
Śūlapāṇi 41, 66
Śūlinī 20n
Sunandā 27, 35, 40-41, 44 and n, 59
Sunandānanda 37, 54n
Sundarānanda 37, 40, 54 and n, 61
Sundarī 37, 40, 48n, 54 and n, 61, 65, 107
Suparṇa 96
Suparṇākhya 32n
Supārśva 27, 68, 96
Surapūjitā 28n
Surasā 29n, 30n
Sureśa 41
Sureśī 41
Sūrya 6 and n
Suvarṇākhya 32n
Suvarṇākṣa 108
Svadhā 29n
Svāhā 27, 31n, 69
Svargadā 29n
Svargalakṣmī 38n
Svargamārga 2 n, 66n, 96
Svargoccheda, °dbheda 29n, 97
Svayambhū-liṅga of Śiva 8
Śvetabandha 41, 97
Śyāmā (Kālī) 48n, 75
Śyāmārahasya of Pūrṇānanda 75-76, 77n
Śyāmasundara 79
Syria 7

Tailaṅga 41, 65, 97
Taittirīya Saṁhitā 29n
Tamoghnī 31n
Tamolipta 31n, 97
Tāmra 40
Tāṇḍyamahābrāhmaṇa 5
Tantracūḍāmaṇi 3, 4 and n, 20n, 39, 42, 48n, 58n
Tantrakaumudī 76
Tantrasāra 4, 7n, 14n, 16, 18n, 20,23 and n, 28n, 48n, 51n, 74-80
Tapasvinī 30n
Tapolakṣmī 38n
Tārā 16, 28, 39, 48n, 69, 97
Tārādyā 62
Taraṅgā 28, 69n, 82
Tārārahasya 25n, 77n
Tārārahasya-vṛttikā 18
Tāriṇī 39
Tarkaratna, Pañcānana 80
Tarkavācaspati, Tārānātha 42
Tathāgata 105
Tattvacintāmaṇididhīti 75
Teshub 20n
Thomas, F. W. 17n
Thuggee 15
Tibet 16
Tilottamā 28, 70
Tippera Dist. 3n, 16
Tīrabhukti, Tirhut in North Bihar 47n
Tirotā 36, 47n, 97
Tīrthika 10, 16
Tīrthasaṅgama 97
Tīvraka 35, 46n
Traipura 27n, 97

Tribal deities 3n
Trihalikāgrāma 66n
Trihuta (Tīrabhukti) 41, 97
Trikūṭa 27, 68, 97
Trimūrti 24
Trinetreśvara 35, 44n
Tripada 97
Tripathi, R. S. 105
Tripura 97
Tripurā 4n, 19, 20n, 36, 41, 47 and n, 48 and n, 60, 63, 97
Tripurākṣa 36, 47n, 60
Tripuramālinī 35, 40, 45, 59, 62, 86
Tripuranāśinī 35, 45n, 59, 86
Tripurā Rājamālā 58n
Tripurasundarī 36, 38n, 43, 47, 63
Tripureśa, Śiva of Tripurā 4n, 36
Tripuṭā 40
Trisandhyā 27, 40, 68, 108
Trisandhyeśvara 35, 44, 59, 62
Trisrotā, Tista river in North-Eastern India 20, 21n, 23n, 36, 38n, 40-41, 47, 63
Triśūlā 107
Triśūlinī 31n
Triveṇī 19 and n, 97
Tṛpti 29n
Tryambaka 35, 40, 44 and n, 47n, 59
Tryambakeśvara temple at Ponabalia 44n
Tuljā Bhavānī 14, 82
Tuljāpura 107
Turjā (Tuljā) Bhavānī, 14, 82
Turkish Musalman 17
Tuṣṭi 28, 69n

Ucchiṣṭacaṇḍālinī 66
Uḍḍīna 22n
Uḍḍīnapura 97
Uḍḍīśa, from *Oḍḍavisa*, same as Orissa 21 and n, 23n, 97
Uḍḍiyāna in Swat Valley 12 and n, 13 and n, 14n, 16, 17 and n, 18, 19 and n, 21 and n, 23n, 30-31, 35, 97, 104
Uḍḍiyānabandha 12n
Udyatparvata 8, 9 and n, 11
Ugra 102
Ugrā 108
Ugratārā 34n, 97
Ujānī, same as Kogrām in Burdwan Dist 35, 40, 46n, 97-98
Ujjani 35, 46n, 98
Ujjayinī 21 and n, 22n, 23n, 35, 38n, 45n, 46 and n, 47, 59, 98
Umā 3 and n, 27, 36, 37, 39n, 41, 53 and n, 64, 69, 72, 105
Umālakṣmī 28, 69n
Umānanda 36, 40, 48
Umāvana 36, 53n, 60
Unmatta 35, 39, 40, 44 and n, 59, 62
Unmatta-bhairava 28n
Upaniṣad 102
Upa-pīṭha 39, 41
Ūrdhvapāda-Vajravārāhī 16
Urjanı 35, 46n, 98
Urjayinī 35, 46n
Urvaśī 28, 70
Uṣas 5
Uṣṇatīrtha 27, 69, 98
Utkala 35, 40, 45, 59, 62, 98
Utpalā 27, 32n, 68
Utpalākṣī 27, 68n, 108
Utpalāvartaka 27, 69, 98
Utsādana 41
Uttarā 41, 98
Uttarakuru 28, 70, 98
Uttaramānasa 29n, 66n, 98
Uttariṇī 41

Vācaspatya 7n, 25n, 43
Vaḍavā 66n
Vagalāsthāna 107
Vāgmatī 19, 20n, 98
Vaidyanātha, Deoghar-Vaidyanāthdhām 19n, 26n, 25n, 27, 35, 40, 45 and n, 59, 62, 69, 98, 107
Vaiṣṇava 22, 75 and n
Vaiṣṇavī 28 and n, 30n, 65, 70
Vaiśravaṇa 28, 70
Vaiśravaṇ-ālaya 98
Vaitaraṇī river 19 and n
Vaivasvata 40, 51n, 98
Vājasaneyi Saṁhitā 24n
Vajradhātvīśvarī 11n
Vajrasattva 11 and n
Vākpatirāja 20, 104
Vakra 40
Vakranātha, 37, 40, 57, 98
Vakratuṇḍa 37, 40, 55 and n, 61
Vakreśvara in Birbhum Dist. 37, 39-40, 43n, 57, 98
Vakreśvarī 40
Vāmācāra 10n
Vāmadeva 41, 64
Vāmana 21 and n, 23n, 36, 48n, 54, 61, 65, 98
Vāmeśa 37, 40, 54n
Vaṁśīdāsa of Mymensing 24n, 34n
Vanamāla, records of 15n
Vandinikā 28, 70n
Vandanīyā 28, 70
Vaṅga 18, 98
Varadā 38n
Varāha 105
Varāha-parvata 25n, 28n, 66n, 98

Varāha-śaila 27, 67
Vārāhī 19, 20n, 28n, 36, 40, 53, 60, 65, 98
Vārāṇasī 17, 18 and n, 19n, 20, 21n, 27n, 27, 33, 34n, 36, 37n, 41, 43n, 51 and n, 64, 66 and n, 98
Varārohā 27, 69
Vardhamāna 98
Vardhamānaka 81
Vareṇya 81, 98
Vasiṣṭha 30n
Vasiṣṭha-tīrtha 26n, 98
Vāstoṣpati 71
Vastrapāda 32n, 98
Vastreśvara 28, 69, 99
Vasu, N.N. 39, 74 and n, 75 and n, 77
Vaṭakeśvara 40
Vaṭaparvatikā 30n, 99
Vaṭīparvatikā 30n, 99
Vatsanābha 37, 56n
Vedagarbhā 40, 64, 87
Vedamastaka 99
Vedamātā 30n
Vedāraṇya 107
Vedaśiras 99
Vedavadana 99
Vedeśa 99
Vedic Rudra 3n
Vegala 27, 69n, 99
Veṇā 99
Veṇīmādhava 40, 50n
Veṇumatī 99
Veṇuvatī 29n
Vetravatī 66n
Vibhāsa 37, 41, 54, and n, 61, 99
Vidiśā, modern Besnagar 45n
Vidyā 31n
Vidyālaṅkāra, Rāmatoṣaṇa 77-80
Vidyāpura 27n, 31n, 99
Vidyābhūṣaṇa, Rāmalobhana 79
Vidyābhūṣaṇa, Rāmalocana 78-79
Vidyābhūṣaṇa, S.C. 75
Vidyāvāgīśa, Kṛṣṇamaṅgala 79
Vijayā 30n, 35, 39n, 40, 45n, 99
Vijayanta 26n, 30n, 99
Vikramāditya 5
Vikṛta, Vikṛtā 37, 55 and n, 61
Vikṛtākṣa 37, 40, 55n
Vilvā 27, 67n
Vilvaka 26n, 27, 66, 99
Vilvala 27, 67n 99
Vilvapatrikā 27, 67
Vilvapīṭha 27n, 38n
Vimalā 19, 20n, 27, 31n, 35-36, 38n, 41, 45 and n, 50 and n, 59, 64-65, 68, 99, 107
Vimaleśvara 31n, 99
Vimukti 30n
Vināyaka 27, 69, 99
Vindhya 21 and n, 23n, 27, 30n, 65, 68, 99
Vindhyācala 107
Vindhyagaṅgā 30n
Vindyagaṅgāsaṅgama 99
Vindhyagiri 19, 20n
Vindhyakandara 99
Vindhyavāsinī, non-Aryan goddess 20 and n; her temple near Mirzapur, U. P. 20, 27, 30n, 35, 41, 68, 104
Vindhyaśekhara 41
Vipāśā 27, 29n, 66n, 68, 99
Vipradāsa 24n
Vipula 27, 68
Vipulā 27, 68, 99
Vīrabhadra 6, 73
Vīrācāra 10n
Virajā 19 and n, 21 and n, 23n, 31n, 33 and n, 38n, 65, 86
Virajākṣetra in Utkala 35, 45 and n, 59
Virajāpura 99
Virāṭa, Virāṭadeśa 39, 43n, 57 and n, 99
Virūpākṣa 41
Viśāla 100
Viśālā 29n
Viśālākṣī, Pīṭha-goddess 18, 19n, 27, 29n, 32n, 33, 34n, 36, 41, 51, 64, 66, 108
Viśālalocanī 33 and n
Viṣṇu 6-7, 10n, 11n, 24 and n, 73-74, 75 n, 104-05
Viṣṇupada 29n, 66n, 100
Viṣṇupriyā 29n
Viṣṇusaṁhitā 66n
Viṣṇuvardhana, Hoysala king 25n
Viśvā 27, 67
Viśvakāmā 27, 67n, 81
Viśvakāyā 27, 67, 81
Viśvamātā 41
Viśvamātṛkā 40
Viśvamukhī 28, 69
Viśvanātha 41, 79
Viśvāsa, Prāṇakṛṣṇa 77
Viśveśa 37, 40, 57
Viśveśī 37, 55 and n, 61
Viśveśvara 27-28, 41, 47n, 67, 69n, 100
Vitastā 66n
Vrajeśvarī 30n, 38n, 83
Vṛndāvana 25n, 27 and n, 36, 41, 53 and n, 68, 100
Vyāghrapura 32n, 100
Vyomakeśa 57n

Watters 10, 16

Yādaveśvarī 30n
Yāgapura 31n

Yāgapurī 100
Yāgeśvarī 38n
Yājapura in Orissa 33 and n, 100
yajña, sacrifice 5
Yajurveda 24n, 102-03
Yamunā 26n, 27, 28n, 69, 100
Yamunā, river of North Bengal 13n
Yamunā-tīra 66n
Yaśaskarī 27, 69
Yaśora, Īśvarīpura in the Khulna Dist. 37, 39, 41, 43n, 57 and n, 100
Yaśoreśvarī 37, 41, 57
Yaśovarman 20, 57n
Yogācāra doctrine 16
Yogādyā 33 and n, 36, 41, 49n
Yogamāyā 3n
Yogapīṭha 11
Yogeśa 37, 56n
Yogeśvarī 107
Yoginī 10n, 11, 28n
Yoginī Tantra 13n
Yogin, ascetic 3n
Yogīśa 35, 37, 41, 56
Yoni 3n, 7-8, 9n, 13n
Yonikuṇḍa 7-8, 9n
Yoni rings 101
Yonistotra 3n
Yoni Tantra 7
Yoni-tīrtha 15
Yugādyā 36, 38n, 39, 41, 49 and n 60, 100
Yugalā, Pīṭha-goddess 18, 19n

Addenda et Corrigenda

Page 1, line 20. *Read*—from *for*—form

,, 2, line 19. *Read*—Mahāpīṭhanirūpaṇa

,, ,, line 21. *Read*—Śivacarita

,, 3, note 2. *Add*—As regards the maiden (Kumārī) aspect, we may note that, in every Bihāl (*vihāra*) of the Newars of Nepal, a young girl having no scar on her body is worshipped as the living form of Kālī or Durgā. There is also a similar Kumārī for the whole kingdom. The State Kumārī is periodically selected from amongst the girls of the Vanra or priestly community on the last day of the Navarātra, after a trying test. The Newars believe that the valley of Nepal belongs to the Kumārī and therefore every year the king has to receive from her a fresh mandate for ruling the country. The Kumārī is replaced by another before she approaches her first menstruation. See Gopal Singh Nepali, *The Newars*, reviewed in *Swarajya*, March 26, 1966, p. 27

,, 5, line 15. *Read*—Uṣas

,, ,, lines 35 ff. *Add references—Bhāgavata Purāṇa*, IV. 2-7; cf. allusion to the story of the destruction of Dakṣa's sacrifice in the *Rāmāyaṇa*, I. 66.9.

,, ,, note 1. *Add*—In the *Tāṇḍyamahābrāhmaṇa* (VII. 9.16), we are told that the gods were once sharing among themselves the animals sacrificed to them in ceremonies, but that they avoided Rudra in this sharing. *Read*—Appendix III.

,, 7, line 5. *Read*—Viṣṇu

,, ,, line 19. *Read*—afterwards

Page 8, lines 9 ff. *Read*—As will be seen below, there is reason to believe....the *Yoni* of the Mother-goddess.

Add note—George MacMunn says, "at Malabar in Bombay, a great cleft in the rock is known as the *Yoni*, and through it pass barren women desirous of child, who travel from far and wide to do so" (*The Underworld of India*, 1933, p. 99).

,, 11, note 1. *Add*—We have also legends connecting holy places with the limbs of other divinities. The *Vāyu Purāṇa* (Chap. 104) relates a story about Vyāsa who is said to have noticed the following holy places and rivers in the limbs of the Vedas incarnate—(1) Mathurā in their heart, (2) Kāśī between the eye-brows, (3) Kāñcī in the organ of generation, (4) Avanti in the navel, (5) Dvārakā in the throat, (6) Prayāga in the life breath, (7) the Gaṅgā and Yamunā on their left and right, (8) the Sarasvatī in the middle, (9) Gayā in the face, (10) Prabhāsa between the jaw and neck, (11) Badarī in the crown of the head, (12) Puṇḍravardhana-pīṭha and Nepāla-pīṭha in the two eyes, (13) Pūrṇagiri-pīṭha on the forehead, (14) Mathurā-pīṭha on the neck, (15) Kāñcī-pīṭha on the loin, (16) Jālandhara-pīṭha on the breast, (17) Bhṛgu-pīṭha in the ear, and (18) Ayodhyā in the nostril. While there are a few cases of repetition (cf. Nos. 1 and 14, 3 and 15), it is difficult to say whether Bhṛgu (No. 17) is the same as Bhṛgukaccha. It may be noted that only Puṇḍravardhana, Nepāla, Pūrṇagiri, Mathurā, Kāñcī, Jālandhara and Bhṛgu are called *pīṭha*, but that Kāmākhyā is a significant omission.

Page 12, note 5, line 16.	*Read*—c. 1159-79 A. D.
,, ,, note 6.	*Add*—p. 13 and notes, and p. 23 and note 3 (refering to the separate mention of Uḍḍīyāna and Uḍḍīśa or Orissa side by side in the same list).
,, 13, note 1, line 4.	*Add*—See below p. 17, note 3. The *Kālikā Purāṇa* (62. 76 ff.) applies the name Kāmeśvarī to the goddess Kāmākhyā.
,, ,, line 13.	*Read*—mountain
,, ,, last line.	*Add*—The goddess worshipped in the Tāmreśvarī temple near Paya in the Lohit District of NEFA is called Dikkaravāsinī in an inscription of Śaka 1364 (1442 A.D.). See *Journ. Anc. Ind. Hist.*, Vol. I, pp. 17ff.
,, ,, note 2, lines 14-16.	*Omit*—For the same confusion...*Mahābhārata*, II. 14.19. *Read instead*—See p. 13 and notes, and p. 23 and note 3 for the separate mention of Uḍḍīśa (Orissa) and Uḍḍīyāna. See Sircar, *Stud. Geog.*, 1971, pp. 181 ff.
,, 16, line 17.	*Read*—*op. cit.*
,, ,, lines 20-21 and some other places in the book.	*Read*—Andhra Pradesh *for*—Madras Presidency
,, 18, line 1 and some other places in the book.	*Read*—Tamil Nadu *for*—Madras Presidency
,, ,, line 23 and elsewhere in the book.	*Read*—Asiatic Society, Calcutta *for*—Royal Asiatic Society of Bengal.
,, 19, note 1, line 3.	*Read*—*Pradyumno*
,, ,, ,, line 7.	*Read*—*Kāmarūpī* (*pā*).
,, ,, ,, line 8.	*Read*—*Gayā* (*yāṁ**).
,, ,, note 2, line 13.	*Read*—*Uḍḍīyānaṁ*
,, 20, line 6, and elsewhere in the book.	*Read*—Uttar Pradesh *for* United Provinces
,, ,, line 8.	*Read*—c. 725-53 A. D.

Page 21, note.	*Add*—Note the separate mention of Uḍḍīśa (Orissa) and Uḍḍīyāna.
,, 23, note 3, line 19.	Read—*hṛdādyudara*
,, ,, note 3.	*Add*—The separate mention of Uḍḍīśa (Orissa) and Uḍḍīyāna is worthy of note.
,, 24, note 3.	*Add*—For the Avatāras, see also Sircar, *Stud. Rel. L. Anc. Med. Ind.*, pp. 41ff.
,, 25, note 1.	*Add*—For the god Puruṣottama-Jagannātha, see now Sircar, *Stud. Rel. L. Anc. Med. Ind.*, pp. 59ff., to note modification in the views.
,, ,, note 2, line 5.	*Read*—c. 725-53 A. D.
,, 30, note, last line.	Read—*Madhurāyāñ = ca.*
,, 31, note, line 33.	Read—*Kurukṣetre.*
,, 33, line 5.	*Read*—S.E.R. *for*—B.N.R.
,, 37, note, line 7.	*Read*—in Kāmarūpa
,, 39, line 13.	*Read*—suggest
,, 43, note 5, line 1.	Read—*mam = āsya vapuṣo*
,, 46, note 4, line 1.	Read—*kurparañ = c = aiva.*
,, 47, note 2, lines 6 and 8 and elsewhere in the book.	*Read*—Tripura State in East India *and* Jabalpur in Madhya Pradesh.
,, ,, note 2.	*Add*—For the correct date of Dharmamāṇikya, see *JAIH*, Vol. V, pp. 32-33.
,, ,, note 7, line 2.	Read—*Umānando = tha.*
,, 49, note 9.	*Add*—See also *JAIH*, Vol. I, pp. 19ff.
,, 53, note 3, line 2.	*Read*—Nagpur in Maharashtra.
,, 55, note 1, line 5 and elsewhere in the book.	*Read*—Kathiawar (Gujarat).
,, ,, note 6, lines 4-5.	*Read*—Nasik region of Maharashtra.
,, 63, note, line 3.	*Read*—Cooch Bihar District of the West Bengal State.
,, 74, note.	Add—*Lola-jihvā ālola-jihvā, lelihāna-jihvā* or *lalaj-jihvā* was really a characteristic of several Tantric gods and goddesses. See *Tantrasāra*, Vaṅgavāsī ed., pp. 301, 462-63, 470, 502, 514, 596.
,, 80, line 38.	*Add*—Vāyu = Vāyu Purāṇa
,, 80, line 44.	*Read*—Achchhabal
,, 81, line 17.	*Omit*—possibly a mistake for Elāpura.

	Read—modern Alampur in the Mahbubnagar District of Andhra Pradesh.
,, ,, line 21 and some other places in the book.	*Read*—Madhya Pradesh *for*—C. P.
,, ,, lines 27 and 46-47.	*Read*—District, Rajasthan *for*—State, Rajputana.
,, ,, line 50.	*Add*—See also Sircar, *Stud. Geog. Anc. Med. Ind.*, 2nd ed., p. 106.
,, 82, lines 9, 25 and 27.	*Read*—West *before*—Bengal.
,, ,, last line.	*Read*—in Maharashtra
,, 83, line 4.	*Read*—in Haryana
,, ,, line 12.	*Read*—Punjab (Pakistan)
,, ,, line 13.	*Read*—in Maharashtra
,, ,, line 49.	*Read*—North Bengal
,, 84, line 8.	*For*—Hyderabad State *read*—Aurangabad District of Maharashtra; may also be a mistake for *Ālāpura*.
,, ,, line 31	*Add*—According to the *Rājataraṅgiṇī* (I.35), it was the Bheḍa hill in Kashmir and the goddess Sarasvatī appeared there in the form of a swan in a lake. The Bheḍa is identified by Stein with Buḍbrār in the valley of the Birnai (trans., Vol. II, p. 472).
,, ,, lines 44-45.	*Read*—South-Eastern Railway.
,, 85, lines 24 and other places in the book.	*Read*—Rajasthan *for*—Rajputana
,, ,, line 48.	*Read*—Jaipur District
,, 86, lines 38-39.	*Read*—region in Maharashtra
,, ,, line 41.	*Read*—West Bengal
,, ,, line 45.	*Read*—District, Bangladesh
,, ,, line 52.	*Read*—Himachal Pradesh *for*—Punjab
,, 87, penultimate and last lines.	*Read*—Tamil Nadu *for*—Madras *and* West Bengal *for*—Bengal
,, 88, line 11.	*Add*—For modern Degām = ancient Kapālamocana in Kashmir, see Stein, *Rājatar.*, trans., Vol. II, p. 472.
,, ,, line 18.	*Read*—in Haryana.

Page ,, line 41.	*Read*—Baroda District, Gujarat
,, ,, penultimate and last lines.	*Read*—modern Bellary District of Karnataka *and* Jodhpur Division, Rajasthan
,, 91, line 31.	*Add reference*—Vāyu.
,, 92, line 41.	*Add reference*—Vāyu.
,, 94, line 5.	*Add reference*—Vāyu.
,, ,, line 17.	*Add reference*—Vāyu.
,, ,, line 35.	*For*—Gaya *read*—Patna
,, 99, last line.	*Add*—See also Sircar, *Stud. Geog. Anc. Med. Ind.*, 2nd ed., pp. 100-01.
,, 101, line 7.	*Add*—See *The Bhakti Cult and Ancient Indian Geography*, ed. Sircar, pp. 36 ff.
,, ,, note.	*Add*—On the same subject, see also *The Vedic Age* (*The History and Culture of the Indian People*, Vol. I), pp. 147 ff.
,, 104, lines 31 ff.	*Add note*—The deity Stambheśvarī is still worshipped by the people of the different castes of Orissa in some parts of the country under the local name Khambeśvarī and in the shape of a post or pillar without any special association with the Śiva-liṅga (*Ep. Ind.*, Vol. XXVIII, p.112).
,, 105, note 2.	*Add*—The autumnal worship of Durgā was prevalent in the Ayodhyā region of U. P. in the seventh century A. D. See *Life of Hiuen-Tsiang*, trans. S. Beal, p. 86; Sircar, *Stud. Rel. L. Anc. Med. Ind.*, p. 230.